FROM MARGIN TO MAINSTREAM

Consulting Editor
Robert A. Divine
University of Texas at Austin

From Margin to Mainstream

American Women and Politics Since 1960

Susan M. Hartmann

The Ohio State University

TEMPLE UNIVERSITY PRESS   Philadelphia

Published 1989 by Temple University Press, Philadelphia

Copyright © 1989 by Alfred A. Knopf, Inc.

Library of Congress Cataloging-in-Publication Data

Hartmann, Susan M.
  From margin to mainstream : American women and politics since 1960 /
  Susan M. Hartmann.—1st ed.
    p.   cm.
  Bibliography: p.
  Includes index.
  ISBN 0-87722-634-2
  1. Women in politics—United States—History—20th century.
I. Title.
HQ1236.5.U6H38   1989
320′.088042—dc19   88–13645
                              CIP

Manufactured in the United States of America

Foreword

The resurgence of political history is one of the most intriguing developments in recent American historical scholarship. In the years immediately following World War II, historians tended to dismiss the study of past politics as mundane and old-fashioned as they focused on cultural, psychological, ethnic, and intellectual approaches to the American experience. But the enduring importance of political events, brought home to scholars as well as journalists by the tumultuous events of the 1960s and the devastating Watergate scandal, led historians to examine the political past anew. Many historians borrowed ideas and techniques from social scientists to probe into such new areas as voting behavior, party fluctuations, and the role of ethnocultural factors in politics. Others relied on more traditional studies of campaign rhetoric and the impact of charismatic leaders on the political process. The result was a new flowering of political history.

Critical Episodes in American Politics is a series of interpretive volumes designed to bring the new scholarship to bear on some important periods and themes in American political history. Departing from the original attempt to provide chonological coverage, the series now emphasizes significant topics that helped shape the course of American political development in the twentieth century. Employing different techniques and approaches, each of the authors focuses on a distinctive pattern of past political behavior to show how it contributed to the evolution of modern American democracy.

In this volume, Susan Hartmann offers an informative account of the role of women in politics, beginning with their marginal position in 1960 and then showing how the feminist movement brought them into the mainstream of American political life in the 1970s and 1980s. By focusing broadly on the

v

various forms of women's political activity, ranging from NOW's drive for the ratification of the Equal Rights Amendment to Phyllis Schlafly's strident opposition, she shows how American politics changed from 1960, when women played a minimal role in the contest between Richard Nixon and John Kennedy, and 1984, when Geraldine Ferraro became the first woman to run on a national party ticket. Just as women began to play a new role in American society, so did they broaden the political agenda, forcing voters to confront such important issues as abortion, domestic violence, and child care. Her book, both comprehensive and balanced in its approach, enables the reader to gain a better understanding of the revolutionary impact of women on American politics over the past quarter century.

Robert A. Divine

Preface

A third era of women's political participation was launched in the 1960s. From the birth of the nation until 1920, women as a group had been barred from customary political activities such as voting, office-holding, and party activities. This is not to say that they were without political influence. Excluded from formal politics, women nonetheless contributed to the shaping of American government and policies through their work in benevolent societies, abolitionism, temperance, women's rights, and a host of other reform movements. They operated in a female political subculture, distinctive in terms of constituency, modes of activism, and objectives. Through participation in their own organizations, women gained skills, self-confidence, political consciousness, and ultimately a commitment to overturn the male monopoly of formal politics.[1]

After winning the vote in 1920, some women were integrated into the male political culture, but not as equals. Individual white women rose to influential positions within the parties and government, but when they succeeded, they did so largely on men's terms. A small group of white women continued to pursue a feminist agenda, but they lacked a mass base of support. Although women sustained their same-sex organizations and pursued some goals that were of special concern to women, their influence on public policies was faint.

In the context of an expanding federal government, the decline of political parties, and widespread social ferment, women's relationships with the political system entered into a third phase in the 1960s. That era was characterized by extensive mobilization of women behind self-defined goals, an in-

[1]Paula Baker, "The Domestication of Politics: Women and American Political Society, 1780–1920," *American Historical Review* 89 (June 1984): 620–647.

creasing voice and presence within the parties and government at all levels, and dramatic changes in public policies concerning women. This book is an account of how women have reshaped the American political system since 1960.

At the center of these changes was the revitalization of feminism, from a small elite-based movement which had persevered after 1920, into a broadly based struggle that achieved legitimacy as a pressure group at all levels from the smallest community up to the federal government.[2] For convenience, I have used the term "feminism," but in doing so I refer to a multifaceted, organizationally diffuse form of activism whose aims were to expand women's opportunities in the public sphere, increase their autonomy and material well-being, and lessen their dependent status in the family.

Similarly, I use the term "women's movement" broadly, referring to a collection of groups organized around particular feminist goals. These many components frequently formed broad coalitions, but they exhibited considerable differences in objectives and strategies. The term "women's political movement" is used to denote a narrower collection of organizations that sought the election and appointment of women to office and the empowerment of women within the political parties.

The first chapter of the book surveys women's political behavior between 1920 and 1960, focusing on voting patterns, relationships with the parties, office-holding, and public-policy aims and accomplishments. Chapter 2 deals with grass-roots political upheaval in the 1960s from women's perspectives, exploring their participation in various social insurgencies of that decade. Chapter 3 provides an account of the revival and early development of the women's movement.

Women's struggle for power within the parties and for greater female representation in government is the focus of Chapter 4. Chapter 5 analyzes feminist pressure for a broad range of public-policy goals at all levels of government. Chapter 6 traces the development of a countermovement in alliance

---

[2]Leila J. Rupp and Verta Taylor, *Survival in the Doldrums: The American Women's Rights Movement, 1945 to the 1960s* (New York: Oxford University Press, 1987).

with the New Right, which attempted to reverse many of the changes effected by the women's movement.

Antifeminism became institutionalized with the election of Ronald Reagan in 1980, and Chapter 7 outlines the ways in which women's advocates shifted priorities and strategies in efforts to preserve the gains and momentum of the previous two decades. The Epilogue assesses the extent to which the increased politicization of women has transformed American politics, government, and public policies.

In addition to altering the political system, the resurgent women's movement has significantly reshaped scholarship, and this book rests heavily on the growing body of research on women that has accumulated over the past fifteen years. I am indebted to research assistants Lisa Chase, Susan Dyer, Phyllis Gorman, Kathleen Laughlin, and Irene Ledesma, who helped me to locate and analyze that scholarship.

The University of Missouri—St. Louis and Ohio State University aided this study in various ways, and the women's studies communities at those universities provided marvelous environments of intellectual stimulation and support. Special thanks are due to Susan Farquhar and Suzanne Hyers, whose good humor and efficiency helped me fulfill my university responsibilities with time and energy to spare for completing this book.

Jo Freeman allowed me to use her work-in-progress and Joan McLean shared information and insights based on her experience in the women's political movement. They along with Joan Huber and Leila Rupp read the entire manuscript, and I am deeply grateful for all of their thoughtful suggestions. I would also like to acknowledge the reviewers, whose critiques were quite helpful to me: Nancy Schrom Dye, Dean, Vassar College, Nancy Woloch, Columbia University, and Patricia Cohen, University of California at Santa Barbara. Finally, I thank Robert Divine and the staff at Knopf, especially Christopher Rogers, Lauren Shafer, and Elizabeth Greenspan for all the ways they have facilitated the production of this book.

Contents

Chapter 1

After Suffrage: New Opportunities and Old Obstacles

From the Seneca Falls convention in 1848, when women as a group first demanded the right to vote, until 1920, when the Nineteenth amendment was ratified, Americans engaged in intense debates about the role of women in politics. So passionately did they hold their positions that both supporters and opponents predicted that women's suffrage would usher massive changes into the body politic. Some suffragists promised a new era of political morality, the abolition of poverty, social injustice and civil strife, and world peace. Anti-suffragists warned that voting would corrupt and unsex women and destroy the home and family.

Neither the optimistic promises of suffragists nor the dire predictions of their opponents materialized. Suffrage did mark a new era for women by placing them in an independent position *vis-à-vis* the state, by challenging male authority and the assumption that fathers or husbands could speak for women, and by opening the door to participation in the entire spectrum of public affairs. Some women gained positions of influence in political parties and public office, and male officials increased their attentiveness to the voices of women.

On the other hand, the vast majority of women did not use the vote to expand their autonomy, and women were rarely elected or appointed in more than token numbers at any level of government. Women continued to organize for political pur-

1

poses, but finding no unifying goal to replace suffrage, their collective power was fragmented and diminished. Winning the most basic right of citizenship required an enormous struggle and represented a tremendous victory for women, but that right did not automatically confer real political power.[1]

POLITICAL PARTICIPATION IN THE PRE-SUFFRAGE ERA

In one sense, winning the vote represented no abrupt break with the past at all, because women had already insinuated themselves into the political process. By the twentieth century they had begun to exercise power in their own interest and especially on behalf of others. Without formal political rights, women had swelled the ranks of Progressive reform and bore considerable credit for local, state, and national measures designed to improve working conditions, eliminate slums, ameliorate poverty, protect consumers, and purify government. Women pursued reform largely through women's organizations like the Women's Christian Temperance Union, the General Federation of Women's Clubs, the National Association of Colored Women, the National Consumers' League, and the National Women's Trade Union League.

Such female-led organizations gave women opportunities to fill leadership and management positions and to develop political skills. From their efforts to improve their communities and nation outside the political mainstream, it was a logical step to demand direct political power. The ranks of suffrage supporters swelled in the twentieth century as women came to view the right to vote not simply as a matter of justice but also as a necessary means to reform society.

Some women exercised formal political power even before

1. William H. Chafe, *The American Woman: Her Changing Social, Economic, and Political Roles, 1920–1970* (New York: Oxford University Press, 1972), pp. 13–22; Ellen Carol DuBois, *Feminism and Suffrage: The Emergence of an Independent Women's Movement in America, 1848–1869* (Ithaca, NY: Cornell University Press, 1978), pp. 15–17, 45–47. For a superb analysis of suffrage and feminism in the 1910s and 1920s, see Nancy F. Cott, *The Grounding of Modern Feminism* (New Haven: Yale University Press, 1987).

Women college graduates march in suffrage parade in New York City in the 1910s. (Schlesinger Library, Radcliffe College)

the Constitution secured the right to vote for all women. By 1900, women had won partial suffrage in a number of states where they could vote in municipal elections and on school, tax, and bond issues; and they enjoyed full suffrage in Colorado, Idaho, Wyoming, and Utah. The suffrage movement entered into its most dynamic and successful stage in the 1910s, and when Congress passed the Nineteenth Amendment in 1919, women already held full voting rights in twenty states.

Long before they supported suffrage, both major parties and third parties were happy to use the skills of women as party workers. Attorney Clara Foltz, for example, campaigned for the Republican party in California in the 1880s and worked for the national committee in 1900. Another lawyer, Ellen Foster, organized the Women's National Republican Association in 1888 and mobilized voters throughout the country. In 1912 Jane Addams seconded the nomination of Theodore Roosevelt as presidential candidate of the Progressive party—a major part of whose platform was women's suffrage—served on the party's executive committee, and campaigned for Progressive candidates.[2]

As the suffrage campaign gained momentum in the 1910s, a number of women won decision-making posts in the federal government. Julia Lathrop headed the U.S. Children's Bureau; Florence Jaffray Harriman served on the Federal Industrial Relations Commission; Helen Gardener was a member of the Civil Service Commission; and Mary Van Kleek directed the wartime agency which became the Women's Bureau. The first female member of Congress, Jeannette Rankin of Montana, took her seat in the House of Representatives in 1917. Twenty-nine women served in state legislatures in 1920.

Ratification of the Nineteenth Amendment was essential to expanding women's hold on such positions, but voting rights would not automatically bring women political equality. If some suffrage advocates had been prone to exaggerate the consequences of women's full citizenship, many leaders tempered inflated hopes with sober recognition of how much it would take to translate a constitutional right into actual equality. Julia Lathrop cautioned, "Suffrage for women is not the final word . . . but it is the next step in equalizing the rights and balancing the duties" of men and women.[3]

Carrie Chapman Catt, who had led the National-American Woman Suffrage Association (NAWSA) to victory, told women that winning the vote was just the first step. Now they must struggle for a place at the apex of power within the parties. "You won't be welcome," Catt predicted, "but there is the place to go. You will see the . . . door locked tight. You will have a hard fight before you get inside . . . but you must move right up to the center."[4]

If Catt understood women's need for political education and men's reluctance to share power, she did not mention other

2. Corinne L. Gilb, "Clara Shortridge Foltz," and Frank L. Byrnes, "Judith Ellen Horton Foster," in *Notable American Women*, Volume I (Cambridge, MA: Harvard University Press, 1971), pp. 642, 652.

3. Quoted in William L. O'Neill, *Everyone Was Brave: The Rise and Fall of Feminism in America* (Chicago: Quadrangle Books, 1969), p. 67.

4. Anne Firor Scott, *The Southern Lady: From Pedestal to Politics, 1830–1930* (Chicago: University of Chicago Press, 1970), pp. 202–203.

obstacles that barred women's full grasp of political power. Most women were still subordinate within the family, occupied with child-care and other domestic reponsibilities, dependent upon fathers or husbands for their livelihood, and socialized to follow the man's lead. Outside of women's organizations and institutions, few women held leadership positions, and neither men nor women were accustomed to seeing women in decision-making roles.

Moreover, as feminist Anna Howard Shaw foresaw shortly after the suffrage victory, it would be difficult to sustain the interest in political activism which had galvanized so many women in the suffrage struggle. "I am sorry for you young women who have to carry on the work for the next ten years," Shaw commented, "for suffrage was a symbol, and now you have lost your symbol." Having won the right to vote, women lost their essential base of unity; no longer sharing as a class their exclusion from political representation, women split apart as they sought to exercise political power.[5]

Even though no longer bound together by their disenfranchisement, however, women continued to share characteristics that distinguished them politically from men. For several decades women voted in different patterns, and they experienced segregation within political parties. While formal power stayed firmly within men's grasp, women sought political influence as women and, though often fragmented, they achieved some public policy initiatives that bore their distinct imprint.

VOTING PATTERNS

In a pattern typical for newly enfranchised groups, women lagged behind men for several decades at the elementary level of political participation. It was estimated that 43 percent of eligible women went to the polls in 1920, and by 1948 when the first national surveys were taken, 56 percent of qualified women voted, in contrast to 69 percent of the eligible men. In

5. Shaw quoted in Lois Banner, *Women in Modern America: A Brief History* (New York: Harcourt Brace Jovanovich, 2nd edition, 1984), p. 139; Cott, *The Grounding of Modern Feminism*, pp. 6–8.

succeeding years, women gradually narrowed the voter turnout gap; in 1964, for the first time more women voted than men, although the turnout *rate* was still slightly higher for men. For both men and women, voter turnout correlated with higher levels of education and income and with professional and white-collar occupational status. As women advanced in income, education, and employment outside the home, their presence at the polls gradually mirrored that of men.[6]

Even though frequently rebuffed by or segregated in women's suffrage groups, a significant number of black women and their organizations had campaigned for the vote, and they resolutely sought to exercise that right. In Baltimore, for example, the black electorate more than doubled after 1920. In the first elections that brought women to the polls, Chicago elected its first black alderman, and New York City elected its first black to the state legislature. The vast majority of blacks, however, continued to reside in the South, and there black women faced the same obstacles that had disenfranchised their fathers and brothers. Though large numbers of black women attempted to register, most were defeated by unreasonable tests, tax requirements, and other tactics that Southern officials had perfected to deny the vote to black men.[7]

Black women also shared with most black men and many white women the lower income, educational, and employment levels associated with low voter turnout. As late as 1952, 87 percent of black women had never voted. In the 1950s, however, the great migration of blacks out of the South to northern and western cities where they could exercise their rights as citizens had begun to transform their voting behavior. By the end of that decade, nearly one-third of eligible black women were voting. Voter turnout among black women lagged behind that of black men, but after 1952 black women increased their turnout rate faster than did black men, white men, or white women.[8]

6. Sandra Baxter and Marjorie Lansing, eds., *Women and Politics: The Invisible Majority* (Ann Arbor: University of Michigan Press, 1980), pp. 20–39.

7. Rosalyn Terborg-Penn, "Discontented Black Feminists: Prelude and Post-script to the Passage of the Nineteenth Amendment," in Lois Scharf and Joan M. Jensen, eds., *Decades of Discontent: The Women's Movement, 1920–1940* (Westport, CT: Greenwood Press, 1983), pp. 261–76.

8. Baxter and Lansing, *Women and Politics*, pp. 73–84, 89.

Along with their lower rates of voting, white women also differed somewhat from men in their political views and in their choice of candidates. While it was not surprising that newly enfranchised women shared the same values as their husbands and consequently tended to express similar political preferences, they also displayed some independence when it came to issues. As the only legislator to vote against American entrance into both world wars, Jeannette Rankin symbolized women's more pacifistic views. Polls consistently demonstrated that women more frequently opposed military intervention and expansion of the military establishment. Many women were also found to be more supportive of government efforts to promote racial equality, assist disadvantaged groups, and alleviate poverty.[9]

A gender gap in candidate preference appeared as early as 1915 when women supported a reform candidate for mayor of Chicago while men voted for the choice of the local machine. The first significant difference in male and female voting in a presidential election occurred in 1952 when women's support for Dwight D. Eisenhower surpassed that of men by six percentage points. Political experts linked that preference for Eisenhower to women's concern about the Korean War and its attendant disruption of the economy and their displeasure with corruption in the Truman administration. In the post-suffrage era, women favored the Republican party slightly more than men did, but that difference was linked to characteristics of the female voting population such as higher income and educational levels, and not to gender. The independent female voting bloc anticipated by some suffragists simply failed to materialize.[10]

WOMEN AND THE POLITICAL PARTIES

The experience of women in party organizations fulfilled Carrie Chapman Catt's forecast of a long struggle before women could exercise real political clout. Growing numbers of women volunteered for local party work—performing secretarial chores,

9. *Ibid.*, pp. 57–60.

10. Chafe, *The American Woman*, p. 26; Baxter and Lansing, *Women and Politics*, pp. 61–62, 66–67.

holding coffee parties for candidates, and serving as canvassers and election clerks and inspectors—but relatively few rose to leadership posts. As late as 1956, when there were more than 3,000 county organizations, women headed fewer than one hundred. Scarcer yet were female chairs of state committees, and their tenure in those positions was usually limited to a year or two. Much more typically, women held the post of vice-chair. Asked about what roles women played in politics, one of these activists responded, "to do the work that men do not have the time to do." Another reported that men "look around for the nearest woman every time there's drudgery to be done, but don't consult them otherwise."[11]

Beginning in the 1920s both parties instituted reforms that gave women nominal equality. National committees included one man and one woman from each state, and women served as vice-chairs of each national committee. Such representation, however, was more token than real. According to Eleanor Roosevelt, "fifty-fifty looks better on paper than it has worked out in practice. Too often the vice chairmen and the committeewomen are selected by the men, who naturally pick women who will go along with them and not give them any trouble. Thus they are apt to be mere stooges. . . ."[12]

By the 1940s women had also won equal representation on the parties' platform committees and other important bodies. Powerful women, such as Democrats Mary (Molly) Dewson and Emma Guffey Miller, and Republicans Katherine Howard and Ivy Baker Priest, occasionally held such posts, but equal representation failed to challenge the male monopoly over real power. Until the 1960s, party conventions rather than primary elections held sway in candidate selection, and in this arena women were woefully underrepresented. Women gradually increased their presence at national conventions, but until the 1970s women never constituted more than 20 percent of delegates at any party convention.[13]

11. Martin Gruberg, *Women in American Politics: An Assessment and Sourcebook* (Oshkosh, WI: Academia Press, 1968), pp. 48–53, 64–70.

12. *Ibid.*, pp. 59–64; Eleanor Roosevelt and Lorena A. Hickok, *Ladies of Courage* (New York: G. P. Putnam's Sons, 1954), p. 16.

13. Susan M. Hartmann, *The Home Front and Beyond: American Women in the 1940s* (Boston: Twayne Publishers, 1982), pp. 152–53.

Victims of double discrimination, black women faced even greater obstacles to exercising power within the political parties. Those few who rose to leadership did so primarily in party units concerned with "colored" voters. Daisy Lampkin, who had organized black women for suffrage in Pittsburgh, went to the Republican national convention in 1928 as an alternate and became vice-chair of the Colored Voters' Division of the national committee. Her fellow Republican, Irene McCoy Gaines, led the Illinois Federation of Republican Colored Women's Clubs and served as Republican state committeewoman. Mary Church Terrell organized black women in the eastern states for the Republican National Committee, and played a similar role in the 1930 Senatorial campaign of Ruth Hanna McCormick. Crystal Fauset served as director of Colored Women's Activities for the Democratic National Committee and in 1938 became the first black woman elected to a state legislature. Fauset served only one term in the Pennsylvania statehouse, and in the 1940s she left the party, feeling that it failed to appreciate black women's aspirations for political participation.[14]

White women found their greatest opportunities for party leadership through a different form of segregation. On the eve of the suffrage victory, both major parties established women's divisions. These bodies suffered the obvious liabilities of separate organizations for women. Their existence made it easier for male leaders to ignore women's concerns in the parties' major decision-making bodies and thus to keep women and their interests "ghettoized." But the women's divisions brought more advantages than disadvantages. Within them women planned and directed their own activities, monopolized leadership positions, and developed political skills. Moreover, the women's divisions eventually proved to male politicians that women could be mobilized as voters and party activists and could make important contributions to party goals.

Molly Dewson orchestrated the most impressive demonstration of women's potential when she took over the Wo-

14. *Ibid.*, p. 154; Terborg-Penn, "Discontented Black Feminists," p. 275; Elizabeth F. Howard, "Daisy Lampkin," in Barbara Sicherman and Carol Hurd Green, eds., *Notable American Women: The Modern Period* (Cambridge: Harvard University Press, 1980), pp. 406–8; Ruth Bogin, "Crystal Fauset," *Ibid.*, pp. 224–25.

men's Division of the Democratic party in the 1930s and molded it into a vital element in Democratic politics. A good friend of Eleanor and Franklin Roosevelt, with experience in reform movements and New York politics, Dewson brought to her job a variety of ideas about how to mobilize women. Under her leadership, the Women's Division recruited 15,000 women to become experts on one aspect of New Deal policy and then to canvass their communities educating voters on that program. The Women's Division published a party magazine, the *Democratic Digest*, increasing its circulation from 1,600 in 1935 to 26,500 in 1938, and wrote and distributed millions of fact sheets which represented 80 percent of the party literature distributed in 1936. In that election Dewson's associates mobilized more than 60,000 women to campaign door-to-door. Regional conferences where women heard from government officials was another Women's Division innovation which provided political education for women and increased their commitment to the party. When the division held a national conference in 1940, 5,000 women paid their own expenses to learn about the Roosevelt administration's progress and future plans.[15]

Republican women also had to struggle to convince men that women could be an effective political force. When Massachusetts Republican Katherine Howard saw her name on a mailing from the state Finance Committee that discussed a meeting to which she had not been invited, she protested: "I was not in the habit of having my name appear on circulars without my consent. . . . I was not giving my time to the Republican party just to be an ornament at the head table." Having established her place on the Finance Committee in fact as well as on paper, Howard organized an extremely effective fund-raising campaign among women. Demonstrations of similar success at fund-raising by women in other states won women three seats on the national Republican Finance Committee where they served for the first time in 1951. In 1948 Howard herself became the first woman elected secretary of the Repub-

15. Chafe, *The American Woman*, pp. 39–41; Roosevelt and Hickok, *Ladies of Courage*, pp. 11–21; Susan Ware, *Beyond Suffrage: Women in the New Deal* (Cambridge: Harvard University Press, 1981), pp. 68–77, 82–86.

lican National Committee, and in 1952 presidential candidate Dwight D. Eisenhower appointed her the only woman on his Campaign and Policy Committee.[16]

While the Women's Divisions in both parties had a measure of autonomy, their budgets and very existence were dependent on the male leadership. After the Democratic defeat in the election of 1952, party officials abolished the Women's Division without even consulting the women; national committee-women first learned about it through the newspapers. Abolition of the Women's Division would save money, and it was billed as a means of "integrating" women into the total party structure. In fact, it destroyed their independent base, redistributed their activities among units controlled by men, and removed the *Democratic Digest* from their control. Within months Republican women experienced a similar defeat.[17]

The cavalier dismissal of the Women's Divisions belied their importance both to women and to the parties. They had provided opportunities for women to develop and use political skills, and they had mobilized thousands of women to contribute to party objectives. These contributions were not offered without cost, for women leaders used them to exact new opportunities. As Molly Dewson claimed after the 1932 campaign, "The Women's Division has something to say about these things. We did a lot to elect [Roosevelt]. I know I did, and he knows I did." Dewson's clout, for example, won Democratic women equal representation on the Platform Committee from which they had been excluded until 1936, and Howard effected a similar coup with the Republican Finance Committee.[18]

WOMEN APPOINTED TO OFFICE

Female party leaders also used their influence to win government appointments for women. A surge of female appointments occurred in the 1930s when Molly Dewson and Eleanor Roosevelt exerted continuous pressure on the president and his

16. Roosevelt and Hickok, *Ladies of Courage*, pp. 19–20, 31, 40–46.
17. *Ibid.*, pp. 29–34; Hartmann, *The Home Front and Beyond*, pp. 155–56.
18. Ware, *Beyond Suffrage*, pp. 57–58.

Mary McLeod Bethune, founder of the National Council of Negro Women and New Deal official, with Eleanor Roosevelt. (Courtesy of the Bethune Museum and Archives National Historic Site)

political advisors to reward women with patronage. Even before Roosevelt won the presidential nomination, Dewson began a campaign for the appointment of Frances Perkins as Secretary of Labor. Perkins's appointment, and those of Ruth Bryan Owen as Minister to Denmark, and Florence Allen to the U.S. Court of Appeals, were all firsts and important symbols for women, but women won numerous executive posts elsewhere in the federal bureaucracy, especially in the New Deal agencies created in response to the Depression. Eleanor Roosevelt also used her influence to secure the first important position in the federal government for a black woman. Mary McLeod Bethune directed Negro affairs in the National Youth Administration and was one of the few blacks with access to the White House. Most of the women who won appointments during the 1930s were veterans of suffrage and social welfare activism, and (with the exception of Bethune) they constituted a Washington network in pursuit of social reform and progress for women.[19]

Bipartisan coalitions of women's organizations formed in the 1940s to press for female appointments; they compiled lists of qualified women, submitted names, and mobilized pressure on appropriate officials. Women appointees, however, owed most to the efforts and skills of female party leaders. India Edwards, as head of the Women's Division of the Democratic National Committee, worked hard and effectively for Harry S Truman's election in 1948. Having won access to the president as well as his confidence, Edwards presented Truman with carefully pre- pared cases for women appointees when high positions became vacant. In response, Truman gave Eugenie Anderson, party leader from Minnesota, the first female diplomatic appoint- ment at the ambassador level. He appointed another party ac- tivist, Georgia Neese Clark as Treasurer of the United States, as well as Anna Rosenberg as Assistant Secretary of Defense, and Freida Hennock to the Federal Communications Commission. Truman refused, however, to appoint a woman to his cabinet, and he vetoed Edwards's recommendation of a woman for the Supreme Court on the grounds that the male judges would not be able to relax around a woman.[20]

When Eisenhower was elected in 1952, Republican women promoted female appointments with equal zeal. Eisenhower named Oveta Culp Hobby Secretary of Health, Education and Welfare, only the second woman to hold a cabinet post; he rewarded Katherine Howard's contributions to his campaign with a high post in the Civil Defense Administration; and he appointed the first woman to the White House staff. In fact, Eisenhower's record on appointing women surpassed Tru- man's, just as Truman's had exceeded that of Roosevelt.[21]

All the fanfare attending these appointments, however, be- lied their negligible effect on the overall political status of women. Few of the presidential appointees identified with is- sues of particular concern to women, and even if they had, their numbers were too few to influence policy. Women never con-

19. *Ibid.*, pp. 6–17, 45–67.

20. Cynthia E. Harrison, *On Account of Sex: The Politics of Women's Issues, 1945–1968* (Berkeley: University of California Press, 1988), pp. 52–58.

21. *Ibid.*, pp. 58–62; Roosevelt and Hickok, *Ladies of Courage*, pp. 33, 46.

stituted more than 3 percent of all appointments requiring Senate confirmation. Nor did they fare any better in Civil Service positions. In fact, federal agencies actually specified that men only were to be appointed to 94 percent of mid- to high-level openings. In 1960, women filled just twenty-four of the 2,050 supergrade positions in the federal bureaucracy, and they held only three of the 425 federal judgeships.[22]

WOMEN IN ELECTIVE OFFICE

Opportunities for women to exercise power in elective office were also severely limited. As would be expected, women did best at the local level, but even in positions more likely to be filled by women, they were vastly underrepresented. In 1960 women comprised just 10 percent of school board members, and more than half of the nation's school boards had no women at all. Women were elected to municipal legislative bodies in Cleveland and New York in the 1920s, but such major cities as Milwaukee, Minneapolis, Philadelphia, and Los Angeles failed to place one woman on the city council before 1950. Occasionally, a woman served as mayor, but usually for a brief term in a small city or town. Lawyer Dorothy M. Lee, veteran of the Oregon house and senate, was an exception, serving as mayor of Portland from 1948 until 1952 when she was defeated by a candidate whose slogan was "a man for a man's job." Women made their greatest gains in municipal government during the 1950s. While ten women occupied the position of mayor in 1952, 112 did so in 1964; the number of women in county positions increased from 10,000 to 20,000, and at the end of the 1950s, women filled 10,000 city posts.[23]

When the Nineteenth Amendment was ratified, sixty women had already won seats in state legislatures, and twenty-nine were serving in 1920. By 1963, women had increased their representation to 351, but this represented less than 5 percent

22. Harrison, *On Account of Sex*, pp. 62–64; Mary M. Lepper, "A Study of Career Structures of Federal Executives: A Focus on Women," in Jane S. Jacquette, ed., *Women in Politics* (New York: John Wiley and Sons, 1974), p. 113.

23. *Ibid.*, pp. 201–18; Roosevelt and Hickok, *Ladies of Courage*, pp. 76–81.

of all state lawmakers. Women frequently moved into state politics from civic activism in women's organizations such as the League of Women Voters, and the majority of successful women served in small states with disproportionately large legislatures. In these states, districts were smaller, it was easier and less expensive for women to campaign, and the large number of seats along with the low salaries attached to these offices reduced the competition. Minority women were virtually absent from state office. Mrs. E. Howard Harper was appointed in 1927 to take her dead husband's seat in the West Virginia legislature, but the first black woman was not elected until 1938 when Democrat Crystal Fauset served briefly in the Pennsylvania Assembly. By 1960 only a handful of black women had won seats in statehouses.[24]

The two women governors before 1960 owed their offices to their husbands. In 1925, Wyoming voters elected Nellie Tayloe Ross to a full term after she had succeeded her husband who died in office. Though she narrowly lost reelection, Ross later became vice-chair of the Democratic National Committee, and when Roosevelt named her Director of the Mint, she joined the network of Democratic women that had formed around the New Deal in the 1930s. Miriam A. ("Ma") Ferguson also succeeded her husband who was still alive but had been impeached. Her slogan was "Two governors for the price of one," and Texas voters had no doubts about who would actually run the administration when she was elected in 1924 and—after two losses—again in 1932.[25]

Husbands were likewise crucial for a large number of the early group of national legislators. In nominating a woman to succeed her husband, the parties could avoid intraparty conflict, gain the sympathy vote, and capitalize on a man's reputation. Around one-third of the women who served in Congress before 1960 filled unexpired terms of their dead husbands and usually lasted no more than one term. But the 1940s witnessed

24. Gruberg, *Women in Politics,* pp. 169–70; Emmy F. Werner, "Women in the State Legislatures," *Western Political Quarterly* 21 (March 1968):42–44; Gerda Lerner, ed., *Black Women in White America: A Documentary History* (New York: Random House, 1972), pp. 321–22.

25. Ware, *Beyond Suffrage,* pp. 152–53; Gruberg, *Women in Politics,* pp. 189–90.

a trend towards increasing longevity, and after 1940 more women won seats on their own. No more than eleven served in Congress at any one time before 1950, but by 1961 they numbered seventeen in the House and two in the Senate.[26]

Women had very few role models for office-holding, and the socialization of both men and women encouraged conceptions of politics as a male field. Public-opinion polls taken in 1945 found women more inclined than men to support women for high office, but among neither sex did a majority favor having women at the highest levels of government. Most important, women with political aspirations at all levels had to overcome the reluctance of party leaders to support them. India Edwards believed that parties usually backed women when "they think it's a lost cause but they know they have to have *some* candidate." When after eight years of service in the House, Margaret Chase Smith wanted to represent Maine in the Senate, she was rebuffed by Republican leaders and had to win the nomination on her own. In fact, voters seemed more supportive of women than did party leaders. Successful women candidates found it much harder to secure the nomination than to win the election.[27]

Women at all levels of government usually served apprenticeships in party work, but a majority also developed political knowledge and skills through leadership in women's organizations. For example, Margaret Chase Smith, who represented Maine in the House from 1940 to 1948 and in the Senate from 1948 to 1972, had been president of her state Federation of Business and Professional Women and member of its national board. Eugenie Anderson had cut her political teeth in the Minnesota League of Women Voters. Before her election to two terms in the Oregon legislature and one in the U.S. Senate, Maurine Neuberger was active in the American Association of University Women (AAUW) as well as the League of Women

---

26. Hartmann, *The Home Front and Beyond*, pp. 149–50; Naomi B. Lynn, "American Women and the Political Process," in Jo Freeman, ed., *Women: A Feminist Perspective* (Palo Alto, CA: Mayfield Publishing Company, 2nd ed., 1979), 419–21.

27. Hartmann, *The Home Front and Beyond*, p. 150; Peggy Lamson, *Few Are Chosen: American Women in Political Life Today* (Boston: Houghton Mifflin, 1968), pp. xxiii, 12–14.

Voters (LWV). Eleanor Roosevelt developed her leadership capabilities, a network of political friends, and her unique commitment to public affairs through involvement in the LWV, the Women's Trade Union League, and the New York City Club.[28]

If the LWV's strict nonpartisanship limited women's impact on electoral politics, the League did serve as a kind of farm club for women politicians. In the 1950s, 300 officers and board members resigned each year to enter partisan politics. Ella Grasso, who would eventually hold Connecticut's highest office, described both the training and motivational functions of the LWV: "It teaches you to understand issues, to formulate programs, and to learn legislative procedures. However, when . . . you want to translate legislative programs into action, then you have to learn to work within the political structure." Elected to the Connecticut General Assembly in 1952, Grasso centered much of her energy on objectives from the League's program.[27]

PRESSURE-GROUP POLITICS

Women's organizations not only motivated and trained women for public office, they also operated as pressure groups. They partially compensated for the small number of women in decision-making posts by mobilizing popular support for public policies of particular concern to women. Women's minimal appearance at centers of power did not mean that women as a group were without influence. In the post-suffrage era substantial numbers of women organized to shape public opinion, mobilize voters behind female-defined issues, and exert direct pressure on legislators and administrators. But diverse organizations never coalesced around a program addressing women's interests that was sufficient to marshal a mass movement.

While dozens of national women's organizations played some role in the political arena, a few were especially active,

28. Hartmann, *The Home Front and Beyond,* p. 14; Roosevelt and Hickok, *Ladies of Courage,* pp. 144–47, 216.

29. Lamson, *Few Are Chosen,* pp. 216–17; Marion Sanders, *The Lady and the Vote* (Boston: Houghton Mifflin, 1956), p. 119.

visible, and influential. Established on the eve of the suffrage victory to replace the NAWSA, the League of Women Voters devoted itself to combating the remaining legal discriminations against women, to educating women to their new responsibilities as members of the electorate, and to training them for party and government leadership. With 100,000 members in the early 1930s, the League mobilized womanpower to further the reform efforts that had engaged so many women since the 1890s. Nationally and in local and state branches, League women sponsored voter education projects; pressed for reforms in governmental structures and practices; campaigned for a variety of measures dealing with labor, children, conservation, and peace; and, especially in the early post-suffrage years, worked for laws to expand women's rights and opportunities.

While the LWV was the direct descendant of the mainstream wing of the suffrage movement, the National Woman's Party (NWP) represented the more militant suffragists. In 1921, its leader Alice Paul pointed out that even with the vote, "women . . . are still in every way subordinate to men before the law, in the professions, in the church, in industry, and in the home." Consequently, the NWP dedicated itself single-mindedly to securing total equality for women, and from 1923 on concentrated its energies on passage of an Equal Rights Amendment (ERA) to the Constitution. Representing only 8,000 women at its peak, and for many years nearly the only advocate for the ERA, the NWP lobbied in every Congress and sought to build up popular support, thereby keeping that issue alive until more propitious times.[30]

A number of other women's organizations had fairly sharply defined foci, though none so narrow as that of the NWP. College graduates organized in the American Association of University Women (AAUW), which emphasized educational reform and educational and career opportunities for women. The National Federation of Business and Professional Women (BPW), comprised mainly of women in white-collar jobs and professions, also emphasized employment opportunity. Like the LWV and NWP, these organizations represented primarily white, middle-class women, and each had around 70,000 members by the 1940s. Promoting the interests of working-class women were

30. Chafe, *The American Woman*, pp. 112–31.

the National Women's Trade Union League (WTUL) and the National Consumers League (NCL). Most vigorous in the pre-suffrage years, these two groups enjoyed successes in the 1920s and 1930s, but declined thereafter. Female pacifists worked through the Women's International League for Peace and Freedom (WILPF), which like the WTUL and NCL reaped gains in the first two post-suffrage decades, but which survived those groups to influence policy again in the 1960s.

With few exceptions, notably WILPF and WTUL, these women's organizations claimed the allegiance of few black women. While a number of white women's groups addressed racial problems, they either barred black members or segregated them. Politically active black women thus worked through their own organizations like the National Association of Colored Women (NACW). Failing to make significant headway in interracial cooperation with white women, they focused attention on race issues and mobilized an especially vigorous attack against lynching. Founded by Mary McLeod Bethune in 1935, the National Council of Negro Women (NCNW) became the largest among black women's organizations. Its concentration on problems of the entire race did not prevent the NCNW from seeking specific opportunities for women, as it did in pressing Roosevelt for the appointment of black women in federal agencies.[31]

A few black women sought civil rights for their race more directly, anticipating the mass protests that would characterize the black freedom struggle in the 1960s. Women participated in the nonviolent resistance activities pioneered by the Congress of Racial Equality (CORE) in the early 1940s, and a group of female students at Howard University staged sit-ins to integrate cafeterias in the nation's capital in 1943 and 1944. Among these young women were Pauli Murray, who subsequently played a leadership role in the feminist movement of the 1960s and 1970s, and Patricia Roberts (Harris), whose political career would culminate with cabinet posts in the administration of Jimmy Carter.[32]

While white and black women pursued political objectives

---

31. Terborg-Penn, "Discontented Black Feminists," pp. 268–74.

32. Pauli Murray, *Song In A Weary Throat: An American Pilgrimage* (New York: Harper and Row, 1987), pp. 198–209, 220–31.

largely along separate paths, white women did achieve intraracial cooperation in pursuit of public policies of benefit to large groups of women. Established in 1919 as a common lobby, the Women's Joint Congressional Committee brought together several women's groups, including the LWV, the BPW, the AAUW, the NCL, and the WTUL, as well as religious organizations like the National Council of Jewish Women, in efforts to enact legislation dealing with education, child labor, peace, maternal health, and other issues. The Committee's greatest triumph was its defeat of the medical lobby to win the 1921 Sheppard-Towner Act, which provided federal funds for maternal and infant health care. Through collective action, women gained objectives in the areas of citizenship rights, child labor, consumer protection, and civil service reform at the national level as well as numerous state and local measures regulating the conditions of women's employment, increasing government protection of children, granting women the right to jury service, and reforming municipal and state governments.[33]

Politically active women could not, however, avoid a severe conflict over the proposed Equal Rights Amendment. The NWP's introduction of that measure in 1923 alienated most active women who opposed such an amendment in large part because it would invalidate state laws governing conditions for employed women. These laws set limits on the numbers of hours women could work, restricted night employment, mandated rest periods, seats, and other facilities, required health and safety precautions, and barred women from some occupations altogether. NWP women believed that such sex-specific legislation obstructed women's advance in employment, cultivated the image of women as weak and vulnerable, and damaged their self-esteem. Opponents of the ERA, on the other hand, argued that these sex-specific laws were essential because the courts had disallowed such protective measures for male workers, and the majority of women workers did not have labor unions to defend their interests. Without these safeguards, they argued, women would face intolerable exploitation in the work-

---

33. For women's activities in one state, see Felice D. Gordon, *After Winning: The Legacy of the New Jersey Suffragists, 1920–1947* (New Brunswick, NJ: Rutgers University Press, 1986).

place. The argument continued through the 1950s, exhausting a large measure of politically active women's energy and diluting female power by contributing to a public impression that no common purpose existed among women.

After a decade of suffrage, women found legislators at all levels less responsive than they had been in the wake of the Nineteenth Amendment. By the end of the 1920s it was clear that a "women's bloc" at the polls, initially feared by many legislators, had not materialized. Women did, however, continue to exert collective pressure: in the 1930s and 1940s they made some headway at the federal level against discrimination against women workers, and they continued to make piecemeal improvements in women's legal status at the state level.

By the post–World War II era, most major women's organizations had diluted their earlier emphasis on obtaining women-specific policies, but four goals continued to claim the energies of some segments of organized womanhood: (1) Coalitions of women's groups and female party leaders pressured male officials to appoint women to high government positions; (2) The National Woman's Party, now joined by a few additional groups such as the National Federation of Business and Professional Women, continued to lobby vigorously for the Equal Rights Amendment; (3) As an alternative to the amendment, opponents called for a federal commission to investigate the status of women and recommend policy changes; (4) A coalition of women's organizations and labor unions pressed Congress for a national equal pay law.[34]

CONCLUSIONS

By the end of the first four post-suffrage decades American women had enlarged their involvement in politics, which had begun even before they enjoyed full citizenship. Women had nearly closed the gender gap in voter turnout. They had volunteered for party work by the thousands, and a few had devel-

34. Leila J. Rupp and Verta Taylor, *Survival in the Doldrums: The American Women's Rights Movement, 1945 to the 1960s* (New York: Oxford University Press, 1987), pp. 45–52.

oped skills, reputations, and power bases sufficient to gain the respect and attention of male leaders. As elected or appointed government officials, women had demonstrated that qualities of political leadership did not depend on gender. And, especially through their single-sex organizations, women had contributed to the shaping of public policies.

What distinguished women from men as political actors was their absence in all but token numbers from the visible, central seats of decision-making. Sex-role socialization continued to define politics as a man's world and to discourage women from careers that typically provided stepping-stones to political leadership. Those women who overcame such barriers to political aspiration still faced male reluctance to share power and popular misgivings about the propriety and capability of women for high office.

If voting rights did not manifestly reshape the lives of most women, by the 1950s other developments had brought more dramatic changes and laid the foundation for women to launch a vigorous attack on the male monopoly of politics and policy. In the years following World War II, women entered the labor force in ever-increasing numbers, a movement especially pronounced among married women. Women also flocked to colleges and universities, attaining new capabilities and expectations that for many could not be satisfied within traditional roles. Although women had more children in the postwar decade—a phenomenon of such significance as to evoke the term "baby boom"—they were completing childbearing at younger ages. Together these developments reduced the domestic claims on women, confronted larger numbers of women with sex discrimination in the public sphere, and formed the preconditions for a profound challenge to the traditional distribution of labor, roles, rights, and privileges according to gender.

Chapter 2

Women in Grass-Roots Movements of the 1960s

Striking changes in women's life patterns combined with dramatic upheavals in the body politic in the 1960s to push women into the political arena with a force not seen since the peak of the suffrage struggle. Ever larger numbers of women entered the work force and attended college. Women had fewer children and experienced greater marital instability, as the birth rate declined and divorce rose sharply. Moreover, the 1960s spawned a host of grass-roots movements that engaged large numbers of women, developed their political skills and self-confidence, and led them to reflect on their own exclusion from formal political power.

Encouraged by the liberal rhetoric of John F. Kennedy's "New Frontier," which promised to "get the country moving again" and to tackle economic and social problems that had accumulated since World War II, large numbers of Americans seized on the possibilities for reform. Especially unique to the politics of the 1960s were the massive use of sit-ins, marches, and other unconventional tactics by pressure groups as well as the tendency to question traditional authority, power relations, economic arrangements, and social values. Most prominent among protest groups, blacks and youths challenged establishment politics and expanded the locus of political conflict and negotiation from the halls of government to the streets.

Women helped to shape these protests, and they in turn saw their lives reshaped by their involvement in the black freedom struggle, the Chicano movement, welfare rights activism, student protests, and movements against the Vietnam War. Women not only joined the struggles on the political spectrum's left, they also counted significantly in the backlash against reform.

THE BLACK FREEDOM STRUGGLE

Of all the movements giving vitality to the politics of the 1960s, the civil-rights movement did most to transform the possibilities for women in the public arena. That movement afforded broad scope for female participation and leadership, and it engaged women at the grass-roots level at rates nearly equal to those of men. It provided the model and inspiration for other disadvantaged groups which derived their ideologies, tactics, and legislative agendas from the civil-rights example. Moreover, in their struggle for racial justice, some women became aware of the limitations they experienced as women and expressed the first stirrings of the women's liberation movement.

Given the centrality of women in black protest and the effects that movement would have on women's aspirations, it is fitting that the Montgomery, Alabama bus boycott—the event by which many historians mark the beginnings of the civil-rights movement—began when a woman, Rosa L. Parks, defied local segregation laws by refusing to give up her bus seat to a white man. Black protest was as old as American racism, and the Montgomery movement had been preceded by earlier boycotts, demonstrations, and sit-ins. But the Montgomery protest mobilized larger numbers, lasted longer, received national publicity, demonstrated the efficacy of massive nonviolent direct action, and launched the leadership of Martin Luther King, Jr. and the Southern Christian Leadership Conference. The civil-rights movement that swept through the entire South a few years later had as its primary aims to end segregation in public places, to attack employment discrimination, and to overthrow the system that denied the vote to most southern blacks.[1]

Rosa Parks's defiance of segregation was consistent with her

1. Aldon D. Morris, *The Origins of the Civil Rights Movement: Black Communities Organizing for Change* (New York: The Free Press, 1984), pp. 1–4, 17–25.

personal history and that of other women in the black freedom struggle. She had been secretary of the local National Association for the Advancement of Colored People (NAACP) since 1943; had organized the NAACP Youth Council and served as its adviser; and had been ejected from seats designated for whites before. Four months before her arrest, Parks had attended workshops at the Highlander Folk School, established at Monteagle, Tennessee in the 1930s as an interracial enterprise designed to empower oppressed people. At Highlander, Parks met Septima Clark, a teacher who became director of education there after South Carolina school officials fired her for her NAACP activities. At the time of the Montgomery boycott, Clark was working with Bernice Robinson, a beautician from Johns Island, South Carolina, to set up citizenship schools where blacks prepared themselves to register to vote.[2]

Other black women assumed prominent roles in organizing the Montgomery boycott. Local professional black women had founded the Women's Political Council (WPC) in 1946 to register black women to vote, and it had previously confronted the City Commission with grievances regarding the bus system, public parks and playgrounds, and public employment of blacks. The WPC was headed by Jo Ann Robinson, an English teacher at Alabama State College who herself had been threatened and humiliated by a bus driver when she inadvertently sat in the white section. Her organization had already discussed plans for a bus boycott, and when Parks was arrested on December 1, 1955, it was ready to move. WPC members consulted with E. D. Nixon, an activist who had headed both the Montgomery NAACP and the local Brotherhood of Sleeping Car Porters. Nixon had worked with Parks for years and was looking for a situation around which to mount a boycott.[3]

While Nixon mobilized support from local ministers, Robinson activated members of the three WPC chapters and enlisted students and faculty at Alabama State College. Overnight they prepared thousands of information sheets and blanketed the

2. *Ibid.*, pp. 51–52, 141–55.

3. David J. Garrow, ed., *The Montgomery Boycott and the Women Who Started It: The Memoir of Jo Ann Gibson Robinson* (Knoxville: University of Tennessee Press, 1987), pp. 15–16, 20–25; Morris, *Origins of the Civil Rights Movement,* pp. 52–63.

black community with them. On December 5, leaders of local
black organizations founded the Montgomery Improvement
Association (MIA), electing King as president. Jo Ann Robinson
served on its Executive Board, was a member of the team that
negotiated with local and state officials, and edited the monthly
MIA Newsletter. The MIA organized an alternative transportation system, marshalled the black community behind a massive
boycott that lasted nearly a year, and mounted a legal challenge
culminating in a United States Supreme Court ruling striking
down the bus segregation laws in November 1956.[4]

In response to the Montgomery movement and protests
springing up in Tallahassee, Birmingham, Little Rock, and
other southern cities, the Southern Christian Leadership Conference (SCLC) was formed to unify and expand the struggles.
Among the initiators of SCLC was Ella Baker, a southerner by
birth who had spent her adult life in New York City. Baker was
a seasoned community organizer who had developed NAACP
chapters throughout the country as its national field secretary
and director of branches. Although male ministers controlled
the SCLC, Baker set up its office in Atlanta, was its first associate
director, and temporarily served as executive director. Along
with her organizational skills, Baker brought a vision of a movement that was democratic and decentralized and relied for
leadership upon developing the skills and powers of ordinary
people at local levels. Such a vision was often at odds with the
charismatic style of leadership exercised and preferred by King
and other prominent pastors. Baker's differences with SCLC
ministers over centralized versus "grass-roots" leadership, her
insistence that women and young people be involved throughout the organization, and the inability of most black ministers
to recognize the potential of women for leadership, all served
to limit the full impact of Baker's talents in the SCLC. Yet she
played a crucial role in its origins and was to be even more
important in the second new civil-rights organization.[5]

Black churches figured prominently in the civil-rights move-

4. Morris, *Origins of the Civil Rights Movement*, pp. 52–63; Garrow, *The Montgomery Boycott*, pp. 43–47, 74, 80, 129.

5. Garrow, *The Montgomery Boycott*, pp. 102–4, 112–15; Paula Giddings, *When
and Where I Enter: The Impact of Black Women on Race and Sex in America*
(New York: William Morrow, 1984), pp. 268–69.

ment, and that prominence circumscribed the potential of black women for leadership in the struggle. The major institution in the black community and the only significant autonomous one, the black church held the allegiance of masses of people, served as the financial base of the movement, provided educated and skilled leaders, and furnished meeting places and a communications network. But while women formed the bulwark of black religion, Baker "knew from the beginning that as a woman, an older woman, in a group of ministers who are accustomed to having women largely as supporters, there was no place for me to have come into a leadership role." Male associates of SCLC confirmed Baker's perception that King and other ministers did not view women as equally worthy and capable of leadership positions.[6]

Along with boycotts, civil-rights activists in the late 1950s increasingly employed the tactic of sit-ins, which they conducted in at least sixteen cities from 1957 to 1960. Usually launched by the Congress of Racial Equality (CORE) or by NAACP Youth Councils which favored a more activist approach than their legalistically oriented parent body, these sit-ins were sometimes led by women. In 1957, for example, high school teacher Clara Luper trained members of the Oklahoma City Youth Council in nonviolent direct action and in 1958 led them in sit-ins at the Katz Drug Store. A few months later, her friend Shirley Scaggins organized sit-ins in Tulsa. These and similar protests formed a precedent for four freshmen at North Carolina Agricultural and Technical College when they sat in at the Woolworth lunch counter in Greensboro, North Carolina in February 1960.[7]

On the second day of the Woolworth sit-in, twenty-five men and four women joined the "Greensboro Four." Two days later, while mobs of white students harassed the protesters, three white women from the University of North Carolina Women's College joined the black students at the lunch counter. Within

6. Morris, *Origins of the Civil Rights Movement*, pp. 4–7; Gerda Lerner, ed., *Black Women in White America: A Documentary History* (New York: Vintage Books, 1973), pp. 350–52; David Garrow, *Bearing the Cross: Martin Luther King, Jr., and the Southern Christian Leadership Conference* (New York: William Morrow, 1986), pp. 141, 655 (fn. 12).

7. Morris, *Origins of the Civil Rights Movement*, pp. 188–93.

two months the sit-in movement spread to more than fifty cit-ies. Most of these demonstrations did not occur spontaneously but were encouraged, planned, and sustained by adult activists linked to SCLC, CORE, or the NAACP. Ella Baker telephoned people she knew at numerous colleges, asking, "What are you going to do? It's time to move." Daisy Bates, who had led the integration of Little Rock High School in 1957, recruited stu-dents from Philander Smith College, whom she trained for local protests.[8]

Uncomfortable with SCLC's caution and perceiving the need for "the development of people who are interested not in being leaders as much as in developing leadership among other people," Baker moved quickly to capitalize on the students' enthusiasm and to prepare them to expand the struggle. With the sponsorship of SCLC, in April 1960 she called a meeting of representatives from the major protest groups, student organi-zations, and civil-rights groups to be held at her alma mater, Shaw University in Raleigh, North Carolina. Encouraged by Baker, the students resisted pressures to join established civil-rights organizations and formed their own Student Nonviolent Coordinating Committee (SNCC). Baker found space for the new organization at SCLC's Atlanta office, recruited Jane Stem-bridge, a white student, to set up the office, and kept SNCC going while an organizational structure was developed. More than twice the age of SNCC's average member, Baker actively participated in its major projects and decisions throughout its lifetime. According to SNCC leader John Lewis, "in terms of ideas and philosophy and commitment she was one of the youngest persons in the movement."[9]

Baker's vision of a movement committed to "group-cen-tered leadership," local control, and opposition to hierarchical authority blossomed in SNCC in the early 1960s. Consequently, SNCC offered more scope for full female participation than any other organization in the movement. Its commitment to greatly intensifying attacks on the color line made any individual—male or female—welcome. In fact, large numbers of women

8. *Ibid.*, pp. 197–203; Clayborne Carson, *In Struggle: SNCC and the Black Awakening of the 1960s* (Cambridge, MA: Harvard University Press), pp. 9–12.
9. *Ibid.*, pp. 19–26.

demonstrated that men had no monopoly over courage, determination, and willingness to put their bodies on the line. In the early 1960s nearly half of the students taking active part in sit-ins and in freedom rides designed to integrate public transportation were women.[10]

When SNCC adopted the tactic of "jail, no bail," to emphasize its refusal to compromise with an evil system, women too filled the southern prisons. Two of the most prominent black women in SNCC, Diane Nash and Ruby Doris Smith, joined two male volunteers in one of the first jail-ins, spending a month in the Rock Hill, South Carolina jail. Later in 1961, Bertha Gober was jailed twice during attacks on the system of segregation in Albany, Georgia. Some teachers at Albany State supported the students, who comprised the majority of the Albany Movement. Trois J. Latimer, for example, urged her students to "get out of here and fight for your rights." But college authorities opposed the demonstrations and expelled Gober, a not uncommon fate for students who defied the conservatism of their black institutions. The most active women endured prison more than once. Arrested in Mississippi in 1962 after she had married and was pregnant, Diane Nash refused bail, asserting, "This will be a black baby born in Mississippi, and thus where ever he is born he will be in prison. I believe that if I go to jail now it may help hasten that day when my child and all children will be free. . . ."[11]

As SNCC members and other activists spread throughout the South and established long-term organizing projects—most notably, the Council of Federated Organizations' (COFO) voter-registration project in Mississippi—they discovered another source of female support for the movement. Especially in rural areas, black women opened their homes to organizers, often in the face of threats from the white community. Mary Dora Jones of Cleveland, Mississippi flouted the warnings of her boss and housed and fed seven black and four white activists.

10. Donald Matthews and James Prothro, *Negroes and the New Southern Politics* (New York: Harcourt, Brace and World, 1966), pp. 412–17.

11. Carson, *In Struggle*, pp. 31–32; Dick Cluster, ed., *They Should Have Served That Cup of Coffee* (Boston: South End Press, 1979), pp. 14–17; Sara Evans, *Personal Politics: The Roots of Women's Liberation in the Civil Rights Movement and the New Left* (New York: Vintage Books, 1979), pp. 39–40.

Confronting her neighbors' fear that whites would burn her house, she responded, "Ain't but one thing 'bout dyin'. That's make sho' you right, 'cause you gon' die anyway." Recalling her courageous decision later, she remarked, "If they had burnt it down, it was just a house burned down." When they sheltered and fed freedom struggle workers, black women transformed their traditional domestic roles into political acts.[12]

Among Jones's counterparts throughout the rural South, some moved from harboring volunteers to leadership in the movement. After housing SNCC leader Muriel Tillinghast, Unita Blackwell joined the Mississippi Freedom Democratic Party (MFDP) established by civil-rights activists as an alternative to the regular Democratic party, which systematically excluded blacks. As MFDP delegate, Blackwell went to the Democratic National Convention in 1964 to challenge the all-white delegation sent by the regular Democrats, and she later won election to mayor of Mayersville, Mississippi. Even more prominent was Fannie Lou Hamer, who lost her home and was the target of racists' guns when she attempted to register to vote in 1962. Moving to Rulesville, Mississippi, she joined SNCC's voter-education project, and in 1963 she was arrested, jailed, and so brutally beaten that she hid her face from her family for a month. Hamer became a field secretary for SNCC, and she helped organize the MFDP and served as one of its leaders at the Democratic National Convention in 1964. Although she lost both the MFDP challenge and her congressional campaign in 1964, she continued as a political leader and community organizer until her death in 1977.[13]

SNCC's emphasis on democratic leadership and the strengths and skills of women themselves brought women more power in SNCC than in any other civil-rights organization. Diane Nash and Ruby Doris Smith had positions of influence and respect in SNCC's inner circles; Robinson served as administrative secretary and then replaced James Forman as executive secretary from 1966 to her untimely death in 1967. Out in

12. Howell Raines, *My Soul Is Rested: Movement Days in the Deep South Remembered* (New York: Penguin Books, 1983), pp. 279–81.

13. *Giddings, When and Where I Enter,* pp. 284–90, 293–95; Raines, *My Soul Is Rested,* pp. 249–55.

Fannie Lou Hamer speaking on behalf of the Mississipi Freedom
Democratic Party before the credentials committee at the
Democratic National Convention in Atlantic City, August 1964.
(Wide World Photos)

the field, Gloria Richardson led the SNCC-centered movement
in Cambridge, Maryland, while Muriel Tillinghast and Cynthia
Washington headed major projects in Mississippi. Eleanor
Holmes Norton, president of the local NAACP while a student
at Antioch, went to Mississippi to promote voter registration
during her summer vacation from the Yale Law School. The
following year she worked on the legal brief supporting the
MFDP and helped coordinate its strategy at the Democratic
National Convention. Although men were usually the public
spokesmen and were better known outside the movement,
black women exercised leadership in individual campaigns, did
major administrative work at headquarters, and held the attention of male leaders when important decisions were to be
made.[14]

14. Evans, *Personal Politics*, pp. 41, 76; Giddings, *When and Where I Enter*,
pp. 290–92, 302; Carson, *In Struggle*, 148; Peggy Lamson, *Few Are Chosen:*

White women too participated in the black freedom struggle, both as demonstrators and in decision-making positions, though on a lesser scale than their black counterparts. Jane Stembridge was SNCC's first office manager, and Casey Hayden and Mary King had major administrative responsibilities. All three women were initially inspired by their religious convictions to work for racial justice, and all three got a large chunk of their early political education from Ella Baker. During the Freedom Summers of 1964 and 1965, around 1,400 northern white students went south to work on community organization and voter-registration projects. Nearly half of those were women, even though women had to overcome much more resistance from parents and were less likely to be sponsored by supportive northern organizations. These women set up libraries, helped prepare blacks for active citizenship by teaching in freedom schools, worked in project offices, and did house-to-house canvassing for voter registration—usually in the midst of threats and harassment from local whites.[15]

The skills and confidence women gained in the civil-rights movement and the values of self-determination, grass-roots leadership, and individual worth that informed SNCC in the early 1960s led Mary King and Casey Hayden to think about women as an oppressed group and to wonder if there was room in SNCC to address these issues. In 1964, King wrote an anonymous paper on the topic for a SNCC retreat, but the majority response was disdain and ridicule. A few black women supported the statement, and some black women had participated in a half-mocking demonstration by women earlier that year at the SNCC office in Atlanta. Yet, while several black women commented retrospectively on the lack of equality for women or their views, most black women did not recognize sexual prejudice at the time, or they felt that the struggle against

---

American Women in Political Life Today (Boston: Houghton Mifflin, 1968), pp. 152–63.

15. Mary King, *Freedom Song: A Personal Story of the 1960s Civil Rights Movement* (New York: William Morrow, 1987) provides an excellent firsthand account by one of the most important white women in the black freedom struggle. See also Mary Aickin Rothschild, "White Women Volunteers in the Freedom Summers: Their Life and Work in A Movement for Social Change," *Feminist Studies* 5 (Fall 1979):466–90, and Evans, *Personal Politics,* pp. 70–73.

racism rendered all other issues insignificant. Ruby Doris Smith, for example, felt that attention to women's concerns was divisive and disruptive. Thus, it was primarily white women whose experiences in the civil-rights struggle led them to a political analysis of their position as women, and who brought insights, ideology, and tactics from black protest into an emerging women's liberation movement.[16]

By the mid-1960s, black insurgency had made inroads into the system of segregation, won considerable sympathy and support from northern liberals, and achieved the two most important federal laws since Reconstruction, the Civil Rights Act of 1964 and the Voting Rights Act of 1965. Yet activists were disillusioned. Progress had been painfully slow and won only at great personal sacrifice and the loss of more than a dozen lives. The federal government had failed even to protect the safety of activists, and in allotting just two seats to the MFDP while seating the all-white delegation, the Democratic Party in 1964 had responded to the Mississippi voter organization project with a slap in the face. Especially in SNCC, leaders began to doubt the efficacy of nonviolent protest and the advisability of working within the system. Embittered by the lack of support from white allies, activists began to feel the necessity for a black movement independent of whites and based on the celebration of black culture.

While the turn to "black power" sent white activists into other movements, at least symbolically and at times in practice, it also undermined the role of black women. The rhetoric of newer, more militant leaders such as Stokely Carmichael, H. Rap Brown, and Eldridge Cleaver emphasized the need for black men to regain their "manhood." Angela Davis, active in the radical community of Los Angeles in the late 1960s, felt that some male leaders confused "their political activity with an assertion of their maleness" and saw women leaders as a threat to that masculinity. As leaders in the local SNCC organization, Davis and other women were attacked for "taking over the organization. . . . By playing such a leading role . . ., some of [the

16. Evans, *Personal Politics*, pp. 76, 84–85; Giddings, *When and Where I Enter*, pp. 302–3, 309–17. I have relied on Mary King, *Freedom Song*, pp. 443–74, which revises Evans's account of the raising of women's concerns within SNCC.

men] insisted, we were aiding and abetting the enemy, who wanted to see Black men weak and unable to hold their own." While the vast majority of black women nonetheless maintained their primary allegiance to the black freedom struggle, some began to identify the need to work against oppression based on both race and gender.[17]

CHICANA ACTIVISM

Black power and the urban racial violence that erupted in dozens of cities in the late 1960s attracted the lion's share of national publicity, but other grass-roots movements emerged that galvanized women into political action. The second largest racial minority, Mexican-Americans, also mobilized with increasing fervency in the 1960s to protest discrimination and economic exploitation. New organizations sprang up all over the Southwest, but the most prominent was the National Farm Workers' Association—subsequently the United Farm Workers (UFW)—founded by Cesar Chavez in 1963 to obtain better wages and working conditions for agricultural laborers.

Women endured the deplorable conditions in agriculture both as laborers in a system that frequently employed entire families, and as homemakers struggling to care for their families in the dilapidated structures and inadequate facilities of most migrant housing. Such conditions characterized the life of Jessie Lopez De La Cruz, who moved from school to school as her family followed the harvests and who finished only the sixth grade. She continued to work in the fields after marriage and the birth of six children, because, as she said, "if it were just the men working . . . we wouldn't earn enough to support a family."[18]

Recruited in 1962 when Chavez visited her home, De La Cruz began organizing farm workers on the job and in their

17. Angela Davis, *An Autobiography* (New York: Random House, 1974), pp. 161, 181.

18. Ellen Cantaro, *Moving the Mountain: Women Working for Social Change* (Old Westbury, NY: The Feminist Press, 1980), pp. 97–122.

homes after work. She reported that women were often more vocal than men at union meetings and participated aggressively in union efforts to keep workers out of the fields during strikes. On one occasion De La Cruz led fifty women to defy company guards and county police and chase scab workers out of a grape field. Later she told her husband, "See? See what women can do? We got all those men out there to come out!"[19]

De La Cruz became an official organizer for the UFW in 1967 and headed a union hiring hall. As her activism expanded beyond strictly work issues, she testified at legislative hearings, promoted bilingual education, and worked on a host of issues affecting Mexican Americans. De La Cruz was appointed to the Fresno County Economic Opportunity Commission and to California's Commission on the Status of Women, and she went as a delegate to the Democratic National Convention in 1972.[20]

Best known among the women of the UFW was Dolores Huerta, daughter of a migrant worker. Her college degree distinguished her from most Chicanas, and she first became active organizing Chicano voters in Stockton, California. Chavez recruited her to become a lobbyist and organizer for the farmworkers, and Huerta rose nearly to the top of the union as its vice president and chief negotiator.[21]

Women played leadership roles elsewhere in the increasingly politicized Chicano community. For example, Virginia Muzquiz helped organize Chicanos in winning representation on the Crystal City, Texas city council in 1963. In 1969, she rallied the community to support a boycott of the Crystal City public schools. Musquiz helped found and served as county chairwoman of the Raza Unida party, a third-party movement of Texas Chicanos; she captured formal political power with her election as Zavala County Clerk in 1974.[22]

19. *Ibid.*, pp. 137–39.

20. *Ibid.*, pp. 96–100, 127–29.

21. Alfredo Mirande and Evangelina Enriquez, *La Chicana: The Mexican-American Woman* (Chicago: University of Chicago Press, 1979), pp. 233–34.

22. Martha Cotera, *Profile on the Mexican American Woman* (Austin, Texas: National Educational Laboratory Publishers, Inc., 1976), pp. 107–8.

THE WELFARE RIGHTS MOVEMENT

Poor, educationally disadvantaged minority women played an even larger role in the welfare rights movement. That cause developed from a growing recognition that civil rights were meaningless without economic security and opportunity, and it drew leadership and support from activists seasoned in the civil-rights struggle. The rise of poverty as an issue of national concern in the early 1960s and the antipoverty programs of the Johnson administration further galvanized such activists to create a national movement to eradicate poverty.[23]

Two social scientists, Richard A. Cloward and Frances Fox Piven, circulated a paper "A Strategy to End Poverty," which called for the mobilization of poor people to demand welfare benefits. Massive enrollments in welfare programs, they believed, would create an enormous strain on the welfare system and force its replacement by a guaranteed income. Their most important recruit was George Wiley, a black activist who had left a university professorship to become associate director of CORE. In 1966 and 1967, Wiley set up the National Welfare Rights Organization (NWRO), became its executive director, and recruited staff, funding, and other support from civil-rights and liberal groups. But while its funding and leadership depended upon middle-class white and black men, its constituency depended upon mobilizing poor people. Poor black women became the human mainstay of the NWRO, and these women eventually challenged both the priorities and the white and male leadership of the organization.[24]

In fact, even before the establishment of the NWRO, black women had begun to mobilize around the issue of welfare. In 1963, Johnnie Tillmon, a mother of six in the Watts area of Los Angeles, was forced to go on welfare when failing health prevented her from doing the menial jobs that had been supporting her family. Her difficult and dehumanizing experience with the welfare system led her to organize welfare mothers in her

23. Guida West, *The National Welfare Rights Movement: The Social Protest of Poor Women* (New York: Praeger, 1981), pp. 19–22.
24. *Ibid.,* pp. 23–32.

neighborhood, and she established Aid to Needy Children (ANC) to push for jobs, education, and child-care services for poor women. Tillmon participated in the founding of NWRO and served as chair, its highest elective office, for several years.[25]

The NWRO was an interracial organization that aimed to mobilize poor people of all races and both sexes to demand jobs for those able to work and adequate income for those who could not take jobs. In practice, however, membership was almost exclusively female, and black women, many of whom were politicized by the civil-rights movement, constituted 80 percent or more of NWRO's membership. Reflecting that constituency, the elected, formal officials—who were volunteers—were black women, along with a few black men, and white and Hispanic women. In contrast, the paid staff and organizers were predominantly white, middle-class, and male.[26]

The male staff, black and white, emphasized priorities at odds with the needs and experiences of welfare mothers. These men assumed that jobs for most welfare mothers were not a realistic possibility and wanted to focus on obtaining adequate income for these "economically immobile" women, along with jobs for men and the strengthening of two-parent families. Women agreed on the goal of adequate economic support within a dignified distribution system, but they also emphasized jobs, training, and child care for welfare mothers. Black welfare mothers like Johnnie Tillmon and Beulah Sanders insisted that poor women wanted decent jobs so that they could support their families. If the nation was unable to provide sufficient jobs with adequate wages, poor women should have the choice of staying home and taking care of their families, an enterprise that society needed to recognize as real work. Thus, in their challenge to the male staff, black women sought to redefine "productive work," to obtain economic independence for women, and to secure child-care services that would help women accommodate employment with their responsibilities as mothers. Anticipating the mainstream feminist movement's

25. *Ibid.*, p. 83.
26. *Ibid.*, pp. 39, 44–47, 53, 57–59.

concern with the "feminization of poverty," which would come a decade later, Tillmon pointed out that "every woman is one man away from welfare."[27]

Welfare mothers not only challenged the ideological and policy orientation of male staff, they also challenged their very power and positions. Faced with demands from its constituency, NWRO administrators began to add poor women to the staff in 1969; in 1971 Tillmon became Wiley's associate director, and, when Wiley left in 1973, she became executive director. The ascendancy of women's priorities and leadership in the NWRO, however, came as the organization was nearing dissolution, a victim of internal conflicts as well as external conditions, especially the declining public interest in the poor. Nonetheless, the organization had mobilized thousands of women (peak membership was around 25,000 in 1969), improved somewhat the material conditions of welfare recipients, influenced government policymaking and public attitudes about poverty, and demonstrated the assertiveness and political potential of poor black women. In addition, these women had developed and articulated a number of ideas that would subsequently be taken up by middle-class feminists.[28]

STUDENT PROTEST

At the same time that the NWRO was getting underway, middle-class feminism was developing in the student protest movement, another struggle which took part of its inspiration and early constituency from black insurgency. An amorphous collection of ad hoc groups that sprang up on college campuses, the student movement of the 1960s reached its highest organizational form in the Students for a Democratic Society (SDS). Created in 1960 out of the remains of an older socialist-oriented student organization, SDS took considerable inspiration from the civil-rights movement, shared its emphasis on participatory

27. *Ibid.*, pp. 47, 82–94.
28. *Ibid.*, pp. 94–95, 113–23, 384–87.

democracy, and found among its constituency many students who had gone south to work in the black struggle. By 1968, between 50,000 and 75,000 students, largely white and upper middle-class, were affiliated with SDS in hundreds of campus chapters, and even more could be counted on to participate in specific actions. Addressing a range of issues that included academic policies and curricula, social and economic justice, militarism, and civil rights, the student protest movement had its greatest impact in mobilizing opposition to the Vietnam War.

Women in the student movement experienced more intensely conditions that had inspired the questioning of sex roles in SNCC. Particularly in the SDS Economic Research and Action Projects (ERAP), begun in 1963 to organize the urban poor in the North, women found role models in strong ghetto women and discovered their own skills and courage. They were not, however, accepted as equals by their male colleagues. According to one activist, "as a woman . . . I was allowed to develop and . . . was given much more responsibility in SNCC than I ever was in SDS." While SDS women frequently proved to be the most effective organizers, all of the project directors in 1964 were men, and only one woman sat on the ERAP executive committee. In the Chicago project, women were sent to earn wages at Woolworths to support the male organizers.[29]

National leadership in SDS paralleled that of the ERAP projects. Women joined SDS and attended its conventions in proportions only slightly lower than their representation among college students. But no woman held a national office until 1966, and not until 1968 did a woman enter the highest ranks. Although the ideal of SDS was "a democracy of individual participation," in practice male leaders infused decision-making with an aggressive, cerebral, competitive, and manipulative style that discouraged female participation. According to one SDS man, he and his fellows were imbued with "arrogance, elitism, competitiveness, machismo, ruthlessness, guilt—replications of

29. Evans, *Personal Politics,* pp. 108, 126–55; James Weinstein, *Ambiguous Legacy: The Left in American Politics* (New York: New Viewpoints, 1975), pp. 132–33.

patterns of domination and mystification we have been taught since the cradle."[30]

As student protest focused more sharply on opposition to the Vietnam War after 1965, women found themselves even more in the background. When draft resistance became a primary vehicle for opposing the war, women could serve as counselors or organizers, but they could not take the ultimate step of defiance. One woman who worked in draft resistance found her role "unbelievably subservient . . . because women couldn't burn draft cards and couldn't go to jail so all they could do was to relate through their men. . . ." That role was expressed in a popular slogan of draft resistance, "Girls Say Yes to Guys Who Say No!"[31]

In November 1965, before Casey Hayden and Mary King left SNCC as black nationalism began to suffuse that organization, they put on paper their emerging feminist analysis. Distributed to women in SNCC and in the ERAP projects, their paper articulated a "sexual caste system" that dictated subordinate roles for women both within and outside the movement. While they considered the chances of starting a women's movement "nil" and assumed that activist women would continue to devote their energies to problems of race, war, and poverty, they hoped that women could begin to talk more openly and "to create a community of support for each other. . . ." Some women in ERAP had already raised the issue of women's roles, and at an SDS meeting in December 1965, the first workshop on women was held.[32]

These discussions enabled women for the first time to express frustrations and even anger at male attitudes and behavior. Women found confirmation for their own perceptions and began to identify a broad range of questions that would ultimately provide the base for a full-scale analysis of women's position in American society. They did not, however, find much support or even interest among men. While radical men sometimes paid lip service to the need for eliminating sexism, and SDS even passed a resolution to that effect in 1967, the

30. Evans, *Personal Politics,* pp. 108–19, 154.
31. *Ibid.,* pp. 179–82.
32. *Ibid.,* pp. 98–100, 235–38.

most consistent responses to women's demands were inattention, ridicule, and hostility. By the end of 1967, radical women had given up on the possibility of addressing their interests within the movement. In part drawing conclusions parallel to those that had spawned the black power movement, women formed independent, informal groups in cities across the country, and the radical wing of the women's movement was born.[33]

ANTIWAR ACTIVISM

Outside of the student-led wing of the antiwar movement, and especially within their own organizations, women found greater opportunities to lead and contribute in ways more coincident with their capabilities. The half-century-old United States section of the Women's International League for Peace and Freedom (WILPF) began to lobby against the United States presence in Vietnam as early as April 1964. The second important women's peace organization, Women Strike for Peace (WSP), was formed to work for disarmament and a nuclear test ban treaty. A loosely organized, non-hierarchical cluster of local groups, WSP mobilized 50,000 women to march for peace in 1961. The new group survived investigation by the House Un-American Activities Committee in 1962, even managing to make that body look ridiculous, and subsequently played a major part in the antiwar movement. Throughout the 1960s it staged demonstrations, often in conjunction with WILPF. Its members, notably Coretta Scott King and Dagmar Wilson, frequently spoke at antiwar rallies, and it was the first peace group to meet formally with representatives of the North Vietnamese. WSP was also the first group to demonstrate at the Pentagon, and it took the lead in protesting the use of napalm against the Vietnamese.[34]

33. *Ibid.*, pp. 161–68, 186–211.

34. Charles De Benedetti, *The Peace Reform in American History* (Bloomington: Indiana University Press, 1980), pp. 111, 166–73; Nancy Zaroulis and Gerald Sullivan, *Who Spoke Up? American Protest against the War in Vietnam, 1963–1975* (Garden City, NY: Doubleday and Company, 1984), pp. 19, 34, 44, 51, 64, 103–4, 114; Amy Swerdlow, "Ladies' Day at the Capitol:

Women also exerted leadership in male-dominated peace actions. Norma Becker, a New York City schoolteacher who had organized for civil rights in Maryland and Mississippi, was a central figure in the New York antiwar coalition. She never spoke at large rallies and consequently received little media attention, but within the peace movement she was an indispensable activist. In 1965 she organized the Fifth Avenue Peace Parade Committee. Throughout the 1960s Becker routinely turned out thousands of demonstrators for marches in New York and Washington, and she was one of the few women who served on steering committees of various national antiwar coalitions as representatives of organizations composed of both men and women.[35]

Women achieved prominence in other antiwar organizations. Bettina Aptheker helped found the Student Mobilization Committee to End the War in Vietnam (SMC), and by 1967 that group had overtaken SDS's primacy in the national student peace movement. Another woman, Linda Dannenberg, organized SMC's national office and served as its first executive secretary. Aptheker initiated the idea for a national student strike, which resulted in one million students boycotting classes on April 26, 1968. An even larger demonstration involved millions of citizens in October 1969. One of the four national organizers of Vietnam Moratorium Day was Marge Sklencar, who had headed SDS at Mundelein College and worked in Senator Eugene McCarthy's presidential campaign. She subsequently served on the steering committee of the National Mobilization Committee to End the War in Vietnam.[36]

Bella Abzug formed a bridge between the grass-roots politics of the 1960s and traditional politics. A founding member of Women Strike for Peace and its Washington lobbyist, Abzug was an activist lawyer and a leader among antiwar Democrats who worked to deny Lyndon Johnson a second term in 1968. In 1970 she successfully challenged the Democratic incumbent for the Congressional seat representing the West Side of Man-

---

Women Strike for Peace Versus HUAC," *Feminist Studies* 8 (Fall 1982):493–516.

35. Zaroulis and Sullivan, *Who Spoke Up?,* pp. 54–55, 214–15, 256, 264, 285, 373, 420.

36. *Ibid.,* pp. 97–98, 150, 168, 264, 280, 298.

Women Strike for Peace demonstration against the Vietnam War, 1971. At center is WSP founder Bella Abzug. (Bettye Lane)

hattan. Her first action in Congress was to introduce legislation calling for United States withdrawal from Vietnam within six months, and she persevered in this effort until the last American departed in 1975.[37]

REACTION FROM THE RIGHT

Issues of race, poverty, and foreign policy activated women on the right as well as on the left of the political spectrum in the 1960s. As legislation and court orders began to attack racial injustice outside the South and as blacks in northern and western cities mobilized against segregation and discrimination in their own regions, opposition to black aspirations grew among non-southerners. Groups that traditionally had opposed federal welfare programs found new adherents as government spending increased to fund the Johnson administration's war on

37. *Ibid.*, pp. 341, 363, 387, 402, 416; Esther Stineman, *American Political Women: Contemporary and Historical Profiles* (Littleton, CO: Libraries Unlimited, Inc., 1980), pp. 1–2.

poverty. And anticommunists grew increasingly restive over government activities on behalf of arms control, the failure of the United States to launch an all-out effort against the North Vietnamese, and what they perceived to be the radical forces behind the politics of protest. Less numerous than those involved on the liberal side and less likely to deviate from traditional forms of political behavior, considerable numbers of women participated in conservative movements, and a few emerged as leaders. None were more prominent than Louise Day Hicks and Phyllis Schlafly.

In choosing the Boston School Committee elections for her entry into electoral politics, Louise Day Hicks embarked on a customary route for women. In other respects she was anything but customary. She credited her political ambitions to her father, a wealthy lawyer, banker, real estate dealer, and judge in South Boston, whose Irish residents revered him. After her father's death, Hicks entered Boston University's law school, where, as a thirty-six-year-old mother, she was one of 9 women among 232 students in her class. Women and blacks constituted her informal study group in law school. After practicing law with her brother for five years, in 1961 she entered the race for the Boston School Committee as a reformer and "the only mother on the ballot," with support from women's groups and the black community. In 1963, she was elected chair of the committee, and that same year the NAACP began to press for desegregation of Boston's schools.[38]

Hicks was initially inclined to reach an accommodation with the NAACP, but she refused to admit any School Committee responsibility for the de facto segregation, and she resolutely opposed busing or redistricting to integrate the schools. Her stand won enormous support in ethnic working-class neighborhoods and guaranteed her three terms on the School Committee, subsequent elections to the Boston City Council, and one term in the United States Congress. Although she lost two bids for mayor, one in 1967 when she failed by 12,000 votes out of 200,000 cast, she was a major force in Boston politics—and the subject of attention in the national media—for nearly two decades. While her name was a byword for racism among liber-

38. J. Anthony Lukas, *Common Ground: A Turbulent Decade in the Lives of Three American Families* (New York: Alfred A. Knopf, 1985), pp. 115–25.

als, she was not a full-blown conservative. She supported the war in Vietnam, but she sided with liberals on many domestic issues, including the Equal Rights Amendment. Moreover, her political success derived not simply from her ability to exploit racism, but also from her identification with working-class whites' sense of powerlessness, attachment to their communities, and rage at the "outside power structure" that threatened what little control they maintained over their neighborhoods.[39]

Phyllis Schlafly (born Phyllis MacAlpin Stewart) did fit the mold of the complete conservative, but she was no less ambitious nor adept at political mobilization than was Hicks. Although her father, an engineer, was unemployed while she was growing up during the Depression, Schlafly's family maintained an intense hostility to the social and economic innovations of the Roosevelt administration. In order to uphold their middle-class status and to provide an education for their daughters at an elite Catholic girls school, her mother took a job. Following her mother's example of industry, Schlafly worked her way through Washington University with a 48-hour-a-week job at a St. Louis defense plant, and in 1945 she received a master's degree in political science from Radcliffe.[40]

The conservatism she imbibed at home was strengthened and honed in her post-college years. Schlafly worked first for the American Enterprise Association (now the American Enterprise Institute), a business-supported organization that did research, analysis, and speechwriting for Congressmen opposed to big government. Returning to St. Louis, she managed a congressional campaign for a conservative Republican, and worked for two banks as librarian, speechwriter for bank officers, and compiler of a monthly newsletter. She met Fred Schlafly, a wealthy lawyer from Alton, Illinois who was deeply committed to combating communists at home and abroad, when he sought out the author of ideas so congenial to his own. In 1949 they married.[41]

While bearing and raising six children, Phyllis Schlafly be-

39. *Ibid.*, pp. 126–37; Ellen Goodman, "Louise Day Hicks," *Ms.* 4 (January 1976):99–103.

40. Carol Felsenthal, *The Sweetheart of the Silent Majority: The Biography of Phyllis Schlafly* (Garden City, NY: Doubleday, 1981), pp. 9–23, 59–68.

41. *Ibid.*, pp. 69–84, 106–9.

came an influential figure in conservative Republican politics. In 1952, she won the Republican primary for the House of Representatives. Following a campaign during which reporters dubbed her the "powder puff candidate," and a local newspaper pictured her cooking her husband's breakfast, she lost the election in her heavily Democratic district. Throughout the 1950s and 1960s she worked for Republicans across Illinois, was elected as delegate to the 1956 Republican convention and as alternate in 1960, and headed the Illinois Federation of Republican Women. In 1964 she wrote *A Choice Not an Echo*, a self-published book calling on "grass-roots" Republicans to wrest control of the party from the "king-makers," the eastern, liberal, internationalist wing of the party. The book sold 3 million copies and helped win the Republican nomination for conservative senator Barry Goldwater.[42]

Schlafly's identification with Goldwater's rout in 1964 diminished her influence in the national Republican party. As first vice president of the National Federation of Republican Women (NFRW), she was in line for the presidency in 1967. But the male leaders of the Republican National Committee, judging her a threat to their plans to edge the party towards the mainstream, engineered her defeat. Bitter in her loss, she made one of her rare acknowledgments that women experienced discrimination: "Many men in the party frankly want to keep the women doing the menial work, while the selection of candidates and the policy decisions are taken care of by the men. . . ."[43]

Schlafly made one more unsuccessful bid for the House in 1970, but after her defeat for the NFRW presidency she channeled most of her political efforts into extra-party nonelectoral activities. In 1967 she began publication of *The Phyllis Schlafly Report* to maintain contact with the 3,000 women who had supported her candidacy for NFRW president, and she established the Eagle Trust Fund to receive contributions for causes favored in the newsletter. In 1968, she began to organize like-minded women by holding annual political-action leadership conferences where she promoted conservative causes and can-

42. *Ibid.*, pp. 152–78.
43. *Ibid.*, pp. 177–97.

didates and taught women how to mobilize behind them. Women, she said, "are tired of doing all the menial work and being told they have to accept the candidate presented to them."[44]

Within a few years, Phyllis Schlafly would achieve even greater power and visibility as she discovered a new cause, that of antifeminism. By 1970, the Equal Rights Amendment had emerged as the major goal of a renewed feminist movement, one which owed a great deal to the protest politics of the 1960s. The movements of the 1960s, and especially the black freedom struggle, had sensitized political officials and the public to various forms of discrimination and economic exploitation. They held out ideals of individual worth, self-determination, and equality, and provided opportunities for many women to develop political skills and self-confidence. It was only a matter of time until these women awakened to the gap between their abilities and their limited opportunities. Drawing heavily on the ideology and strategies of the groups that fashioned the turbulent politics of the 1960s, they helped to create a mass women's movement that dramatically reshaped women's relationships with the political process.

44. *Ibid.*, pp. 195–97, 266–69.

Chapter 3

Origins and Politics of the New Feminism

It was not only in the "new politics" of the 1960s that women's presence manifested itself more intensely than at any time since the suffrage movement. While some women were taking to the streets, others became increasingly assertive in traditional politics, most importantly in the halls of the federal government. Many of these women were "old hands" at politics with years of experience in women's organizations, party politics, labor unions, or, in a few cases, federal office. Capitalizing on the climate of reform shaped in part by the Kennedy and Johnson administrations and even more so by the grass-roots movements of the 1960s, a relatively small group of women played leading roles in establishing new federal policies concerning women. With passage of the Equal Pay Act of 1963 and Title VII of the Civil Rights Act of 1964, women became the subject of national legislation for the first time since the 1920s.

Defying the conventional process of interest-group politics, these new laws preceded the development of a mass movement of women. To be sure, the efforts of seasoned women activists supported by traditional women's organizations were critical to their passage, but the Equal Pay Act and Title VII succeeded without significant grass-roots pressure on lawmakers. On the contrary, it was the new federal laws which, in conjunction with the development of feminist consciousness among women in the New Left, sparked a revived women's movement. By the end of the 1960s, women had established themselves as a force that politicians could not ignore, and they had laid the groundwork for a significant expansion of their political presence in the 1970s.

As it began, the decade did not appear auspicious for women's claims on the political process. On the one hand, more and more of them, especially married women, had been joining the work force, so that by 1960, 35 percent of all women were employed and constituted one-third of the labor force. Their numbers in higher education also increased during the 1950s, and by 1960 women made up 36 percent of all undergraduates. In addition, the birth rate began to decline, and the advent of the contraceptive pill gave women unprecedented control over childbearing.

Yet the vast majority of women worked in low-paying, low-status jobs, and many of those who attended college soon found themselves stifled in the isolation and routine of domesticity. Thus women's growing presence in the labor market and in higher education failed to challenge traditional attitudes about their appropriate roles. The conventional norm that designated homemaking and childrearing as women's primary responsibilities also kept them out of political office. In 1963, just 351 women served in state legislatures, constituting a scant 5 percent of the total, and only 13 held congressional seats, down from a peak of 19 in 1961. Underlying their inferior position was the fact that it was perfectly legal to discriminate against women in nearly all aspects of life.[1]

Nor did the three major goals promoted by organized womanhood since the 1940s—an equal pay law, an ERA, and the appointment of a woman to federal office—seem any closer to realization. A coalition of women's organizations, labor unions, and civic groups had lobbied for a federal equal pay bill since 1950, but could not even persuade Congress to hold hearings. The smaller group of women's organizations pushing for an Equal Rights Amendment obtained favorable reports from Senate committees in the 1950s, but that was all they got. While

1. Myra Marx Ferree and Beth B. Hess, *Controversy and Coalition: The New Feminist Movement* (Boston: Twayne Publishers, 1985), pp. 4–14; Emmy E. Werner, "Women in Congress: 1917–1964," *Western Political Quarterly* 19 (March, 1966): 28.

women's organizations evinced some satisfaction in appointments of women to high government posts, neither Truman nor Eisenhower allotted more than 2.4 percent of the positions that they controlled to women.[2]

THE PRESIDENT'S COMMISSION ON THE STATUS OF WOMEN

Even these token achievements seemed threatened when John F. Kennedy took office in 1961. Kennedy failed to consult important women in the Democratic party, nor did he respond to their recommendations that he make noteworthy appointments of women. Criticism and pleas from such party activists as India Edwards, Emma Guffey Miller, and even Eleanor Roosevelt failed to move him. Columnist Doris Fleeson remarked, referring to the theme of his presidency, " . . . it appears that for women the New Frontiers are the old frontiers." Kennedy's failure in the matter of female appointments was due in part to his goal of attracting "the best and the brightest," which assumed that such talent would be drawn from the elite educational and corporate institutions where few women were to be found.[3]

Although the New Frontier embraced no goals that had specific relevance to women, the tone of Kennedy's administration and the substance of his program held promise. In calling for economic revitalization, initiatives to diminish poverty, a national health program for the elderly, and federal aid to education, Kennedy conditioned the country to see change as desirable. His sympathy with Martin Luther King, Jr., and aspects of the black freedom struggle, though far from overwhelming, surpassed any previous administration's support for civil rights and helped to legitimize efforts to promote equality.

When Kennedy did pay attention to women's concerns, he listened to Esther Peterson, an early Kennedy supporter and

2. Patricia G. Zelman, *Women, Work, and National Policy: The Kennedy-Johnson Years* (Ann Arbor, MI: UMI Research Press, 1982), 13–14, 19–21.

3. Cynthia Ellen Harrison, *On Account of Sex: The Politics of Women's Issues, 1945–1968* (Berkeley: University of California Press, 1987), pp. 75–81.

President John F. Kennedy with Eleanor Roosevelt *(left)* and
Esther Peterson at a meeting of the President's Commission on the
Status of Women, February 1962. (Abbie Rowe photograph in the
John F. Kennedy Library, Boston)

experienced labor organizer and lobbyist. Appointed to the
post of Assistant Secretary of Labor and Director of the
Women's Bureau, Peterson was much more interested in promoting policy initiatives for working women than in securing
female appointments. She had long supported equal pay legislation while opposing an Equal Rights Amendment. In the 1940s
Peterson had worked with the coalition of women's organizations calling for a commission to investigate the status of women
as an alternative to an Equal Rights Amendment. She used her
clout with President Kennedy to commit him to an equal pay
bill and a federal commission on the status of women.[4]

Peterson persuaded the president that establishment of a
commission would demonstrate his concern for women's problems and dampen the persistent demands for an equal rights
amendment from the National Woman's Party (NWP), the National Federation of Business and Professional Women's Clubs

4. *Ibid.*, pp. 85–88.

(BPW), and their allies. In December 1961, Kennedy established the President's Commission on the Status of Women (PCSW). Chaired by Eleanor Roosevelt, the commission was composed of eleven men and fifteen women, including cabinet officers, Congressmen and women, and leaders in labor, religion, education, and other professions. The commission created a number of subcommittees so that ultimately more than one hundred individuals, mostly women, were involved in its work. The goals were to design proposals that would combat sex discrimination in government and private employment, and to recommend services that would enable women "to continue their role as wives and mothers while making a maximum contribution to the world around them. . . ."[5]

In accordance with its goals, the commission's report presented proposals for ameliorating disabilities suffered by women because of their sex, while at the same time reaffirming the primacy of women's maternal role. Although the PCSW ignored the inherent contradiction between greater opportunities for women in the public sphere and their primary responsibilities for homemaking and child care, it did recommend significant changes in government policies and employment and educational practices. Opponents of the Equal Rights Amendment far outnumbered supporters on the commission, but they agreed on a compromise that left open the possibility for future consideration of an amendment. The commission supported an alternative route to equality for women, a proposal developed by legal scholar Pauli Murray, who had a long history of civil-rights activism. Murray believed that the Fourteenth Amendment prohibited sex discrimination just as it did race discrimination, and she suggested that women press the Supreme Court for such an interpretation. Incorporating Murray's proposal, the commission's report stated that a constitutional amendment was not necessary "now," but it urged the filing of suits against discriminatory laws in an effort to obtain

5. Leila J. Rupp and Verta Taylor, *Survival in the Doldrums: The American Women's Rights Movement, 1945 to the 1960s* (New York: Oxford University Press, 1987), pp. 168–69; Margaret Mead and Frances Balgley Kaplan, *American Women: The Report of the President's Commission on the Status of Women and Other Publications of the Commission* (New York: Charles Scribner's Sons, 1965), pp. 66, 207–13, 254–65; Harrison, *On Account of Sex*, pp. 109–15.

Supreme Court rulings that would establish women's right to equal treatment under the Fifth and Fourteenth Amendments.[6]

Besides providing an agenda for change, the commission brought visibility and legitimacy to women's concerns and consciousness raising among women themselves. When the PCSW completed its work in October 1963, Kennedy followed its recommendations and appointed a Citizens' Advisory Council (CAC) on the Status of Women and an Interdepartmental Committee on the Status of Women (ICSW) composed of cabinet officials. The BPW and other groups of women began to press governors to establish state commissions, and within a few years the PCSW had spawned parallel commissions in forty-nine states. Composed primarily of women, these commissions extended the documentation of women's unequal status begun by the PCSW. In 1964 members of state commissions began to meet at annual conferences, thereby forming a national network of individuals with information about and heightened awareness of sex discrimination. By the middle of the decade, hundreds of women shared copious data and growing concerns about sex discrimination as well as expectations that at least some of those inequities would be corrected. Pauli Murray spoke for many of the women involved in the commissions when she called that experience "an intensive consciousness-raising process leading directly to my involvement in the new women's movement."[7]

THE EQUAL PAY ACT AND TITLE VII

Before 1963, employers could with impunity pay a woman less for doing exactly the same job as a man. The blatant injustice of such a practice had made equal pay legislation a priority of women's organizations, and that became Esther Peterson's second objective after persuading the president to form the

---

6. *Ibid.*, pp. 125–34; Pauli Murray, *Song in A Weary Throat: An American Pilgrimage* (New York: Harper and Row, 1987), pp. 347–53.

7. Rupp and Taylor, *Survival in the Doldrums*, pp. 173–74; Murray, *Song in a Weary Throat*, pp. 347–48.

PCSW. Armed with skills and contacts she had developed as a lobbyist for organized labor and with the full backing of the administration, Peterson spearheaded the drive for congressional action. She directed the collection of data, coordinated the lobbying activities of unions and women's groups, and effected the compromises necessary to achieve passage of the Equal Pay Act in 1963.[8]

The Equal Pay Act, which required employers to pay men and women equally when they performed equal work, remedied only part of the discrimination borne by women in the labor force. Women who worked full-time earned just about 60 percent of what men did, but that gap derived primarily from the sex-segregated labor force. The vast majority of women worked in different jobs from men, and predominantly female occupations usually paid less than predominantly male ones. The Equal Pay Act would not touch this discrepancy, for it applied only where men and women were doing the same work. Nonetheless it was of tremendous import. Besides enabling hundreds of thousands of women to file wage discrimination charges against employers and to win wage increases and back pay, it drew public attention to sex discrimination. Moreover, it set a precedent for government intervention in the economy on behalf of equity for women and boosted morale among the still relatively small group of women concerned with improving women's opportunities.

The next federal initiative on behalf of employed women covered not just wages, but all aspects of employment. Title VII of the Civil Rights Act of 1964 owed its passage above all to an improbable combination of conservative legislators who opposed civil rights legislation and women activists. Responding to the demands of the black freedom struggle, when Lyndon B. Johnson succeeded Kennedy in November 1963 he made passage of a comprehensive civil-rights bill a legislative priority. While the bill was before the House Judiciary Committee, National Woman's Party members persuaded Howard W. Smith to introduce an amendment to Title VII that would prohibit discrimination in employment on the basis of sex, as well as race,

8. Harrison, *On Account of Sex*, pp. 89–105; Zelman, *Women, Work, and National Policy*, pp. 30–32.

color, religion, and national origin. Smith, a Democratic Representative from Virginia who sat on the Judiciary Committee and chaired the powerful House Rules Committee, was an inveterate opponent of civil-rights legislation and a longtime sponsor of the Equal Rights Amendment. Although Smith insisted that he was serious about women's right to legal protections, he undoubtedly grasped the amendment's potential for killing the entire civil-rights bill.[9]

While a number of male Representatives vied to see who could make the best jokes about it, five Congresswomen seriously urged passage of the sex provision. Its most ardent supporter was Martha Griffiths, a Democrat from Michigan who had intended to introduce such an amendment herself. Referring to the tone of the debate thus far, she argued that "if there had been any necessity to have pointed out that women were a second-class sex, the laughter would have proved it." Griffiths herself indulged in the racist argument that without the sex provision, Title VII would disadvantage white women because employers would prefer black women in order to avoid charges of race discrimination.[10]

Spearheading the opposition to the amendment was Edith Green, who had sponsored the Equal Pay Act and served on the PCSW. Representing the views of Esther Peterson and other administration officials and of liberal legislators who strongly supported attacks on racial discrimination, she warned that the sex amendment could prevent passage of the entire section of the bill. Despite this opposition, the amendment adding sex discrimination to Title VII passed by a vote of 168 to 133, and the House approved the entire bill 290 to 130. Nearly all of the men who had spoken for the sex provision voted against the bill itself thus suggesting that they had supported the sex provision as a means to kill the bill.[11]

Once the House had passed the bill with the sex provision

9. Carl M. Brauer, "Women Activists, Southern Conservatives, and the Prohibition of Sex Discrimination in Title VII of the 1964 Civil Rights Act," *Journal of Southern History* 49 (February, 1983):41–51; Zelman, *Women, Work, and National Policy,* pp. 58–67.

10. Brauer, "Women Activists, Southern Conservatives, and the Prohibition of Sex Discrimination," pp. 48–50.

11. *Ibid.,* pp. 52–56; Zelman, *Women, Work, and National Policy,* pp. 58–67.

intact, the administration decided to support the amended bill in order to avoid negotiations between the House and Senate over different versions. With active lobbying by NWP members and determined leadership from Margaret Chase Smith (Republican of Maine), the Senate too accepted the sex clause. In the absence of a strong women's movement, a small group of women, assisted by conservative men who had their own reasons, achieved a second major policy advance. The politically savvy Peterson termed it "a sudden jump through many stages of history." Because it applied not just to wages, but to all aspects of employment including hiring and promotion, Title VII of the Civil Rights Act of 1964 laid a much firmer basis for employment equity for women than did the Equal Pay Act. Moreover, it helped to generate a movement that would ultimately promote changes unimaginable to the law's supporters.[12]

ORIGINS OF MAINSTREAM FEMINISM

While Congress debated the Civil Rights Act of 1964, *The Feminine Mystique* hit the best-seller lists. Published in 1963, that book grew out of Betty Friedan's study of what had happened to members of her Smith College graduating class of 1942. Friedan found considerable dissatisfactions among these women, whose lives did not conform to the cultural model of the happy housewife. Her book indicted the social scientists, doctors, educators, and advertisers who fashioned and hyped that ideal and blamed women if they did not find fulfillment in the roles of wife and mother. Although *The Feminine Mystique* ignored the conditions of minority and working-class women and failed to probe deeply into the web of constraints that limited women, it struck a responsive chord among thousands of educated, middle-class housewives who embodied a contradiction between the intellectual and social stimulation of their college years and the isolation and routine of domesticity.[13]

12. Zelman, *Women, Work, and National Policy,* pp. 57, 68–71.
13. Betty Friedan, *The Feminine Mystique* (New York: Dell Publishing Company, 1963).

As these women began to look outside themselves to understand their discontent, women already involved in politics—in Congress, the executive branch, women's organizations, labor unions, and Status of Women commissions—became more assertive about sex discrimination. An early target was President Johnson's War on Poverty, launched in 1964. At congressional hearings on administration bills, Edith Green questioned officials about their seeming lack of concern for poor *women*, and she obtained a promise that in the job-training program for poor youths there would be a Job Corps for women. A few women also criticized the administration's report, *The Negro Family: The Case for National Action*, written by Daniel Patrick Moynihan, Assistant Secretary of Labor. Not only did the report neglect the problems of black women, it seemed to suggest that black women enjoyed greater opportunities than did black men, and that their position as "matriarchs" emasculated men and weakened the family. Although the War on Poverty continued to emphasize programs and opportunities for men, women leaders had achieved some recognition of female poverty and had also increased their sensitivity to government's chronic blindness to women's interests.[14]

That sensitivity became more acute as women observed the government's implementation of Title VII. Charged with handling complaints of discrimination under Title VII and with establishing guidelines for implementation of the law, the Equal Employment Opportunity Commission (EEOC) treated sex discrimination with disdain and derision. One executive director, for example, called the sex provision a "fluke . . . conceived out of wedlock." The commission's refusal to rule that Title VII invalidated labor laws that applied only to women infuriated the NWP and other ERA supporters; however, most women's organizations were satisfied with the EEOC's inclination to retain such protective legislation. What provoked near unanimous outrage was the EEOC's failure to outlaw want ads listing positions by sex. Pauli Murray, who had lobbied for the sex provision in Title VII, suggested that it might be necessary for women to demonstrate, like blacks, for their rights. Martha Griffiths, on the House floor in June 1966, charged the EEOC

14. Zelman, *Women, Work, and National Policy*, pp. 78–88.

with "contempt [and] flat hostility to the human rights of women."[15]

Women's Bureau official Catherine East, who was also Executive Secretary of the Interdepartmental Committee on the Status of Women, had Griffiths's speech circulated among representatives of state status of women commissions meeting that month in Washington. A number of those women responded by drafting a resolution demanding across-the-board enforcement of Title VII. When officials at the conference told them that they could not introduce such a resolution, they concluded that women needed a new organization committed exclusively to eliminating sex discrimination. Women in the government were sensitive to women's concerns and had done nearly all they could to articulate them, but they suffered the constraints inherent in their official positions. Consequently, before they left the conference, proponents of the resolution channeled their frustrations into plans for a new women's rights organization that could pressure the government from the outside.[16]

THE NATIONAL ORGANIZATION FOR WOMEN

Three hundred individuals had joined by October 1966, when the National Organization for Women (NOW) held its first formal meeting. The thirty women and men at the founding meeting included longtime advocates of women's rights, women whose consciousness had been raised during service on commissions on the status of women, labor union activists, and educational leaders. Marguerite Rawalt, for example, was an NWP member, former president of the Business and Professional Women, and lobbyist for the ERA. Another NWP member, Caruthers Berger, was a federal employee, as were Mary Eastwood and Catherine East. Caroline Davis and Dorothy Haener from the United Auto Workers (UAW) brought a labor perspective to the new organization. Pauli Murray and Kathryn Claren-

15. *Ibid.*, pp. 92–105.
16. Betty Friedan, *It Changed My Life: Writings on the Women's Movement* (New York: Random House, 1976), pp. 75–83.

bach had experience on status of women commissions, as did most of the other founders.

Betty Friedan had initiated the groundwork for NOW and became its first president. Two former EEOC commissioners sympathetic to women's demands, Richard Graham and Aileen Hernandez, were chosen as vice presidents, and Caroline Davis of the UAW became secretary of the new organization. Clarenbach headed the board of directors, which included officials in universities, unions, and government, business executives, representatives of state commissions on women, and members of religious orders. Establishing as its purpose "to take action to bring women into full participation in the mainstream of American society now . . . in truly equal partnership with men," NOW promised to support claims for equality for all deprived groups, and "to mobilize the political power of all women and men intent on our goals." NOW called for equal participation and treatment of women in employment, education, and government, for establishing new institutions to facilitate public roles for women, for true equality in marriage, and for destroying false images of women. Task forces were set up to address seven areas: employment, education, religion, the family, the mass media, politics, and female poverty.[17]

Within a year, NOW could celebrate its first major achievement. In 1965 President Johnson had issued an Executive Order to prohibit discrimination by the federal government and by private employers with federal contracts, and to require both to establish affirmative action programs. Like the original Title VII, the order included race, creed, color, and national origin, but not sex. Within a month of its founding, NOW joined BPW in calling for a sex provision to be added to the order. NOW began to petition federal officials, and in 1967, the ICSW, CAC, and a study group composed of women in the executive branch all recommended amendment of the original executive order, and Johnson followed that advice in October.[18]

17. *Ibid.*, pp. 84–91; Harrison, *On Account of Sex*, p. 196; Jo Freeman, *The Politics of Women's Liberation: A Case Study of an Emerging Movement and Its Relation to the Policy Process* (New York: David McKay Company, 1975), p. 75.

18. Zelman, *Women, Work, and National Policy*, pp. 110–17; Friedan, *It Changed My Life*, pp. 98–99.

The inclusion of women in affirmative action policy indicated that the claims of feminists had some force among federal officials. Moreover, the new executive order in conjunction with Title VII signaled that it was appropriate for federal policy to treat sex discrimination as it did racial discrimination. This would facilitate the inclusion of sex equity throughout federal policy by enabling feminists to "piggy-back" onto measures promoted by the civil-rights movement. But it also alienated black women, who feared that white women would benefit more than black people who had fueled the movement making equity measures possible in the first place.[19]

To comply with affirmative action, firms with government contracts and the government itself had to do more than simply cease discriminating. They were required to take forceful action to hire, train, and promote women and minority men; and they had to establish goals and prove that they were making all necessary efforts to achieve those goals. Failure to comply produced no legal penalties, only the threat of losing a government contract. Enforcement varied from administration to administration, but in general affirmative action helped significant numbers of women and minority men gain employment in areas that had been closed to them, and move in larger numbers into middle-management ranks.

Affirmative action was one of the most controversial programs aimed at promoting equity. Popular misconceptions about it abounded. It did not require the setting of absolute quotas, nor did it mandate the hiring or promotion of unqualified candidates. Nonetheless, these beliefs, fed in part by opponents who claimed that affirmative action meant "reverse discrimination" against white males, limited popular support for affirmative action. It nonetheless remained federal policy and withstood attempts by succeeding administrations to weaken or kill it.

In her 1967 President's Report, Friedan proposed that NOW extend its activism to electoral politics. Outlining a Bill of Rights for Women for 1968, she advocated its presentation to the political parties and major candidates with the promise that "we . . . cross party lines to work for and support those

19. Paula Giddings, *When and Where I Enter: The Impact of Black Women on Sex and Race in America* (New York: Bantam Books, 1984), p. 308.

candidates who will commit themselves to our Bill of Rights and defeat those who are its enemies." She also urged that women begin to run for office themselves. NOW members concurred with the need for involvement in the 1968 elections but disagreed with the specifics of the proposed Bill of Rights. Although the NOW convention ultimately approved the list, serious divisions rose over two demands: for an Equal Rights Amendment, and for reform of laws restricting abortion. Labor women were concerned about the ERA: many of them had come to believe in the need for an amendment, but their unions remained adamantly opposed to any measure that would wipe out protective labor legislation for women. When NOW put the ERA on its agenda, union women were forced to withdraw from active participation. Other members did not see abortion as a women's rights issue, and they feared that NOW's stand would lose support for the young organization.[20]

Those and other differences could not be contained, and in 1968 various groups of women left NOW to start new organizations. Believing that a more conservative organization was needed to appeal to women in the nation's heartland, Elizabeth Boyer, an Ohio lawyer and NOW founder, left to form the Women's Equity Action League (WEAL). According to its president, Nancy Dowding, WEAL avoided issues "that polarize people—like The Pill or abortion or husbands washing dishes." The new organization attracted women who viewed abortion as too controversial for a women's rights organization and who wanted to focus on just three areas: employment, education, and taxation.[21]

On the other hand, some younger women found NOW's approach too timid. They especially disliked its structure which, dominated by the national leadership, left little scope for local initiatives and few opportunities for the sharing of power. Led by Ti-Grace Atkinson and others mostly from the New York chapter, these women walked out of NOW to form The Femi-

20. Friedan, *It Changed My Life*, pp. 101–6.

21. Anne N. Costain and W. Douglas Costain, "Strategy and Tactics of the Women's Movement in the United States: The Role of Political Parties," in Mary Fainsod Katzenstein and Carol McClurg Mueller, eds., *The Women's Movements of the United States and Western Europe: Consciousness, Political Opportunity, and Public Policy* (Philadelphia: Temple University Press, 1987), pp. 199–201.

nists, adopting a structure conducive to equal participation of all members. That nonhierarchical structure characterized the myriad of local groups that were beginning to form around women newly converted to feminism by their experiences in protest movements.[22]

THE EMERGENCE OF RADICAL FEMINISM

As NOW was beginning to perfect the tools of feminist activism, an entirely separate movement concerned with women's oppression was developing throughout the country. The experiences that had led women in the civil rights and student protest movements to begin to question sex roles were being replicated throughout the protest groups that formed the New Left politics of the 1960s. By the end of 1967, many of these women abandoned hope that their claims would be recognized by the men who dominated the radical groups. When in September 1967 the National Conference for a New Politics—a gathering of 200 civil-rights, antiwar, and various radical organizations—dismissed women's demands as "trivial" compared to the needs of other oppressed groups, it effectively told women to form their own movement. Jo Freeman, civil-rights and students' rights activist, started an independent women's group in Chicago, and Shulamith Firestone began one in New York. Similar groups rapidly appeared in San Francisco, New Orleans, Boston, and Washington, D.C. In November 1968 this "women's liberation" arm of the movement held a national conference in Chicago which attracted more than 200 women from twenty states and Canada.[23]

Thus, by the end of 1968, women had formed two distinct types of groups to politicize their own interests. The type represented by NOW and WEAL has been variously termed the older branch, the moderate wing, or the bureaucratic strand; it

22. Judith Hole and Ellen Levine, *Rebirth of Feminism* (New York: Quadrangle Books, 1971), pp. 88–90, 95–96; Freeman, *The Politics of Women's Liberation*, pp. 80–82.

23. Freeman, *The Politics of Women's Liberation,* pp. 103–7; Sara Evans, *Personal Politics: The Roots of Women's Liberation in the Civil Rights Movement and the New Left* (New York: Random House, 1979), pp. 193–211.

has been called reformist, moderate, and women's-rights oriented. The type that grew out of radical protest politics has been called the younger branch or the collectivist strand; it defined itself as radical and its goal, "women's liberation." Initially, the two wings were alike only in that white, middle- and upper-middle class, relatively well-educated women comprised the overwhelming majority of their adherents.[24] In other respects the two movements differed significantly. Women in the moderate strand were older, in the middle years of lives devoted to professional careers and/or to volunteer work in traditional women's organizations and mainstream politics. They were accustomed to pursuing objectives in hierarchically organized structures, to employing the tactics of conventional interest groups, and to working through the courts, legislatures, and executive agencies. While aware of the limitations imposed on women by their home and family roles, these women were most conscious of the relatively overt discrimination encountered when women attempted to operate in public institutions dominated by men.

In contrast, the younger women's approach to feminism had been shaped by their activities in radical protest movements. In the New Left they had imbibed the concepts of participatory democracy and the empowerment of ordinary people. Their bitterness at the male refusal to implement these principles where women were concerned heightened their resolve to create structures in which every woman had a voice and an opportunity to develop her skills and employ her talents. Forswearing hierarchical structures, they rotated leadership positions, shared tasks, and made decisions only after obtaining consensus. They took over slogans from the civil-rights movement, changing "brotherhood of all peoples" into "sisterhood" and "black pride" into "female pride." Finally, they brought from radical politics the instrument of "consciousness raising."

That tool was crucial to the development of feminism because it enormously expanded the movement's political agenda. The idea behind consciousness raising was that "the personal is political," i.e., that an individual's experiences and

24. Ferree and Hess, *Controversy and Coalition*, pp. 48–49.

feelings are important; that what appear to be personal problems are often common to all women and are shaped by social institutions; and that those problems are susceptible to political solutions. Analyses of women's situation that emerged from small, informal, politically oriented discussions called "rap groups" went beyond exposing discrimination in formal institutions to uncovering oppression embedded in sex-role socialization and the private experiences of family life and sexuality. Much more inclined than the moderate branch to probe deeply into the structures that promoted sexual inequality, women on the left made major theoretical and ideological contributions to the emerging feminism.[25]

The younger branch of the movement also veered sharply from the older in its view of the appropriate means to promote social change. Convinced by their New Left experiences of the futility of working within the system, women's liberation activists concentrated on creating alternative institutions. Believing that established institutions were not amenable to the reforms promoted by their counterparts in NOW through the avenues of traditional politics, radical feminists created collectives controlled by women and designed to meet their needs. Throughout the country, they organized community women's centers, health clinics, bookstores, day-care centers, music collectives, rape crisis centers, and the like.[26]

Finally, the radical women differed from the moderates in their inclination to engage in flamboyant tactics. Before the end of the decade, local groups had mounted a number of activities crafted to attract public attention and shake conventional attitudes. At the Miss America contest in 1968, women threw underwear, cosmetics, and false eyelashes into a "freedom trash can" and crowned a sheep Miss America. Later that fall, a group called WITCH (Women's International Terrorist Conspiracy from Hell) hexed the New York Stock Exchange, whose index subsequently dropped five points. Other events designed to startle the public included a protest at a Bridal Fair exposition and a hairy legs demonstration. While such events drew public

25. *Ibid.*, pp. 62–64.
26. Maren Lockwood Carden, *The New Feminist Movement* (New York: Russell Sage Foundation, 1974), pp. 75–77.

attention to feminist issues, they also subjected the movement to public ridicule.[27]

Disagreement over tactics was just one of the conflicts that erupted both between and within the two strands of the new movement. Those in the more moderate branch were angered by the radicals' tactics and some of their ideas, which they feared would alienate women from the suburbs and hinterlands. The issue of how much the women's movement should identify itself with lesbian rights arose in 1970 and remained divisive for several years. Even within the radical groups, dissension developed as they struggled with the meaning and practice of a collective process.

Yet far from weakening the emerging feminism, its very diversity resulted in new energy and resilience. The proliferation of groups enabled individual women to find one most suited to their own interests. Moreover, the two major wings of the movement came to exchange ideology, tactics, and even personnel. For example, by 1972 WEAL had come to support women's right to abortion and had declared itself in favor of "responsible rebellion." NOW chapters began to set up consciousness-raising groups, and the national organization moved to stronger positions on issues such as abortion and lesbian rights as it embraced new goals rising from the analyses of the women's liberation groups. NOW had already staged sit-ins at all-male bars and, on Mother's Day in 1968, it demonstrated in front of the White House, calling for "Rights, Not Roses," and dumping aprons into a trash pile. Increasingly, the older strand adopted both tactics and aims from the younger one, exemplified most strikingly by NOW's new slogan, "Out of the mainstream—and into the revolution."[28]

At the same time, women's liberation activists became more involved in the mainstream of traditional politics. While continuing to employ more radical tactics and ideologies, they too began to seek reform of laws and established institutions. For example, they lobbied for new abortion laws and child-care centers, and they worked for implementation of antidiscrimina-

27. Ferree and Hess, *Controversy and Coalition*, pp. 62–74; Hole and Levine, *Rebirth of Feminism*, pp. 123–29.

28. Costain and Costain, "Strategy and Tactics of the Women's Movement," p. 201; Friedan, *It Changed My Life*, pp. 108–9; Evans, *Personal Politics*, pp. 215, 225; Freeman, *The Politics of Women's Liberation*, pp. 83–84.

Women's Strike for Equality, New York City, August 1970.
(Bettye Lane)

tion measures. The new strength and possibilities for united action amidst diversity were demonstrated in August 1970. On the fiftieth anniversary of women's suffrage, thousands of feminists of all persuasions responded to NOW's call for a Women's Strike for Equality. They marched, picketed, and held rallies across the country in the largest mass action for women's rights in the nation's history and the first demonstration of the new movement to receive serious and substantial press coverage.[29]

FEMINIST PRESSURES ON THE WHITE HOUSE AND CONGRESS

While demonstrations became an increasingly important tool of feminist politics, women continued to press their concerns in more conventional ways. Although the war in Vietnam preoccupied presidential candidates in 1968, NOW's determination

29. Freeman, *The Politics of Women's Liberation*, pp. 83–84; Friedan, *It Changed My Life*, pp. 146–51; Carden, *The New Feminist Movement*, pp. 78–81.

to make officials accountable on issues of women's rights had its effect. Hubert Humphrey called the ERA a "vital issue," and Richard Nixon also affirmed his support. Even American Party candidate George Wallace spoke in favor of the amendment.[30]

Once in office, Nixon confronted more pressure on women's issues, as Congresswomen themselves became more assertive. In July 1969, four Republican Congresswomen sent a memo charging his administration with having "done absolutely nothing of significance in the field of women's rights, responsibilities and opportunities." Not only had his record of female appointments failed to match "the inadequate action of past Administrations," but it had also failed to make "a single important policy decision or legislative recommendation. . . ." Although the Nixon administration never took the initiative on women's issues, Nixon eventually appointed more than one hundred women to high-level positions, and he created the post of Special Assistant to the President on Women's Affairs. His more immediate response to the Congresswomen's demands was to create a Task Force on Women's Rights and Responsibilities.[31]

Appointed to the task force were a number of individuals already identified with a strong concern for women's rights, including its chair Virginia Allan, former president of the Business and Professional Women, which of all the older women's organizations was second only to the National Woman's Party in its advocacy of women's rights. The administration received the task force's report in December 1969, and then did nothing even when pressed by women activists to release it. After it was leaked to the press and had appeared in several newspapers, the report was officially released in June 1970. For the most part, its specific recommendations stayed within the framework established by that of the PCSW, but it stressed the urgency of action and called for the government to be "as seriously concerned with sex discrimination as with race discrimination." Most notably, it was the first government statement in support of the Equal Rights Amendment.[32]

Concurrent developments were also bringing the ERA to

30. Harrison, *On Account of Sex,* pp. 206–7.
31. Freeman, *The Politics of Women's Liberation,* pp. 205–7.
32. *Ibid.,* pp. 207–8; Hole and Levine, *Rebirth of Feminism,* pp. 49–51.

the forefront, and that measure would serve as a powerful mobilizing and unifying force for the women's movement. A number of federal courts had struck down protective labor laws for women as a violation of Title VII, and in 1969, the EEOC issued a guideline agreeing that such laws were in conflict with Title VII. Since the ERA's threat to protective legislation had disturbed traditional women's organizations, labor unions, and liberal groups concerned about women's working conditions, the court decisions and EEOC guidelines eliminated a major base of opposition to the ERA. Although the AFL-CIO dragged its feet until 1973, in 1970 the United Auto Workers endorsed the ERA, as did the Citizen's Advisory Council on the Status of Women, and the Department of Labor. That same year, Congress began to give serious attention to the amendment.[33]

The fate of the amendment would rest in overwhelmingly male hands, but the arrival of new women in Congress augmented the ranks of such women as Edith Green, Martha Griffiths, Patsy Mink, and Margaret Chase Smith, who had pushed for previous equity measures. In 1966, Margaret Heckler challenged the Massachusetts Republican party, defeating former Republican House leader Joseph W. Martin and winning election to Congress. She was one of the four Republican Congresswomen who took Nixon to task for his neglect of women's concerns. Two years later, Shirley Chisholm became the first black woman to win election to the House of Representatives. Schooled in the Democratic party, the League of Women Voters, and grass-roots community groups, Chisholm served her legislative apprenticeship in the New York Assembly. In gaining her House seat she defeated James Farmer, a founder of CORE who ran on both the Republican and Liberal party tickets, and stressed in his campaign the need for "a strong male image" and "a man's voice in Washington." That, no doubt, was one of the experiences that led her to insist that in politics she felt the sting of sexism to be stronger than racism.[34]

1970 brought two more supporters of women's rights to the House. Bella Abzug, the other most outspoken feminist besides Chisholm, moved to Congress from party work among liberal

33. Freeman, *The Politics of Women's Liberation,* pp. 186–87, 212–13.

34. Hope Chamberlin, *A Minority of Members: Women in the U.S. Congress* (New York: New American Library, 1973), pp. 326–29, 332–38.

New York Democrats and from the Women Strike for Peace, which she had founded. Ella Grasso emerged from more conventional politics in Connecticut, where Democratic party leader John Bailey had cultivated her rise from League of Women Voters work through floor leader of the state House, Democratic National Committeewoman, and Connecticut secretary of state. Though she did not identify herself as a feminist, Grasso had chaired the planning committee for the Governor's Commission on the Status of Women and was sympathetic to women's issues. Her congressional service positioned Grasso to become in 1974 the first woman governor elected in her own right.[35]

While Abzug and Chisholm were the only two new Congresswomen whose victories derived in part from the new politics of the 1960s—particularly the antiwar and civil-rights movements—those grass-roots movements had motivated thousands of women to make unprecedented claims for equality. Combined with mainstream feminists inspired by the initiatives against sex discrimination in the Kennedy and Johnson administrations, these women formed a diverse movement whose political clout increased rapidly. From little more than 1,000 members in 1967, NOW grew to over 4,000 by 1970, and in 1972 would have nearly 15,000 members in more than 200 chapters. Although it did not seek a mass membership, WEAL nonetheless had forty chapters by 1973. Other feminist organizations had been founded to represent women in various professions, and traditional women's organizations like the AAUW and LWV moved women's issues to higher places on their agendas. Moreover, by 1970 this growing movement had found in the ERA an issue capable of mobilizing and uniting even larger numbers of women.[36]

Whether the new movement could unite women across class and racial lines, however, remained problematic. NOW recruited a number of prominent black women, including Pauli Murray, Fannie Lou Hamer, Shirley Chisholm, and Addie L. Wyatt, a leader of the Amalgamated Meat Cutters Union; and

35. Esther Stineman, *American Political Women: Contemporary and Historical Profiles* (Littleton, CO: Libraries Unlimited, Inc., 1980), pp. 50–51.

36. Carden, *The New Feminist Movement*, pp. 105, 134–36, 194.

it elected Aileen Hernandez to succeed Friedan as president in 1970. Individual women and a black feminist group, the Third World Women's Alliance, participated in the August 1970 mass demonstrations, and the National Council of Negro Women was an early supporter of the ERA. Yet the emerging women's movement maintained its overwhelmingly white, middle-class cast, and many minority women remained indifferent or hostile. To them, the movement appeared concerned primarily with the interests of elite women; and while it capitalized on the achievements of the civil-rights movement, it threatened racial unity with its anti-male tone.[37]

Mexican-American women resented the tendency of scholars and some white feminists to stereotype the Chicano family as characterized by extreme male dominance, or "machismo," and the total subordination of women. Moreover, they insisted that feminist issues needed to be addressed within the context of their experiences as Mexican-Americans. As Anna Nieto-Gomez put it, "When a Chicana talks about birth control and abortion, she does so in the context of understanding the cultural genocidal acts of this country," referring to the forced sterilization undergone by many minority women. Similarly, she pointed out, proposals for day care must incorporate the demand that child-care centers be bilingual and bicultural if Chicanas were to mobilize around that issue.[38]

That they did not flock to the new white-dominated organizations did not mean that minority women ignored their gender-based oppression. Just as white women had left feminist organizations to form new ones more conducive to their particular concerns, minority women created their own organizations. In 1970, for example, women from forty-three tribes organized the North American Indian Women's Association. Six hundred Mexican-American women gathered at the first national Chicana conference in 1971 and adopted strong resolutions criticizing the Catholic Church and calling for free legal abortion. 1972 saw the founding of the Conference of Puerto

37. Giddings, *When and Where I Enter,* pp. 303–11.

38. Martha Cotera, *Profile on the Mexican American Woman* (Austin, Texas: National Educational Laboratory Publishers, Inc., 1976), pp. 152–54, 173–76.

Rican Women, and in 1973 Eleanor Holmes Norton and others organized the National Black Feminist Organization.[39]

As women of diverse races and ethnic groups moved to more active engagement in formal politics, they gained a political education and a sense of their capabilities. A Pennsylvania feminist, for example, confessed that she initially didn't even know that one could use a phone book to find one's local representative. As they worked to get a state equal rights amendment, however, she and fellow members of her local NOW chapter soon knew more about the political process than did a legislator they were lobbying.[40] While their feminism initiated them into political activities, women soon came to realize the limitations of seeking to influence male officials. In the 1970s, feminists continued to make demands on legislators and administrators, but they also labored to put women themselves into party and government positions.

39. *Chicana Women Speak Out* (New York: Pathfinder Press, 1971), pp. 3, 13; Ellen Sweet, "A '70s Chronology," *Ms.* 8 (December 1979):60, 66, 68.

40. Carden, *The New Feminist Movement*, pp. 109–10.

Chapter 4

A New Presence in Mainstream Politics

The new movement launched by women in the late 1960s came into its own in the next decade and helped to shape changes of such import as to constitute a new era in American politics. Popular attitudes became more favorable to female political candidates and more supportive of women's policy concerns. Collectively, women became more agressive, demanding power within the parties, seeking influence with lawmakers and public administrators, and organizing on behalf of female candidates. More women were inspired to run for office, and their numbers grew, especially at the state and local levels of government.

CHANGING POLITICAL ATTITUDES AND BEHAVIOR

The resurgence of feminism in the 1960s made itself felt in the realm of mass political behavior in the 1970s. Due largely to women's increasing presence in the labor force and to their rising levels of education, the gender gap in various forms of political participation had been declining for several decades. By the 1970s the differences between men and women in such activities as voting, belonging to a political organization, and working in a campaign were rarely large enough to be statistically significant. In general, sex-related differences no longer characterized mass political participation.[1]

Some features of women's mass political behavior were linked to the feminist movement. Most women who engaged in campaign activities or who initiated contact with public officials strongly supported equality for women in politics, employment, and social roles. Feminist convictions pushed some women into politics, and political activism often heightened women's consciousness of sexual inequality. As would be expected, support of feminist issues and degree of political participation were highest for college-educated women.[2]

According to polls, the absolute numbers of women participating in campaign activities declined between 1960 and 1976 (as it did for men), but the intensity of participation increased among women who worked outside the home. Between 1968 and 1972, just when the women's movement began to claim national attention, the mean number of campaign activities increased for employed women; blue-collar workers and younger employed women registered the largest increases in involvement in political campaigns.[3]

Feminism had an even larger impact on political attitudes among men and women. In just a few years, public opinion polls registered dramatic changes in popular beliefs about women's capabilities and rights. A particularly sharp change occurred in response to the Gallup poll question, "If your party nominated a woman for president, would you vote for her if she were qualified for the job?" In 1969, more men (58 percent) than women (49 percent) responded positively; but two years later women surpassed men, with 67 percent in

1. Karen Leigh Beckwith, *American Women and Political Participation: The Impacts of Work, Generation, and Feminism* (Westport, CT: Greenwood Press, 1986), pp. 17–33, 147–48.

2. *Ibid.*, pp. 95–113; Susan B. Hansen, Linda M. Franz, and Margaret Netemeyer-Mays, "Women's Political Participation and Policy Preferences," *Social Science Quarterly* 56 (March 1976):576–90.

3. Kristi Andersen, "Working Women and Political Participation, 1952–1972," *American Journal of Political Science* 19 (August 1975):445–49.

agreement, compared to 65 percent of the male respondents.[4]

Feminist issues did not, however, exert a substantial influence on presidential campaigns during the 1970s. Even though feminists were active in both parties' national conventions in 1972 and 1976, women's issues were peripheral to the national elections. Presidential candidates evinced no significant differences on women's issues; in 1976, for example, both Republican Gerald Ford and Democrat Jimmy Carter supported the Equal Rights Amendment and opposed abortion, the two most prominent feminist issues, which will be discussed in the next chapter. Presidential candidates did not seek to appeal to the electorate on women's issues, and most voters did not perceive differences in their positions on women's rights. Major feminist organizations remained neutral in the presidential campaigns.[5]

THE NATIONAL WOMEN'S POLITICAL CAUCUS

In 1971, the growing feminist movement launched a vehicle for transforming women's place in electoral politics. A goal of the pre-eminent feminist organization, the National Organization for Women, was to increase women's presence in politics, but NOW devoted more of its energies to lobbying, consciousness raising among its members, and staging public demonstrations. While not disputing the need to change public attitudes and put pressure on policymakers, other women felt that it was time to concentrate on enabling feminists to make policy themselves. These women came from a variety of backgrounds. Elly Peterson of Michigan had been vice-chair of the Republican National Committee. Democrat Mary Ann Krupsak of New York was one of the new breed of women state legislators. Political writer Gloria Steinem was active in the left wing of Democratic politics and soon-to-be founder of *Ms.*, the first mainstream feminist

4. Audrey Siess Wells and Eleanor Cutri Smeal, "Women's Attitudes Toward Women in Politics," in Jane L. Jacquette, ed., *Women in Politics* (New York: John Wiley and Sons, 1974), pp. 56–57.

5. Ethel Klein, *Gender Politics: From Consciousness to Mass Politics* (Cambridge, MA: Harvard University Press, 1984), pp. 144–57.

Founders of the National Women's Political Caucus, July 1971.
Left to right: Gloria Steinem, Bella Abzug, Shirley Chisholm, and
Betty Friedan. (Wide World Photos)

magazine. Party regulars, some NOW activists, women labor
leaders, and women from other grass-roots movements decided
that a new organization was necessary. With Bella Abzug, Shirley Chisholm, Betty Friedan, and Gloria Steinem serving as
spokespersons, they called a national conference for July 1971.[6]

More than 300 women came to Washington, D.C. to found
the National Women's Political Caucus (NWPC). The leaders
had determined to make their movement broad-based, and
they attracted to the meeting not just publicly identified feminists but also women from organized labor, religious groups,
traditional women's organizations, and a variety of ethnic
groups. Civil-rights activist Fanny Lou Hamer, for example, was
among the keynote speakers, and women from diverse groups

6. Betty Friedan, *It Changed My Life: Writings on the Women's Movement*
(New York: Random House, 1976), pp. 166–83; Bella Abzug, *Bella! Ms. Abzug
Goes to Washington* (New York: Saturday Review Press, 1972), pp. 160–61,
163–64, 177, 197–204.

were elected to the National Policy Council, the governing board of the new organization. Along with self-identified feminists and women from both major parties were LaDonna Harris, Indian rights leader; Dorothy Height, head of the National Council of Negro Women; Olga Madar from the United Auto Workers; welfare rights leader Beulah Sanders; and Lupe Anguiano, a Chicana activist.[7]

The founders deliberately structured the organization to represent a broad spectrum of women, and in subsequent years the caucus revised its bylaws to increase the representation of minority women. It took great pains to be bipartisan, requiring that members of both parties be represented in leadership positions and that the national chair be rotated between a Republican and a Democrat. Recognizing the party attachments of most members, in the mid-1970s the NWPC created Republican and Democratic women's task forces to enable members to work on partisan issues.[8]

Electing women to office and increasing their voice in party affairs was a major caucus goal, but the NWPC was not founded simply to promote female candidates. Nor would it support any candidate just because she was a woman. Rather, the caucus established as its purpose the combating of sexism, racism, institutional violence, and poverty. It would achieve these goals by promoting party reform, working for the election and appointment of women to public office, and supporting women's issues and feminist candidates of both sexes and across party lines. In guidelines that the caucus adopted for local and state units to use in endorsement decisions, it committed itself to work for "sweeping social change." "Women's issues" were defined broadly, for the guidelines listed not only such concerns as equal treatment, child care, and reproductive rights, but also a host of policies that included opposition to the war in Vietnam, environmental measures, and arms control. These were guidelines, however, rather than absolute rules, and state and local chapters had considerable autonomy in deciding which candi-

7. Rona F. Feit, "Organizing for Political Power: The National Women's Political Caucus," in Bernice Cummings and Victoria Schuck, eds., *Women Organizing: An Anthology* (Metuchen, NJ: The Scarecrow Press, 1979), pp. 184–85, 207.

8. *Ibid.*, pp. 185, 191–93.

dates to endorse. But when the NWPC established national endorsement guidelines in 1977, it made support for the Equal Rights Amendment, for the 1973 Supreme Court decision affirming women's right to abortion, and for publicly funded child care the *sine qua non*s for caucus support.[9]

The NWPC's founding conference attracted substantial media attention, most of it favorable. *Newsweek*, for example, reported that the founders had created a "plausible definition and a strategy for a women's political movement where none had existed before." Comments from the pinnacle of power were not so positive. Secretary of State William Rogers remarked that a photograph of four Caucus leaders looked "like a burlesque," to which President Nixon replied, "What's wrong with that?"[10]

Undaunted, and perhaps spurred by the derision from the White House, caucus founders fanned out through the country to establish local and state groups. Within a couple of years, almost every state had a caucus and more than 500 local units had been formed. In early 1973, the NWPC had a mailing list which exceeded 30,000, many of whom were newcomers to feminist activism. Thousands more were estimated to belong to local caucuses. Local groups enjoyed election victories as early as 1972, even though at the time caucus support usually took the form of volunteer labor rather than financial contributions. It was not until 1976 that the national caucus had funds to allocate to candidates it endorsed.[11]

Meanwhile, women created a second organization to elect women to public office. Founded in 1974, the Women's Campaign Fund (WCF) began to raise money for female candidates, focusing on congressional elections. Like the caucus, the WCF cut across party lines, and it was led by co-chairs from each of the major parties. Unlike the NWPC, the fund would support only female candidates, and its criteria for selecting candidates were initially less rigorous, requiring that a candidate have a realistic chance of winning and that she take a position on issues

9. *Ibid.*

10. *Ibid.*, p. 185; Maren Lockwood Carden, *The New Feminist Movement* (New York: Russell Sage Foundation, 1974), p. 162.

11. Carden, *The New Feminist Movement,* p. 139.

"affecting the quality of life and human needs . . . substantially more progressive than that of her opponent." Subsequently, the WCF too insisted that its candidates take affirmative stands on the ERA and abortion.[12]

In its first year, the WCF supported women in twenty-two federal and six state campaigns; thirteen of its candidates were elected to Congress, and four to state legislatures. Ten years later, the fund could count nearly 200 women elected with its help, and more than twenty other political action committees had been established at the national, state, and local levels to raise money and generate support for female candidates. As political action commitees (PACs) grew to exert an inordinate influence in American politics, those designed to support women and feminist candidates never matched the vast sums expended by PACs representing business, labor, and other interests, but in many cases, they did make a difference.[13]

The NWPC remained the most visible agency for women's integration into mainstream politics. Its membership resembled that of other women's movement organizations. Most participants were between thirty and fifty years old, and as was true of political elites in general, they were highly educated with above-average incomes. A large majority had been involved in politics before, and an even larger majority were Democrats who placed themselves on the liberal end of the political spectrum.[14]

Most NWPC members were political veterans, and most female politicians, perhaps fearing an association with feminism, never became members. Nonetheless, the caucus did draw new women into political activism and it raised feminist consciousness among those already engaged. In Iowa, for example, where the state caucus claimed 300 members just three months after its founding, one-fourth of those members identified themselves as independents, half of whom had never par-

12. Katherine E. Kleeman, *Women's PAC's* (New Brunswick, NJ: Center for the American Woman and Politics, 1983).

13. *Ibid.*

14. Barbara Burrell, "A New Dimension in Political Participation: The Women's Political Caucus," in Marianne Githens and Jewel L. Prestage, eds., *A Portrait of Marginality: The Political Behavior of American Women* (New York: David McKay, 1977), pp. 244–51; Feit, "Organizing for Political Power," pp. 194–95.

ticipated in political activities before. For Madeline Kunin, a Vermont Democrat who had served on the state's Commission on the Status of Women, the caucus served as catalyst. Kunin had entertained the idea of running for office "someday when my kids were older." In 1972 she was part of a group which started a local branch of the caucus, and "with the support of my women friends, I decided to go ahead." Kunin's election to the Vermont House in 1972 set her on a path to the governor's office, which she won ten years later. For women already experienced in politics, the caucus served to ignite their feminism. Ann F. Lewis came from a career in Democratic politics to the founding conference of the NWPC where she experienced an awakening to feminist concerns. Similarly, Norma Paulus, a Republican elected to the Oregon House of Representatives in 1970, did not see herself as a feminist. She had not even heard of the National Women's Political Caucus, but when she accepted an invitation to an Oregon caucus meeting in 1971, she too became caught up in feminism.[15]

FEMINISM AND THE POLITICAL PARTIES

Besides engaging more women in politics and awakening veterans to women's concerns, the NWPC exerted a dramatic impact on the national party conventions in 1972. Early that year, the caucus established a Women's Education for Delegate Selection (WEDS) project designed to increase the numbers of women delegates to the conventions. As WEDS conducted conferences to instruct women about delegate selection processes, caucus Democrats and Republicans met with their national committees to press for equal representation of women as delegates.[16]

15. Burrell, "A New Dimension in Political Participation," p. 246; Ruth B. Mandel, *In the Running: The New Woman Candidate* (Boston: Beacon Press, 1981), pp. 13–14; Margaret W. Freivogel, "Ann Lewis Turned Interest in Politics into Profession," *St. Louis Post Dispatch,* December 24, 1984; *Women State Legislators: Report from a Conference, June 17–20, 1982* (New Brunswick, NJ: Center for the American Woman and Politics, n.d.), pp. 35–36.

16. Jo Freeman, *The Politics of Women's Liberation* (New York: David McKay, 1975), pp. 160–61.

Democratic women were aided by reforms already under way. In response to the bitter conflicts at their 1968 convention in Chicago, where police attacked antiwar protesters and activists voices were supressed by party bosses, the Democrats created a Commission on Party Structure and Delegate Selection, commonly known as the McGovern-Fraser Commission. Referring specifically to underrepresentation of women, blacks, and youth, the commission issued guidelines for states to take affirmative action in delegate selection so that representatives of these groups would attend the 1972 convention in numbers roughly proportionate to their presence in the population at large. This dramatic departure from tradition—in which party regulars attended party conventions—provided the vehicle for women to press their claims. NWPC Democrats did not achieve their goal of 50 percent women in each delegation, but they did increase the overall presence of women from 13 percent in 1968 to 40 percent in 1972. In a sampling of convention delegates, more than one-third of the women reported that they had been active in the women's liberation movement, and 84 percent said that it had affected them.[17]

Although women exercised collective political clout for the first time at the Democratic National Convention, they also confronted the limits of their emerging power. In the first place, not all politicians who identified with women's concerns attended the convention. Congresswoman Edith Green, for example, agreed with other party regulars that "the Democratic party was taken over by the kooks," and stayed home. There were also conflicts among feminists. While most of the women delegates favored the presidential candidacy of George McGovern, leading caucus members such as Martha McKay of North Carolina came pledged to other candidates. Betty Friedan, who attended as a reporter, not a delegate, charged that Steinem and Abzug were using the caucus as a

17. Ibid.; Jeane Kirkpatrick, "Representation in the American National Conventions: The Case of 1972," *British Journal of Political Science* 5 (July 1975): 275–81; Wilma E. McGrath and John W. Soule, "Rocking the Cradle or Rocking the Boat: Women at the 1972 Democratic National Convention," *Social Science Quarterly*, 55 (June 1974):143.

tool for nominating George McGovern and failing to let all women be heard.[18]

More problematic was the response of the women's movement to the presidential race of NWPC founder and black Congresswoman Shirley Chisholm, the first woman to seek the highest spot on a major party's ticket. Chisholm entered the race late and with little financial or organizational support. Some white feminists, including NOW president Wilma Scott Heide, threw theselves into her campaign. But others equivocated. Steinem and Abzug, for example, attempted to support both Chisholm and McGovern. They no doubt viewed the defeat of Nixon as the top priority and did not want to "waste" their clout on a candidate who could not win. Fannie Lou Hamer, Lupe Anguiano, and other minority women in the NWPC, however, provided vigorous support. In Chisholm's view, white feminists were tentative because they were uncomfortable fighting for a lost cause. Minority women, on the other hand, with long years in civil rights struggles, were "used to taking up seemingly impossible challenges . . . and in the process increas[ing] the chance that success would come, someday." Though not as painful as the rebuff to Chisholm's campaign from black men, the lukewarm response from white feminists further discouraged black women about the sensitivity of the women's movement to black women's concerns.[19]

White feminists who put the nomination of McGovern above a strong show of support for Chisholm may have wondered if it was worth it. McGovern appointed women to key posts in his campaign, including actress Shirley MacLaine as liaison with women's groups, and Anne Wexler and Jean Westwood as floor managers, but these women were not known as feminists. Worse, they stood behind McGovern when he sacrificed women's concerns to ensure his own nomination. Feminists believed that they had been promised the appointment of a woman as co-chair of the convention. California Congress-

18. Susan and Martin Tolchin, *Clout: Womanpower and Politics* (New York: G. P. Putnam's Sons, 1974), p. 33; Friedan, *It Changed My Life*, pp. 175–79; Abzug, *Bella!*, pp. 160–61, 199–203, 219–20.

19. Shirley Chisholm, *The Good Fight* (New York: Harper and Row, 1973), pp. 71–77.

woman Yvonne Braithwaite Burke was selected, but as vice-chair, a position which feminists believed maintained the tradition of women serving as token figureheads. Even more galling was McGovern's failure to support the caucus's challenge to the South Carolina delegation, which included only 25 percent women. Finally, women felt betrayed once more when, in deference to McGovern's wishes, the convention defeated, 1,572 to 1,101, a platform plank in support of women's reproductive freedom.[20]

Despite these defeats, Democratic women enjoyed some notable achievements at the 1972 convention. In the vice presidential nomination, they mobilized 420 votes for Frances (Sissy) Farenthold, a former Texas legislator who had come close to winning the gubernatorial primary. The first woman seriously considered by the Democrats for the national ticket, Farenthold won 13 percent of the vote. Moreover, the Democratic platform included fifteen women's rights planks; and the convention elected Jean Westwood as chair of the Democratic National Committee, another first for women. In all, feminists had learned some lessons about politics, not least of which was the necessity of an independent presence and the withholding of support for candidates until they had given firm commitments on women's concerns. Donna Brunstadt, a delegate from Connecticut, reported that the McGovern camp assumed women would follow him "to hell and back." Reflecting that most women would have done so, she concluded, "I no longer would do that for any man."[21]

Although their party instituted no procedural reforms, Republican women also increased their share of representation, from 17 percent at the 1968 convention, to 30 percent in 1972. Most of these women (60 percent, by one poll) were not sympathetic to the feminist movement, and few controversial issues surfaced as the convention renominated Nixon. Nonetheless the new political movement did make an impact. Jill Ruckelshaus, a White House aide, who had been named caucus spokeswoman for the Republican convention, along with NWPC members Bobbie Greene Kilberg and Doris Meissner, called a

20. Susan and Martin Tolchin, *Clout,* pp. 40–49.
21. *Ibid.,* pp. 49–59.

meeting of the fifty-four female members of the Platform Committee. Cool at first to the idea of expressing women's concerns, the women began to speak of how they felt left out of major party decisions. A smaller group met the next day and decided to press for a platform plank in support of day care. Led by Congresswoman Margaret Heckler, these women defied White House opposition, and their plank prevailed. In addition, caucus women obtained a rule calling for more equal representation of women as convention delegates. Two years later, Republican feminists rejoiced when Mary Louise Smith, a founder of the Iowa Women's Political Caucus, won appointment as the first female chair of the Republican National Committee.[22]

Before the next presidential election, caucus members of both parties developed more formal structures. In 1974, Democrats organized the Democratic Women's Task Force, which combined with the Women's Caucus of the Democratic National Committee to push women's concerns at the 1976 convention. Women's share of delegates fell to 34 percent, but their political savvy made up for their smaller numbers. They prevailed on nearly all of their platform demands, including a plank opposing a constitutional amendment banning abortion. While that plank represented a compromise, it was an advance over the 1972 convention's silence on reproductive freedom. Women also compromised on female representation at future conventions in exchange for presidential nominee Jimmy Carter's promise to campaign for the ERA and to appoint significant numbers of women to his administration. Subsequently, Democratic women won 50–50 representation at the 1978 midterm convention as well as procedures assuring equal representation in 1980.[23]

The Republican Women's Task Force, organized in 1975, led a successful fight at the 1976 convention to retain a pro-ERA

22. Kirkpatrick, "Representation in the American National Conventions," p. 310; Feit, "Organizing for Political Power," pp. 195–96; Margaret W. Freivogel, "Activist Chose Children over Job with Clout," *St. Louis Post-Dispatch*, December 25, 1984.

23. Jo Freeman, "Whom You Know versus Whom You Represent: Feminist Influence in the Democratic and Republican Parties," in Mary Fainsod Katzenstein and Carol McClurg Mueller, eds., *The Women's Movements of the United States and Western Europe: Consciousness, Political Opportunity, and Public Policy* (Philadelphia: Temple University Press, 1987), pp. 215–44.

plank in the platform. Republican feminists managed to pass a minority report supporting women's reproductive freedom, but they lost a floor vote that put an anti-abortion plank in the Republican platform for the first time. With just over 31 percent representation in 1976, Republican women persuaded party chairman George Bush to establish a commission to study the issue of delegate selection. That commission called for more women as delegates, and at the 1980 convention women constituted 40 percent of the total. Although their party had far fewer feminists and much less commitment to women's issues, Republican women did exercise influence on behalf of women's concerns.[24]

The usefulness of parties in furthering feminist goals remained problematic. Feminism gave its last gasp within the Republican party in 1976. By 1980, conservatives had wrested control of the party and, although women were well represented as delegates, feminist concerns were not. Feminists retained and even increased their power within the Democratic party, but that occurred as the influence of parties was declining. Popular primaries rather than party conventions now chose presidential nominees, and candidates depended more on nonpartisan political action committees (PACS) for financial support than they did on parties. Feminist planks in party platforms were of symbolic importance, but candidates did not feel firmly bound to platform positions.

THE DRIVE FOR POLITICAL OFFICE

While women strived for a larger voice within the parties, they also demonstrated a burgeoning interest and a growing success rate in holding public office. The extremely low base of female office-holding in the early 1970s made their gains especially dramatic. Women's share of county governing board seats, for example, doubled between 1975 and 1981. The number of women in state legislatures grew by more than 100 percent between 1971 and 1981, and the number of legislative seats

24. *Ibid.;* Freivogel, "Activist Chose Children over Job with Clout;" Mandel, *In the Running,* pp. 211–12.

held by black women nearly doubled. Women increased their proportion of seats in Congress only marginally, but, as at the state and local levels, important qualitative changes occurred. As we will see, these changes brought women closer to the centers of power and increased their attention to policy issues of particular concern to women.[25]

From a base of around 10 percent which remained constant between 1920 and 1970, women's share of local school board seats jumped to almost 33 percent by 1981. Female membership on city councils grew from less than 10 percent in 1975 to 13 percent by the end of the decade, and women doubled their representation on county governing boards, from 3 to 6 percent. Although feminism played little or no role in the political aspirations of these new council members, once in office a number of them became sensitized to their inferior status. At the 1972 Congress of the National League of Cities (NLC), one hundred women formed a caucus to push through a resolution promoting greater participation of women in policymaking positions in the NLC and state municipal leagues.[26]

Local council membership paved the way to higher office for some women. Janet Gray Hayes served her political apprenticeship with the League of Women Voters before winning a seat on the San Jose, California city council in 1971. Three years later, she was elected mayor, the first woman to head a city with a population of 500,000. Dianne Feinstein became mayor of San Francisco in 1978 after nearly a decade of service on the city's Board of Supervisors. As protégé of Chicago boss and mayor Richard Daley, Jane Byrne's path to power led through Democratic party politics. After Daley's successor fired her from her cabinet position, she ran against him and was elected mayor in

25. Robert Benenson, "Women and Politics," *Editorial Research Reports* 11 (September 17, 1982):707–8; Jewel L. Prestage, "Black Women State Legislators," in Githens and Prestage, *A Portrait of Marginality, p. 405;* Susan J. Carroll and Wendy S. Strimling, *Women's Routes to Elective Office* (New Brunswick, NJ: Center for the Study of the American Woman and and Politics, 1983), p. 141.

26. *Women on School Boards* (Evanston, IL: National School Board Association, 1974), p. 2; Albert K. Karnig and B. Oliver Walter, "Election of Women to City Councils," *Social Science Quarterly* 56 (March 1976):607; Benenson, "Women and Politics," p. 708; "City Councilwomen: A Different Perspective," *Nation's Cities* 11 (September 1973):24–31.

1979. Kathryn Whitmire became the first female officeholder in Houston, Texas in 1977 when she was elected city controller. Two years later two women won city council seats in Houston for the first time, and Whitmire moved up to the mayor's office in 1981. In smaller cities and towns, the gains were equally impressive. By 1980, there were more than one thousand female mayors. Among cities with populations of at least 30,000, the number headed by women grew from seven in 1971 to seventy-two in 1981.[27]

As state legislators, women had seen their ranks diminished during the 1960s. From a peak of 351 in 1961, the number of women in statehouses fell to 293 in 1971. Two years later women had regained the loss, with 424 women filling 6 percent of the seats; and by 1981, 906 female legislators represented more than 12 percent of the total. In ten legislatures, women held 20 percent or more of the seats, and in Oregon and New Hampshire nearly one-third. Although the number of women in statewide elective offices grew only from 10 to 11 percent between 1975 and 1981, two women were elected governor during the decade. Recalling that the previous women governors were elected to succeed their husbands, Ella Grasso identified herself as the "first lady governor who was not first a governor's lady" when Connecticut voters put her in office in 1974. Two years later, Dixie Lee Ray, scientist and former head of the Atomic Energy Commission, became governor of Washington.[28]

A number of factors contributed to the upsurge in female office-holding that began in the 1970s. The increasing number of direct primaries and consequent loosening of party control over nominations provided opportunities for women in areas where parties continued to ignore women as potential candidates. In addition, the declining public trust in government

27. Barbara Williams, *Breakthrough: Women in Politics* (New York: Walker and Company, 1979), pp. 8, 51–65; Esther Stineman, *American Political Women: Contemporary and Historical Profiles* (Littleton, CO: Libraries Unlimited, 1980), pp. 22–24, 42–43; Susan A. MacManus, "A City's First Female Officeholder: 'Coattails' for Future Female Officeseekers?" *Western Political Quarterly* 34 (March 1981):89, 98; Benenson, "Women and Politics," p. 707.

28. Carroll and Strimling, *Women's Routes to Elective Office*, pp. ix, 4; Benenson, "Women and Politics," p. 707; Grasso quoted in Williams, *Breakthrough*, p. 10.

following revelations about the conduct of the Vietnam War and the Watergate scandals made voters more likely to support "outsiders." Mary Anne Krupsak, for example, won the office of New York Lieutenant Governor on the campaign slogan, "She's Not Just One of the Boys."[29]

Even more important was the influence of feminism, though much of that influence was indirect. As Carol Mueller has argued, NOW, NWPC, WCF and other of the new feminist organizations could claim scant direct credit for the rise of women in public office, at least before the late 1970s. Feminist organizations did not provide the bulk of the funds or other support for most of the newly elected women. What feminist groups did was to raise public consciousness, to change popular attitudes. Voters became more receptive to the idea of women in office, and women themselves developed greater self-confidence, higher aspirations, and a sense of their right to roles formerly monopolized by men. More direct links between feminism and the election of women to political office, such as feminist organizations' support for women's candidacies, candidates' attitudes about feminism, and candidates' attention to women's issues in their campaigns, varied considerably among women, although these links strengthened over time.[30]

Two studies conducted under the auspices of the Center for the American Woman and Politics illuminate these connections. The first was a survey of major-party candidates for state legislative seats, state offices, and Congress in 1976. Subjects of the second survey were women office-holders at local and state levels in 1981. While these two surveys are not exactly comparable since only the first included losers as well as winners, they do suggest a growing connection between the women's movement and female office-holders.[31]

29. Susan J. Carroll, *Women As Candidates in American Politics* (Bloomington, IN: Indiana University Press, 1985), pp. 25–26; Stineman, *American Political Women*, p. 98; Mandel, *In The Running*, p. 232.

30. Carol McClurg Miller, "Collective Consciousness, Identity Transformation, and the Rise of Women in Public Office in the United States," in Katzenstein and Mueller, *Women's Movement*, pp. 96–104.

31. Carroll, *Women As Candidates;* Carroll and Strimling, *Women's Routes to Elective Office.* The 1981 survey is summarized along with results of other studies in Kathy A. Stanwick and Katherine E. Kleeman, *Women Make a Difference* (Center for the American Woman and Politics, 1983).

The surveys indicate that political parties played a larger role than women's organizations in recruiting and/or supporting women candidates in both 1976 and 1981. By 1981, however, women's organizations had become increasingly influential in women's campaigns and had actively recruited one-fifth and supported nearly one-half of the successful female candidates. The efforts of women's groups were even more central to black candidates. In 1981, more than half of the black women legislators were encouraged to run by women's organizations, and the latter supported nearly two-thirds of the black women who ran.[32]

Women's issues played a relatively small role in the campaigns of the women who ran in 1976. More than 20 percent of the candidates for state legislatures did not discuss women's issues at all, and only around 10 percent initiated discussion on those subjects. That reticence undoubtedly reflected strategic considerations more than it did their interest in public policies concerning women, for these candidates held overwhelmingly positive attitudes towards the women's movement and women's issues. Of those who ran for a state legislature or statewide office, more than 80 percent reported that they felt very or somewhat positive towards the women's movement and its goals. Similarly, between 60 and 100 percent of these candidates gave a feminist response to a series of questions about the Equal Rights Amendment, abortion, child care, and the like. While Democratic women were more favorable towards women's issues, their Republican counterparts responded with majorities or near-majorities to most of those concerns. Strong identification with feminist goals held also for the 1981 office-holders: they were much more supportive of the Equal Rights Amendment and opposed to a constitutional ban on abortions than were male office-holders, and black women were the most strongly feminist of all.[33]

By 1981, women in office had stronger connections with feminist and other women's organizations. Where only 20 per-

32. Carroll, *Women As Candidates,* pp. 31–32; Stanwick and Kleeman, *Women Make A Difference,* pp. 26–29; Carroll and Strimling, *Women's Routes to Elective Office,* pp. 183–86.

33. Carroll, *Women As Candidates,* pp. 102, 144–49; Stanwick and Kleeman, *Women Make A Difference,* pp. 13–15.

cent of the women candidates surveyed in 1976 were members of feminist organizations such as NOW or NWPC, around half of those in the 1981 study belonged to at least one explicitly feminist group, and more than 75 percent were members of a major women's organization such as the LWV or AAUW. Again, the connections between black legislators and the women's movement were even greater: more than 80 percent belonged to women's organizations, and more than two-thirds held memberships in feminist groups.[34]

A "NEW BREED" OF OFFICE-HOLDERS

Important changes also occurred in women's attitudes and behavior in political office. In 1972, the Center for the American Women and Politics at Rutgers University held the first conference for women legislators. Most of the fifty women who attended were aware of the difficulties women experienced in male-dominated statehouses, but few registered anger at their second-class status or a belief that they could change the system. They tended to be disdainful about wheeling and dealing, uncomfortable about exercising power, and resigned to the fact that women could not crack the male monopoly of leadership positions. Most were reluctant to identify themselves as women or to attach themselves to women's issues, and more than half expressed opposition to the women's liberation movement.[35]

The women who gathered at a second conference ten years later were considerably more familiar with and adept at using the political system. Like their earlier counterparts, they recognized that an association with women's issues might jeopardize their standing with male colleagues. Nonetheless, most of them identified with major goals of the women's movement and had worked for specific bills in their legislatures. They no longer saw themselves as above power politics, and their increased political

34. Carroll, *Women as Candidates*, p. 141; Carroll and Strimling, *Women's Routes to Elective Office*, pp. 87, 183.

35. Jeane J. Kirkpatrick, *Political Woman* (New York: Basic Books, 1974), pp. 124–25, 132–34, 164–67; *Women State Legislators: Report from a Conference, June 17–20, 1982* (New Brunswick, NJ: Center for the American Woman and Politics, n.d.), pp. 15, 16, 19.

sophistication and confidence led them to seek and win leadership positions. Cleatha Deatherage, for example, a Democrat
and founding member of Oklahoma's Women's Political Caucus, was instrumental in the election of the Oklahoma House
speaker. In return, she demanded and got appointment as chair
of the Appropriations and Budget Committee. Other women
held positions as speaker of the Oregon House, majority floor
leader of the Maine House, and Democratic minority whip in
the Illinois House. In all, by 1982 women held 8 percent of
leadership positions in state legislatures.[36]

By the end of the 1970s, women office-holders had also
begun to marshal their power by forming blocs that crossed
over party lines. In some states women were unable to overcome partisanship or differences over abortion and other issues,
but most female lawmakers were involved in bipartisan networks. Most typically, these were informal groups that met
regularly for a meal or social gathering, and their major func-
tion was to provide support enabling women to operate effectively in office. But these meetings might also involve the
exchange of political information, and sometimes women
would coalesce in support of a particular bill. Twenty women
in the Missouri legislature, for example, joined together on behalf of rape law reform. Six states had formal women's caucuses,
and in others, like Missouri, women formed ad hoc coalitions
around specific bills, coordinating strategy and dividing the
tasks necessary to achieve their objectives.[37]

Although the numbers of women in Congress remained
small in the 1970s, qualitative changes similar to those witnessed among state legislators occurred at the national level.
From a peak of nineteen in 1961, women's ranks in Congress
had declined to just eleven in 1971. In 1981, eighteen women
Representatives were sworn in, and the 1982 elections increased that number to twenty-one. The defeat of Margaret
Chase Smith for reelection in 1974 reduced women's presence
in the Senate to zero. While a couple of women were appointed
to fill unexpired terms, it was not until 1978 that another
woman, Republican Nancy Landon Kassebaum of Kansas, was

36. *Women State Legislators* pp. 15–21.
37. *Ibid.*, pp. 57–81.

elected to the Senate in her own right. Paula Hawkins, a Republican from Florida, joined her in 1980.

If their numbers did not distinguish them sharply from their predecessors, the women who served in the 1970s and 1980s were sufficiently different in backgrounds and behavior to constitute a "new breed" of Congresswomen. Fewer of them were widows filling the seats of deceased husbands, and more had held prior elective office. They were somewhat younger and more likely to be married with school-age children. Yvonne Braithwaite Burke bore a child during her first term in Congress, and Colorado Democrat Patricia Schroeder's young children often turned up in the Capitol. While motherhood differentiated them from their male colleagues, the previous careers of the new breed of Congresswomen tended more to resemble those of men; almost half of the women who served in the 1970s had law degrees. Finally, Black women began to fill a larger proportion of women's seats, as Yvonne Braithwaite Burke, Barbara Jordan, and Cardiss Collins followed Shirley Chisholm into the House in the early 1970s.[38]

The careers of these black Congresswomen resembled the various paths to office and legislative styles of their white counterparts. In filling her dead husband's seat in 1973, Cardiss Collins followed a traditional female pattern. She had, however, worked in state government and served as Democratic committeewoman in her Chicago ward, and she held on to the seat in her own right throughout the 1970s and 1980s. Barbara Jordan worked her way up the political ladder in Texas, performing lowly tasks in the 1960 elections, running two unsuccessful races for the legislature, and finally winning election to the Texas Senate in 1966. Jordan belonged to the NAACP but never became involved in the direct action tactics of the civil-rights movement, nor did she employ her legal qualifications in defense of jailed protesters. Rather it was her enormous determination, formidable political skills, consummate oratorical abilities, and cultivation of the patronage of Lyndon B. Johnson and other establishment politicians that led to her success in state politics and to election to the House in 1972. Yvonne

---

38. Irwin N. Gertzog, *Congressional Women: Their Recruitment, Treatment, and Behavior* (New York: Praeger Publishers, 1984), pp. 34, 39–43.

Braithwaite Burke, on the other hand, had defended blacks arrested during the Watts riots of 1965 and served on the commission investigating the conditions that led to the riots. After three terms in the California assembly, she won her House seat in 1972. Burke and Chisholm were outspoken advocates for blacks and women, and Collins worked more quietly on their behalf. Jordan, on the other hand, resisted being identified on the basis of sex or race: "I am neither a black politician nor a female politician. Just a politician. A professional politician." Despite their varied styles, however, all four consistently voted for measures promoted by black and feminist activists.[39]

This "new breed" of Congresswomen also began to shed their status as "outsiders." Women continued to be excluded from unstructured gatherings where groups of Congressmen talked over drinks, met in the House gymnasium, or got together for a golf or hunting party organized by lobbyists. But women penetrated formerly male enclaves, even the congressional swimming pool, which Abzug integrated over the objections of men reluctant to don bathing suits. More significantly, Congresswomen in the 1970s belonged to almost all of the structured informal groups including the various caucuses and the party clubs organized around particular ideological positions, such as the Conservative Democratic Forum, the Republican Study Committee, and the Good Guys, a Republican group which retained its name but admitted women.[40]

Congresswomen also gained greater access to formal leadership positions, though this was much more true of Democrats than Republicans. New York Republican Katherine St. George had been appointed one of three regional whips and had served on the House Rules Committee, but after her retirement in 1964, no Republican woman held such posts until 1983. Seven Democratic women served as whips between 1969 and 1985, and six held seats on the Steering and Policy Committee. Shirley Chisholm broke the male monopoly of the House Rules

39. Stineman, *American Political Women*, pp. 19–21, 31–32; William Broyles, "The Making of Barbara Jordan," *Texas Monthly* (October 1976), pp. 127–33, 198–99.

40. Gertzog, *Congressional Women*, pp. 76–90; Geraldine A. Ferraro with Linda Bird Francke, *Ferraro: My Story* (New York: Bantam Books, 1985), pp. 41–42.

Committee in 1977. While these were significant gains, women's small numbers, relative lack of seniority, and exclusion from the unstructured group network kept them confined to leadership at the secondary level. No woman served as Speaker, floor leader, Chief Whip, or chair of a major House or party committee.[41]

Women's ability to influence national policy increased as they began to serve on a broader range of committees. Generally their predecessors had been restricted to committees dealing with health, welfare, education, and similar concerns to which women were assumed to be uniquely fitted. Congresswomen in the 1970s continued to be well represented on such committees. Referring to the appointment to the Education and Labor Committee of five of the twelve women who served in the Ninety-second Congress, Bella Abzug opined, "Maybe they figure if they get us all in one place we'll cause less trouble." But women also branched out, serving on the prestigious House Appropriations, Rules, and Ways and Means Committees, as well as on those dealing with military affairs, space exploration, business, and commerce. When Barbara Jordan and Elizabeth Holtzman won seats on the House Judiciary Committee, they demonstrated women's competence on national television, which carried hearings on the impeachment of Nixon in 1974.[42]

Women's access to such appointments depended to some extent on their newfound agressiveness and willingness to violate the rule that new members accept whatever assignments were handed them. Shirley Chisholm, for example, rebelled when she was named to the House Agriculture Committee and its subcommittee on forestry. When her unprecedented challenge won her reassignment to the Veterans Affairs Committee, she accepted it with the remark that, "There are a lot more veterans in my district than there are trees." While the Democratic leadership rebuffed Abzug's bid for the Armed Services Committee, she was gratified two years later when Patricia Schroeder won that assignment and became a strong liberal voice on the committee. Initially frustrated when she sought a

41. Gertzog, *Congressional Women*, pp. 92–122.
42. *Ibid.*, pp. 127–41.

seat on the same body, New Jersey Republican Millicent Fenwick joined the Armed Services Committee in 1981.[43]

Congresswomen also became more assertive in challenging chauvinistic and patronizing remarks from their male colleagues, and they noted the decline of such behavior. While some women were willing to overlook harassment or take it as a joke, others chastised Congressmen for condescending or demeaning remarks. Responding to a woman's request to speak at a House committee meeting, a male member said, "In just a minute cutie pie." The Congresswoman then interrupted him, called him "Congressman cutie pie," and made it clear that such language was unacceptable. Turning the tables was the tactic of another woman when a male Senator patted her shoulder, touched her dress, and exclaimed how pretty it was. She responded, "My what a lovely suit you're wearing. You *are* handsome."[44]

Congresswomen of the 1940s and 1950s were willing to champion legislation benefiting women, but they resisted an identification with women's interests. Margaret Chase Smith, for example, declared, "I definitely resent being called a feminist." In contrast, an increasing number of their successors were self-identified feminists. Although Bella Abzug was first to gain national recognition as a a vocal feminist, Hawaii Democrat Patsy Mink, who was elected to the House in 1964, recognized that as one of the few women in Congress she had "an obligation to respond to the needs and problems of women in the nation." When congressional candidates were asked for their positions on six feminist issues in 1976, between 61 and 90 percent gave positive responses. Some Congresswomen like Democrat Marilyn Lloyd from Tennessee minimized their identification with women, but they were outnumbered by a coterie of self-styled feminists, including Republican Margaret Heckler, and Democrats Shirley Chisholm, Elizabeth Holtzman, Yvonne Braithwaite Burke, Patricia Schroeder, Mary Rose Oakar, and Barbara Mikulski. Some women underwent a con-

43. *Ibid.*, pp. 127–40; Shirley Chisholm, *Unbought and Unbossed* (New York: Avon Books, 1971), pp. 94–102; Bella Abzug with Mim Kelber, *Gender Gap: Bella Abzug's Guide to Political Power for Women* (Boston: Houghton Mifflin, 1984), p. 164.

44. Gertzog, *Congressional Women*, pp. 51–75.

version after their elections. Claudine Schneider, elected as a Republican from New Jersey in 1980, "never considered myself a feminist before I got this job." Once in Congress, her conception of her responsibility grew from representing the men and women in her district to representing "all American women." Similarly, Geraldine Ferraro did not consider herself a feminist when she ran for Congress in 1978, but within a few years she had become one.[45]

THE CONGRESSWOMEN'S CAUCUS

Indeed, Congresswomen registered significantly higher degrees of feminism than state and local office-holders. Their high levels of ambition made these women more sensitive to discrimination within the political system, and that consciousness helped them to perceive constraints on women in other areas. Congressional voting patterns reflected this new consciousness. In the 1970s Congresswomen of both parties voted more as a bloc than had their predecessors, and they developed a formal mechanism for promoting attention to women's interests, the Congresswomen's Caucus.[46]

Black legislators had formed a caucus in 1971, and in the early 1970s lobbyists from major feminist organizations urged Congresswomen to do likewise. However, difficulties in working out a structure, opposition to the idea by three senior representatives, Leonor Sullivan, Julia Butler Hansen, and Edith Green, and the unwillingness of some to be formally associated with the brash and flamboyant style of Abzug, delayed its formation until 1977. With the departure of these women, Republican Margaret Heckler, and Democrats Elizabeth Holtzman, Shirley Chisholm, and Barbara Mikulski assumed leadership in

45. *Ibid.,* pp. 159, 247; Abzug, *Gender Gap,* p. 188; Carroll, *Women as Candidates,* pp. 146–47; Andy Plattner, "Various Legislative Styles, Philosophies . . . Found among Congress' 23 Women," *Congressional Quarterly Weekly Report* 41 (April 23, 1983):784.

46. Kathleen A. Frankovic, "Sex and Voting in the U.S. House of Representatives, 1961–1975," *American Politics Quarterly* 5 (July 1977):319–29; Carol Mueller, "Feminism and the New Women in Public Office," *Women and Politics* 2 (Fall 1982):11–14.

organizing the caucus. Fifteen of the eighteen women in the House joined in 1977, although for some, like Barbara Jordan, membership was little more than token.[47]

The Congresswomen's Caucus abetted the women's movement in a variety of ways. It provided for the exchange of information, not just among Congresswomen, but between them and administration officials as well as feminist organizations. At caucus meetings, Congresswomen gave exclusive attention to women's needs and enjoyed opportunities to validate or revise their own positions and to obtain encouragement and practical assistance. The caucus monitored implementation of legislation, organizing support for particular bills and facilitating the division of labor required for their enactment. As we shall see, the caucus mobilized support for a number of new policy initiatives and achieved a stunning victory in getting Congress to extend the time limit for ratification of the Equal Rights Amendment.[48]

Along with these achievements, the representation of women's concerns in Congress suffered major setbacks, not least of which was the loss of key congresswomen. Both Abzug and Mink abandoned their seats to run for the Senate in 1976, and both lost. Yvonne Burke left Congress in 1978 to run for Attorney General in California, a race she lost to George Duekmejian. Caucus faithfuls Martha Keys and Helen Meyner were defeated for reelection in 1978, and Elizabeth Holtzman gave up her House seat to wage an unsuccessful race for the Senate in 1980. The victories of Ferraro and Republican Olympia Snow in 1978 only partially offset these losses. Departures of key caucus members and the arrival of some Republicans with little interest in female solidarity diminished the effectiveness of the caucus, though it carried on until a major reorganization in the 1980s.

WOMEN IN APPOINTED POSTS

While activists tended to concentrate on electoral and legislative politics, women also pressed officials to appoint more

47. Gertzog, *Congressional Women*, pp. 164–87.
48. *Ibid.*, pp. 192–206.

Civil rights activist and Secretary of Housing and Urban
Development, subsequently Secretary of Health and Human
Services, Patricia Roberts Harris *(right)* with her parents and
President Jimmy Carter. (Jimmy Carter Library)

women to office. In many states they created informal structures or formal coalitions that presented lists of qualified
women to executive officials and lobbied for particular women.
Organized under the National Women's Political Caucus, the
Coalition for Women's Appointments exercised pressure at the
national level. Although only slight gains were made under
Nixon and Ford, Carter fulfilled his promise made to feminists
at the 1976 Democratic convention and appointed significantly
more women to high-level posts than had any of his predecessors. He named Patricia Roberts Harris first to head the Department of Housing and Urban Development and later to head the
Department of Health and Human Services, Juanita Kreps Secretary of Commerce, Eleanor Holmes Norton chair of the Equal
Employment Opportunities Commission, and Shirley Hufsted-
ler Secretary of Education. These women in turn practiced
affirmative action in their own appointments, increasing dramatically the number of executive-level women in the agencies
that they led. Kreps even took the occasion of Carter's press

conference at which he introduced his cabinet to chide men for their failures in appointing women to top posts. Carter also responded to feminists' demands for judicial positions, appointing forty women to the federal bench. They represented 16 percent of his total appointments, in contrast to less than 2 percent of those of his three predecessors.[49]

CONCLUSION

The 1970s were notable for women's increasing force in public affairs, particularly in party politics and public office. That development in turn owed much to the resurgence of feminism, which swelled into a mass movement by the early 1970s and which altered public consciousness about women's roles and rights. Popular sentiment became more favorable to women in positions of power, and larger numbers of women themselves grew confident about their right to—and capability of—political decision-making.

Mainstream feminists created more sharply focused organizations to put women in power and facilitate their effectiveness in office. The National Women's Political Caucus and its affiliates, the Women's Campaign Fund, the women's task forces in the Democratic and Republican parties, the Congresswomen's Caucus, and its counterparts in state legislatures all promoted the empowerment of women throughout the political system.

Aided by and working through these new structures, women developed political clout within their parties and became especially influential in Democratic politics. Their political aspirations grew apace, and though continuing to face considerable obstacles not experienced by men, women became increasingly visible and vocal in public office. Their cohesion as an interest group was mirrored in the development of female voting blocs in state legislatures and the House of Representatives. These developments, in turn, helped to shape major changes in public policies concerning women.

49. Stanwick and Kleeman, *Women Make A Difference,* p. 46; Barbara Sinclair Deckard, *The Women's Movement: Political, Socioeconomic, and Psychological Issues* (New York: Harper and Row, 2nd ed., 1979), p. 373; Peggy Lamson, *In the Vanguard: Six American Women in Public Life* (Boston: Houghton Mifflin, 1979), pp. 38–41.

Chapter 5

The Impact on Public Policy

As vigorously as they sought greater representation in their parties and in government positions, women made accelerating demands on the public-policy process. They organized new groups to articulate and lobby for their interests, and they shifted the priorities of traditional women's organizations towards feminist goals. The efforts of organized women and their allies enormously expanded the antidiscrimination legislation initiated with the Equal Pay Act of 1963 and Title VII of the Civil Rights Act of 1964. They also secured congressional approval of the Equal Rights Amendment, nearly fifty years after it was first introduced. Finally, the women's movement focused public attention on a host of new issues, including rape, wife beating, sexual harassment, child care, and displaced homemakers, thereby substantially enlarging the public-policy agenda and effecting changes at every level of government as well as in the judicial system.

THE WOMEN'S POLICY NETWORK

As women promoted their policy concerns through traditional women's organizations and new feminist groups like NOW, WEAL, and NWPC, they also developed new structures that focused on research, litigation, and lobbying. One of the earliest agencies established to gather and analyze information was the Center for Women Policy Studies (CWPS). Founded in 1972 with initial funding from Ralph Nader's Public Citizen organization and the Ford Foundation, the center grew to house a professional staff of ten who investigated a range of issues from credit discrimination to violence against women. Other policy agencies included the Center for Research on Women in Higher Education and the Professions, the International Center for Research on Women, and the Women's Research and Education Institute, a spin-off from the Congressional Women's Caucus. In 1981, such centers joined with women's research units attached to universities to form the twenty-one member National Council for Research on Women.[1]

Another new organization, the Women's Rights Project of the American Civil Liberties Union, headed by Ruth Bader Ginsburg, became the premier litigator on behalf of women's rights in the federal courts. It was joined by several other organizations launched by feminist lawyers to effect change in the judicial arena. NOW incorporated its Legal Defense and Education Fund in 1971, and WEAL added a legal counterpart in 1972. By 1974, feminist litigation was also being conducted by the Women's Legal Defense Fund, the Cleveland-based Women's Law Fund, the Women's Rights Project of the Center for Law and Social Policy, the Reproductive Freedom Project of the American Civil Liberties Union (ACLU), and by organizations like the Southern Poverty Law Center and the International Union of Electrical Workers, which pursued specific issues concerning women.[2]

Women developed parallel organizations to press their claims before legislators. Women's organizations had lobbied for the Equal Pay Act, and small ad hoc groups had lobbied in succeeding years, but it was not until the 1970s that a full-fledged women's lobby existed in Washington. The first new organization was the Women's Lobby, Inc., founded in 1972 by Washington, D.C. NOW members Carol Burris and Flora Crater. Growing out of the final effort for Congressional approval of the ERA, the Women's Lobby defined itself as "a lobby of

1. Jane Roberts Chapman, "Policy Centers: An Essential Resource," in Irene Tinker, ed., *Women in Washington: Advocates for Public Policy* (Beverly Hills, CA: Sage Publications, 1983), pp. 163, 177–90.

2. Karen O'Connor, *Women's Organizations' Use of the Courts* (Lexington, MA: Lexington Books, 1980), pp. 93–115.

women who believe in feminist principles and work to put those principles into law." To operate more effectively in national politics, WEAL moved its national headquarters from Ohio to Washington in 1972, and one year later both NOW and NWPC established national offices in the capital. In 1978, *Time* magazine counted thirty-three women's lobbies operating in Washington.[3]

More important than the activities of any single group was the ability of women's groups to unite in both formal and informal coalitions organized around specific policy issues or areas. These alliances involved not only the new feminist organizations, but also traditional women's groups as well as labor unions and civil-rights organizations. The older women's groups contributed "respectability" and decades of experience in lobbying. Both the American Association of University Women (AAUW) and League of Women Voters (LWV), for example, provided training for women in newer organizations. Moreover, the traditional groups usually had larger memberships for which they could claim to speak and which they could mobilize behind women's interests. Even by the late 1970s, when NOW claimed 125,000 members and the NWPC 50,000, they were outmatched by the AAUW which had 190,000 members, the LWV with 115,000, the National Federation of Business and Professional Women's Clubs (BPW) with 154,000, and United Methodist Women (UMW) with more than one million members.[4]

Coalitions varied in size, strength, duration, and according to the issues they addressed. Ad hoc unions, like the Campaign to End Discrimination Against Pregnant Workers, worked on a specific bill and disbanded upon achieving victory. The National Coalition for Women and Girls in Education, and the National Women's Health Network, were examples of more formal alliances; they were ongoing and lobbied for a range of

3. Anne N. Costain, "Representing Women: The Transition from Social Movement to Interest Group," *Western Political Quarterly* 34 (March 1981):106–7; Arvonne S. Fraser, "Insiders and Outsiders: Women in the Political Arena," in Tinker, ed., *Women in Washington,* p. 132.

4. Costain, "Representing Women," p. 109; Joyce Gelb and Marian Lief Palley, *Women and Public Policies* (Princeton, NJ: Princeton University Press, 1982), pp. 27–28.

bills related to educational equity and health. In some coalitions, groups that opposed each other on one issue might cooperate on another. Both the anti-abortion American Citizens Concerned for Life and the pro-choice National Abortion Rights Action League, for example, cooperated to end discrimination against pregnant women. Most alliances brought together both social movement groups and traditional women's organizations. NOW and WEAL cooperated with the AAUW, UMW, and the National Council of Jewish Women (NCJW) to promote abortion rights, and the network pushing for child-care legislation included the BPW and NCJW as well as NOW and NWPC.[5]

Of critical importance to the new women's lobbies were their allies within government. Congresswomen and a handful of sympathetic Congressmen sponsored and oversaw floor management of most of the women's rights legislation. Especially in the early days when feminist groups entered the public policy arena as amateurs, congressional staffs frequently coordinated and directed lobbying efforts. Women who worked in the executive branch were equally important to the emerging women's policy system. They had access to information and to the ears of key policymakers, they could keep a close watch on implementation of legislation, and they could alert women's groups when policy changes were in the making.[6]

In the 1970s women also began exercising their political muscle on the state and local levels. Some of that clout was developed by Commissions on the Status of Women, which existed in forty-nine states by 1973. While three states subsequently dissolved their commissions, forty-five county and forty-three municipal commissions were still at work in 1977. As official advisory bodies to policymakers, these commissions identified needs and provided information and publicity about women's concerns. Independent lobbies for women also appeared at the state level. In Oregon, for example, women's organizations formed a loose network that cooperated with fe-

5. Anne N. Costain, "The Struggle for a National Women's Lobby: Organizing a Diffuse Interest," *Western Political Quarterly* 33 (December 1980):486–88; Gelb and Palley, *Women and Public Policies,* pp. 58–61.

6. Costain, "Representing Women," pp. 111–12; Tinker, ed., *Women in Washington,* pp. 10–11.

male legislators to press for a broad range of reforms relating to prostitution, inheritance law, displaced homemakers, and violence against women. Like the national women's lobby, state and local efforts involved coalitions that included feminist and traditional women's groups, organized labor, religious groups, and public-interest organizations.[7]

THE EQUAL RIGHTS AMENDMENT

Congressional approval of the Equal Rights Amendment in 1972 was the first major achievement of the broad-based lobbying effort launched by women in the 1970s. Nurtured by the National Woman's Party for nearly fifty years, that cause had picked up support from some women's organizations, notably the BPW and the General Federation of Women's Clubs, but most women's organizations, liberal groups, and labor unions continued to oppose the amendment. These groups feared that the ERA, in requiring state and federal laws to treat men and women equally, would wipe out protective labor laws that applied only to women. In the late 1960s, however, federal courts began to strike down protective laws applying to women only because they violated the ban against employment discrimination in Title VII of the Civil Rights Act of 1964. Consequently, these groups began to reverse their historical opposition to the ERA.

In 1970, the United Auto Workers endorsed the amendment and several other unions followed suit in 1971. By 1972, traditional women's organizations such as the American Association of University Women and the League of Women Voters had done an about-face, and liberal groups including the American Civil Liberties Union and Americans for Democratic Action had also reversed themselves. An official thumbs up for the ERA came in 1970 from the Department of Labor, from the Citizens' Advisory Council on the Status of Women and from the Presi-

7. *The Book of the States, 1978–1979* (Lexington, KY: The Council of State Governments, 1978), p. 264; *Women State Legislators: Report from a Conference, June 17–20, 1982* (New Brunswick, NJ: Center for the American Woman and Politics, n.d.), pp. 36–41.

NOW members keep a vigil on the Capitol steps, pressing for Senate passage of the Equal Rights Amendment, October, 1970. (UPI/Bettmann Newsphotos)

dent's Task Force on Women's Rights and Responsibilities, which President Richard Nixon had appointed.[8]

Strongholds of opposition remained, however, among opinion leaders and lawmakers. Objections were based on fears that the ERA would subject women to the military draft, or predictions that it would cause judicial confusion and chaos, or beliefs that men and women were naturally suited for different functions and that those differences should be embodied in law. In Congress the opposition was led by Representative Emmanuel Celler, New York Democrat, and by Sam Ervin, Democratic Senator from North Carolina. These men headed the House and Senate judiciary committees where action on the amendment had to originate, and they did all they could first to keep the amendment locked up in committee and, that failing, to cripple it with amendments.[9]

8. Marguerite Rawalt, "The Equal Rights Amendment," in Tinker, ed., *Women in Washington,* pp. 62–65; Catherine East, "Newer Commissions," in Tinker, ed., *Women in Washington*, pp. 37–38.

9. Rawalt, "The Equal Rights Amendment," pp. 63–65; Gilbert Y. Steiner, *Constitutional Inequality: The Political Fortunes of the Equal Rights Amendment* (Washington, DC: The Brookings Institution, 1985), pp. 12–21.

To overcome this opposition, a network of activists, women newly politicized by the resurgent women's movement as well as those who had been active before the rebirth of feminism, employed a variety of strategies. In early 1970, NOW members disrupted a Senate subcommittee hearing testimony on the eighteen-year-old vote to demand that the Senate schedule hearings on the ERA. Congresswoman Martha Griffiths took the politically dangerous risk of challenging Celler's hold on the House Judiciary Committee. Using her clout as member of the House Ways and Means Committee, Griffiths persuaded more than 200 legislators to sign a discharge petition freeing the amendment for action on the House floor. The House voted overwhelmingly for the amendment in August 1970, but supporters in the Senate delayed a vote when the opposition added crippling provisions to the measure.[10]

In pushing the ERA to the floor of the House, Griffiths did not work alone. Especially vital in mobilizing pressure on Congress was longtime ERA advocate Marguerite Rawalt, a Washington lawyer who had headed the national BPW, served on the President's Commission on the Status of Women, and was a founder of NOW. Rawalt worked with the BPW and the General Federation of Women's Clubs in enlisting their members to send letters and telegrams urging their representatives to sign the discharge petition. She also recruited Geri Joseph, Vice Chair of the Democratic National Committee, and Gladys O'Donnell, who had defeated Phyllis Schlafly for the presidency of the National Federation of Republican Women. These women organized pressure campaigns among women in both major parties. Members of a Washington, D.C. consciousness-raising group, many of whom worked in congressional offices, organized the Ad Hoc Committee for the ERA and exerted direct pressure on Congressmen.[11]

Activists generated millions of letters urging legislators to

10. Rawalt, "The Equal Rights Amendment, pp. 63–65; Berenice Carroll, "Direct Action and Constitutional Rights: The Case of the ERA," in Joan Hoff-Wilson, ed., *Rights of Passage: The Past and Future of the ERA* (Bloomington: Indiana University Press, 1986), p. 68.

11. Fern S. Ingersoll, "Former Congresswomen Look Back," in Tinker, ed., *Women in Washington*, pp. 199–201; Jo Freeman, *The Politics of Women's Liberation: A Case Study of an Emerging Social Movement and Its Relation to the Policy Process* (New York: David McKay, 1975), pp. 209–21.

vote for the ERA. Fifteen hundred letters a month flooded some congressional offices. More than twenty women conducted a personal lobbying campaign, going from office to office on Capitol Hill. Once the House passed the amendment again in 1971, by a vote of 354–24, Griffiths herself lobbied Senators. Senate approval came in March 1972 by a vote of 84–8.[12]

A number of factors accounted for passage of the ERA nearly five decades after it was first introduced. The persistence of the NWP and its allies in the BPW and other organizations had developed a core of supporters in Congress. The black freedom struggle had provided a climate of sensitivity to equal rights, and the ideas of the emerging feminist movement were beginning to resonate among large numbers of women already involved in women's organizations, party politics, and grassroots movements, as well as those who became politicized when they encountered feminism. The efforts of traditional women's groups, party activists, and new feminist organizations succeeded with Congress because the traditional opposition had dissipated and new opposition had yet to coalesce.

The amendment was passed without riders, stating simply that "Equality of rights under the law shall not be denied or abridged by the United States or by any State on account of sex." Two more brief sections provided that Congress would have enforcement powers, and that it would take effect two years after ratification. A separate enabling resolution set the time limit for ratification at seven years.

Hawaii, the first state to ratify, did so within hours after passage, and within three months, eighteen more states had jumped on the ERA bandwagon. At the end of 1972, twenty-three states had ratified, and eight more folowed suit in 1973. In that year the last major opposition to the ERA fell as the AFL-CIO shifted its stance to one of support. But then prospects began to darken. Nebraska lawmakers had second thoughts, and its legislature became the first of several to attempt to rescind its approval. Moreover, as we shall see in the next chapter, the amendment began to encounter formidable new opposition spearheaded by Phyllis Schlafly.[13]

12. Freeman, *The Politics of Women's Liberation*, pp. 209–21.
13. Rawalt, "The Equal Rights Amendment," pp. 66–68.

LITIGATION FOR WOMEN'S RIGHTS

Even before the ERA passed Congress, women were pursuing an alternate route to constitutional equality. In response to a suit argued by the ACLU and supported by WEAL, NOW, and BPW which filed *amicus curiae* (friend of the court) briefs, the Supreme Court for the first time struck down a state law on the ground of sex discrimination. Its 1971 decision in *Reed v Reed* held that an Idaho law preferring men over women as executors of wills violated the equal protection clause of the Fourteenth Amendment. Two years later, in *Frontiero v Richardson*, argued by the ACLU's new Women's Rights Project (WRP), the Court overturned a law granting male military personnel benefits for their families greater than those available to female personnel.[14]

In *Frontiero*, four justices argued that sex classifications should be subject to the same "strict scrutiny" that the Court had established for racial classifications. According to that doctrine any racial categories were considered inherently "suspect"; to sustain them the state had to prove an overwhelming public purpose and to show that no alternative ways existed to accomplish that purpose. Advocates for women's rights, however, were never able to persuade a majority of the Supreme Court to treat sex as it did race. Instead, the Court developed a less rigid test for laws that made sexual distinctions: the classification had to serve "an important governmental objective" and to be "substantially related to the achievement of [that] objective."[15]

Nor was the Court receptive to efforts challenging laws that were seemingly sex-neutral, but that in operation had a disparate effect on women. In *Personnel Administrator of Massachusetts v Feeney* (1979), the Court held that a law giving veterans a lifetime preference in civil service jobs did in fact operate "overwhelmingly to the advantage of males," because the vast

---

14. O'Connor, *Women's Organizations' Use of the Courts*, p. 96; Wendy W. Williams and Judith L. Lichtman, "Closing the Law's Gender Gap," *The Nation* 239 (September 29, 1984):281.

15. Williams and Lichtman, "Closing the Laws Gender Gap," p. 128; Margaret A. Berger, *Litigation on Behalf of Women* (New York: The Ford Foundation, 1980), pp. 16–18.

majority of veterans were men. Nonetheless, the Court ruled the law constitutional because it found no legislative *intent* to discriminate against women.[16]

Despite their failure to obtain full application of the equal protection clause to women, feminist litigators successfully whittled away at laws treating men and women differently. In doing so, they significantly altered a legal system that had been based on the premise that men were breadwinners and women homemakers. In a series of cases in the 1970s, the Supreme Court ruled that women were entitled to the same benefits for their families under Social Security, welfare, and workers compensation programs as men; that the legal age for adulthood should not be higher for men than for women; that responsibility for alimony should not be exclusively male; and that sons and daughters of divorced couples should be treated equitably with regard to child support. It should be noted that women were not the exclusive beneficiaries as the legal system moved towards a single standard for both sexes. With regard to alimony and child support, for example, women lost old "privileges," and men were the primary beneficiaries.[17]

ECONOMIC AND EDUCATIONAL EQUITY

In general women found legislators more hospitable to their claims than Supreme Court justices, especially in the early part of the 1970s. If the Equal Rights Amendment was the grandest victory for women during the Ninety-second Congress, it was not the only one. With little support—and sometimes outright opposition—from the Nixon administration, advocates of women's rights were able to strengthen and expand substantially federal anti-sex-discrimination policy.

In 1972, Congress amended the Equal Pay Act to cover administrative, executive, and professional positions. Extended coverage was also a feature of the Equal Employment Opportu-

16. Berger, *Litigation on Behalf of Women*, p. 18; Williams and Lichtman, "Closing the Law's Gender Gap," p. 284.

17. Williams and Lichtman, "Closing the Law's Gender Gap," p. 282; O'Connor, *Women's Organizations' Use of the Courts*, pp. 96–98; Berger, *Litigation on Behalf of Women*, pp. 19–20.

nity Act of 1972, which enlarged the EEOC's jurisdiction to include educational institutions and state and local governments, and which empowered the EEOC to initiate suits on its own against employers who discriminated. In addition, antidiscrimination provisions were written into revenue sharing, public works, and a host of other federal programs. Many of these amendments were the work of feminist leader and New York Congresswoman Bella Abzug, who carried around a standard anti-sex-discrimination clause which she jumped to insert at every possible opportunity.[18]

A far-reaching addition to public policy initiatives for women in the Ninety-second Congress was the Educational Amendments Act, whose Title IX for the first time banned sex discrimination in education. Educational equity was a high priority for the Women's Equity Action League (WEAL), and WEAL had a powerful ally in Edith Green, who chaired the House Special Subcommittee on Education and sat on WEAL's advisory board. In an atmosphere of public and congressional sensitivity to women's rights, the bill, sponsored by Green and Senator Birch Bayh, passed with relative ease and with little lobbying. Green in fact dissuaded lobbyists, believing that to call attention to the bill would only alert potential opposition.

After enactment of Title IX, that opposition did develop, whereupon women from a variety of organizations including WEAL, NOW, NWPC, AAUW, and the Women's Lobby, organized to defeat weakening amendments and to secure an implementing regulation with teeth in it. In so doing, they defeated a lobby of the male sports establishment, which viewed educational equity as a threat to men's intercollegiate athletics. As a result, Title IX provided that no federal funds would go to educational institutions that practiced sex discrimination in any of its programs, including admissions, athletics, financial aid, counseling, facilities, and employment practices. While the women's lobby made some compromises and never secured complete enforcement, it did demonstrate for the first

18. Jo Freeman, *The Politics of Women's Liberation* (New York: David McKay, 1975), pp. 175–76, 202–4.

time the potential of collective female power even when the opposition was formidable.[19]

Advocates for sex equity in education achieved two more federal policy initiatives in the 1970s. The Women's Educational Equity Act (WEEA) was conceived by a group of women representing among others WEAL, AAUW, the National Education Association, the National Council of Jewish Women, and Capitol Hill staff who secured sponsorship of Patsy Mink in the House and Walter Mondale in the Senate. Like her colleague Edith Green, Mink was a shrewd student of legislative politics. Instead of pressing for separate legislation, she had her bill hidden as an amendment to a multibillion-dollar education bill that passed in 1974. Going beyond the ban on discrimination enacted in Title IX, WEEA provided federal funds for schools and organizations to create programs and materials that would actively counter sex-role socialization and stereotyping. When the program expired in 1978, it was renewed and its funding more than doubled.[20]

Believing that WEEA was insufficient to deal adequately with sex bias in vocational education, women next addressed the acute disparities between men and women in that area. With most of the vocational-education establishment cool to sex-equity provisions, the Coalition for Women and Girls in Education worked with legislators and staff to incorporate their aims into the Vocational Education Act of 1976. Sponsored by Shirley Chisholm and Walter Mondale, the provisions called for each state vocational education program to have a sex-equity coordinator, for women to be appointed to state advisory commissions, and for states to demonstrate provision of equal opportunities for women as a condition for receiving federal funding.[21]

Amendment of the Fair Labor Standards Act to include domestic workers was another victory for women in the early

19. Mary Ann Millsap, "Sex Equity in Education," in Tinker, ed., *Women in Washington,* pp. 97–101; Gelb and Palley, *Women and Public Policies,* pp. 95–124.

20. Gelb and Palley, *Women and Public Policies,* pp. 96–97, 109–11; Arvonne S. Fraser, "Insiders and Outsiders: Women in the Political Arena," in Tinker, ed. *Women in Washington,* pp. 130–32.

21. Millsap, "Sex Equity in Education," pp. 104–7.

1970s, one which indicated the capacity of the feminist movement to reach beyond the interests of more privileged women. Shirley Chisholm, chief sponsor of the bill, orchestrated a multi-faceted coalition that included NOW, NWPC, the Women's Lobby, BPW, and women's religious organizations as well as civil rights and social action groups and organized labor. She mobilized thirteen of the fifteen Congresswomen, who in a strong letter of support effected one of their earliest collective actions. (The other two women Representatives ultimately voted for the bill.) With Senate approval already in hand, the House passed the bill for the first time in June 1973, by a vote of 225–192. Nixon vetoed the measure as "inflationary," but in 1974, Congress mustered enough votes to override a presidential veto, and domestic workers came under protection of the minimum-wage law. The legislation represented the first successful alliance of feminist groups and organized labor since passage of the Equal Pay Act in 1963.[22]

Between 1972 and 1975 women also marshalled their networks to promote women's equal access to credit. They noted in particular that employed wives' incomes were not fully counted in credit applications, that single women routinely faced discrimination, and that divorced or widowed women had difficulty establishing credit in their own names. The NOW task force on credit and the Center for Women Policy Studies provided background information and technical expertise, while AAUW, BPW, NWPC, WEAL, and NCJW mobilized lobbying campaigns. Senate action was spearheaded by William Brock, a conservative Republican from Tennessee. Brock's sympathy with women's credit difficulties was influenced by his feminist aide, Emily Card, who also served as liaison with women's groups. Republican Margaret Heckler and New York Democrat Edward Koch led the effort in the House, which resulted in the Equal Credit Opportunity Act of 1974. As they had with Title XI, women remained mobilized, shifting their efforts to the administrative branch where they secured an acceptable regulation for implementation of the law. The equal-credit legislation represented a departure from prece-

---

22. Susan and Martin Tolchin, *Clout: Womanpower and Politics* (New York: G. P. Putnam's Sons, 1976), pp. 135–47.

dent. It was the first piece of sex-equity policy that did not build on prohibitions already in effect for race.[23]

Economic and educational equity for women were simultaneously pursued through litigation. NOW and WEAL filed sex-discrimination suits against hundreds of corporations and educational institutions based on the Equal Pay Act, Title VII of the Civil Rights Act of 1964, and the executive orders prohibiting discrimination by federal contractors. WEAL also moved to force compliance with equity legislation by the federal government itself. Noting that no federal funds had ever been withdrawn from educational institutions for noncompliance with antidiscrimination laws, the Center for Law and Social Policy's Women's Rights Project filed suit on behalf of WEAL against the Department of Health, Education and Welfare (HEW). In 1977, it won a court order directing HEW and the Department of Labor to begin enforcement proceedings.[24]

Advocates for women's rights successfully challenged Social Security, welfare and workers' compensation programs that treated men and women differently, and they also directed their attention to inequities in pension programs. On the grounds that women as a group lived longer than men, many retirement programs required women to pay more money than men into pension funds. Plaintiffs representing women argued that they should be treated as individuals rather than being lumped together in actuarial tables, and the Supreme Court in *City of Los Angeles v Manhart* (1978) agreed that higher pay-ins for women violated Title VII.[25]

In the mid-1970s feminists put a label on an old form of on-the-job discrimination. As long as they had worked outside the home, women had been subject to unwanted sexual attention. It took many forms, ranging from direct sexual advances by employers or co-workers to unwanted physical contact and suggestive sexual references in conversations. Radical feminists,

23. Gelb and Palley, *Women and Public Policies*, pp. 63–94; Jane Roberts Chapman, "Policy Centers: An Essential Resource," in Tinker, ed., *Women in Washington*, pp. 177–85.

24. Berger, *Litigation on Behalf of Women*, p. 45.

25. *Ibid.*, pp. 31–32.

who brought the issue to the public-policy agenda, argued that such behavior constituted discrimination against women, and they called it sexual harassment.

Working Women United, a grass-roots group in Ithaca, New York, held a speak-out on sexual harassment in 1975, and NOW subsequently established a Sexual Harassment in Education Project to offer legal aid to students and faculty subjected to unwanted sexual attention. Beginning in 1977, federal appeals courts began to rule that such behavior constituted sex discrimination under Title VII and to hold employers liable for harassment on the part of supervisors and co-workers. State courts began to follow federal court guidelines and to rule that individuals who left their jobs because of sexual harassment were entitled to unemployment insurance. In 1980, women's groups prevailed upon the EEOC to issue guidelines and regulations. Besides defining harassment and establishing liability, the guidelines also called on employers to instruct their work force about the issue and to establish grievance procedures.[26]

WOMEN AND THE MILITARY

The unanimity of feminists on most equity issues splintered on the subject of military service. Promotion of peace was a high priority for many feminists and several traditional women's organizations. They worked for a world in which neither men nor women would have to be soldiers, and they saw little use in promoting greater opportunities for women in military service. Others, however, sought equity across the board, and they wanted women to have equal access to the educational and job-training benefits that attended military service. WEAL, the ACLU's Women's Rights Project, and the Center for Women Policy Studies gave high priority to women's military status, and their efforts were substantially boosted when the United States

26. Laura J. Evans, "Sexual Harassment: Women's Occupational Hazard," in *Jane Roberts Chapman* and Margaret Gates, eds., *The Victimization of Women* (Beverly Hills, CA: Sage Publications, 1978); Joy A. Livingston, "Responses to Sexual Harassment on the Job: Legal, Organizational, and Individual Actions," *Journal of Social Issues* 38 (1982):5–9, 17.

ended the draft in 1973 and military leaders turned to women to offset potential deficits of male recruits.[27]

In fact, several policy changes were initiated by the defense establishment itself. For example, as the war in Vietnam devoured ever larger numbers of men, in 1967 the military lifted the 2 percent quota on enlisted women, opened the ranks of colonel and captain to women on a permanent basis, and allowed women to become generals and admirals. Women's groups, on the other hand, took the initiative in lobbying for admission of women to the service academies, and Congress complied over the Pentagon's objections. In 1977, a diverse group of organizations, including NOW, WEAL, the NCJW, the LWV, the Girl Scouts, and the ACLU established a National Coalition for Women in Defense. The coalition succeeded in opening nontraditional assignments to women and in winning veteran status for women who had served as Women's Air Force Service Pilots during World War II. It failed, however, to end the ban against women in combat positions and to make women subject to military registration, as men were.[28]

Advocates for women in the military also sought equity through the courts. In reponse to a suit filed by the Women's Rights Project (WRP) against the Department of Defense, the military abandoned the policy of dismissing a servicewoman because she was pregnant. Equalization of benefits for male and female personnel was achieved in the *Frontiero* case. In 1978, WRP and WEAL obtained a ruling that the Navy policy of confining women's sea duty to hospital ships and transports was a violation of the equal protection clause. And, a year later a WRP suit toppled the higher standards the Army had set for women enlistees.[29]

27. Carol C. Parr, "Women in the Military," in Tinker, ed., *Women in Washington*, pp. 240–4l; Martin Binkin and Shirley J. Bach, *Women and the Military* (Washington, DC: The Brookings Institution, 1977), pp. 13–14.

28. Judith Hicks Stiehm, "Women, Men and Military Service: Is Protection Necessarily a Racket?" in Ellen Boneparth, ed., *Women, Power and Policy* (New York: Pergamon Press, 1982), pp. 285–86; Parr, "Women in the Military," pp. 240–49.

29. O'Connor, *Women's Organizations' Use of the Courts*, p. 125; Parr, "Women in the Military," p. 239; "ACLU Wins Suit Against Army," *The Spokeswoman* 9 (August 1979):3.

EQUAL TREATMENT FOR PREGNANT WORKERS

Where military issues divided women's advocates, the issue of discrimination against pregnant workers brought a remarkable alliance of organizations. It also succeeded in reversing a Supreme Court decision. In 1974, in a suit brought by the Women's Law Fund with supporting briefs from NOW, WRP, and the International Union of Electrical Workers (IUE), the Supreme Court ruled that compelling pregnant women to take unpaid maternity leaves violated the due process clause of the Fourteenth Amendment. Two years later, however, the Court decided in *Gilbert v General Electric* that employers' refusal to include pregnancy in comprehensive disability plans did not constitute sex discrimination under Title VII. The GE plan, ruled the Court, eliminated pregnant *persons* from coverage, and thus did not discriminate against women. Immediately following the decision, organized labor, women's organizations, civil-rights and religious groups, and even some anti-abortion organizations joined together in the Campaign to End Discrimination against Pregnant Workers and began pressure on Congress to enact the Pregnancy Disability Act.[30]

In obtaining congressional approval, the campaign faced not only opposition from business groups, but also conflicts within its ranks. Feminists wanted the bill to mandate coverage of abortion as well as pregnancy, while anti-abortion groups wanted abortion excluded. In the end a compromise was effected: the bill did not require an employer to pay disability benefits for abortion, except when abortion was necessary to preserve the life of the mother, but it did allow employers to provide abortion benefits if they chose. Feminist and pro-choice groups were more satisfied with the compromise than were anti-abortion groups, but the campaign as a whole achieved a major policy advance for women in the Pregnancy Disability Act of 1978 which amended Title VII to

---

30. Berger, *Litigation on Behalf of Women,* pp. 22–23, 26; Patricia Huckle, "The Womb Factor: Pregnancy Policies and Employment of Women," *Western Political Quarterly* 34 (March 1981):116–21; Gelb and Palley, *Women and Public Policies,* pp. 154–61.

prohibit discrimination against pregnant women in all areas of employment.[31]

EXTENSION OF THE ERA RATIFICATION DEADLINE

Undoubtedly the most difficult achievement of the policy network on women's concerns was passage of a congressional resolution to extend the time limit for ratification of the Equal Rights Amendment. By 1977 the ERA was in trouble. It needed approval by only four more states, but just two states had ratified since 1974, and the time would run out in March 1979. Thus, in October 1977 Representative Elizabeth Holtzman introduced a joint resolution extending the time limit by seven years, and Birch Bayh introduced a companion measure in the Senate. Although Congress had passed some previous Constitutional amendments without time limits, it had never considered a time extension. Along with the unprecedented nature of their goal, ERA supporters also had to overcome the belief among some legislators that the Holtzman resolution should require a two-thirds vote and that states that had already ratified should have the opportunity to rescind their approval.[32]

Holtzman and her colleagues, Margaret Heckler, Patricia Schroeder, Barbara Mikulski, and Gladys Spellman, orchestrated a campaign that overcame these obstacles. They worked with leaders of feminist organizations and other groups supporting the ERA to forge a powerful lobbying campaign, which among other activities turned out 100,000 supporters in the capital to constitute the largest feminist demonstration in history. Congresswomen also persuaded fellow legislators to vote with them on crucial amendments, such as the one regarding rescissions, even if those same legislators would ultimately vote against the resolution. While feminists had to be content with

31. Gelb and Palley, *Women and Public Policies*, pp. 161–66; Huckle, "The Womb Factor," pp. 124–26.

32. Irwin N. Gertzog, *Congressional Women: Their Recruitment, Treatment, and Behavior* (New York: Praeger, 1984), pp. 202–6.

a three-year extension rather than a seven year one, they won their other points when both houses passed the resolution in 1978. Their victory would turn out to be a Pyrrhic one, but in achieving what no one thought possible at the outset, they demonstrated the collective power that women could wield in the national policy-making arena, and the political skills of women who had entered that realm.[33]

THE NATIONAL WOMEN'S CONFERENCE

Congresswomen also organized their forces behind legislation that laid the groundwork for development of a national policy agenda for women. In response to the United Nations' declaration of 1975 as International Women's Year, Bella Abzug, Patsy Mink, and Margaret Heckler introduced legislation to hold a national women's conference. Congress passed the bill and allocated $5 million to fund the National Women's Conference, which was held in Houston, Texas in 1977. More than 2,000 women, elected at special meetings in their communities and states, debated and voted on a twenty-five-plank National Plan of Action. Members of racial and ethnic groups attended in proportions larger than their numbers in the general population, but overall the delegates represented a cross-section of American womanhood, including a sizable number of antifeminists who controlled several state delegations.

The resolutions adopted at Houston covered every significant issue raised by women in the previous decade. They addressed specific issues such as violence against women, women in media, child care, welfare, the ERA, and reproductive freedom, and they incorporated problems of specific groups of women, including older women, racial minorities, lesbians, homemakers, rural women, and criminal offenders. The National Plan of Action reflected how far women had moved in the preceding decade to articulate a new range of policy issues, and it established a national agenda for policymaking on women's concerns for the future. In addition, federal sponsorship and

33. *Ibid.*

funding of the conference legitimated the women's movement at the highest levels of power.[34]

Many of the Houston delegates had already been engaged in efforts to promote women's policy concerns at the state and local levels. Particularly in the area of antidiscrimination legislation, developments on the state level frequently mirrored laws passed by Congress. By the end of the 1970s seventeen states had passed equal rights amendments, and almost every state had equal pay laws and/or statutes prohibiting sex discrimination in employment. Sixteen states passed equal credit measures before Congress approved the Equal Credit Opportunity Act of 1974, and forty states barred discrimination in credit by 1975. A number of states that failed to ratify the Equal Rights Amendment protected women from discrimination in specific areas.

States tended to follow the federal example in anti-sex-discrimination policies, but they took the lead in other areas of concern to women, especially those most conducive to a local approach. While mainstream feminists tended to concentrate on national policies, radical feminists were most active at the local level. Many of the issues addressed in the National Plan of Action, such as abortion rights, rape, and domestic violence entered the public-policy agenda in large measure because of the efforts of the radical branch of the women's movement.

REPRODUCTIVE FREEDOM

Even before the Supreme Court decided in favor of women's right to abortion in 1973, a number of states had liberalized their abortion laws. Abortion reform antedated the feminist movement and was not initially raised as a women's issue. Rather, it originated in the early 1960s as an effort by concerned professionals, especially doctors and lawyers who wanted to allow abortions for specific reasons such as the presence of a severely damaged fetus or a threat to a woman's men-

---

34. Alice S. Rossi, *Feminists in Politics: A Panel Analysis of the First National Women's Conference* (New York: Academic Press, 1982), pp. 24–34, 387–408; Myra Marx Ferree and Beth B. Hess, *Controversy and Coalition: The New Feminist Movement* (Boston: Twayne Publishers, 1985), pp. 123–24.

Pro-abortion demonstration, New York City, May 1972.
(Bettye Lane)

tal or physical health, and who wanted to protect physicians'
right to practice medicine according to their best judgment. By
1970, twelve states had so reformed their abortion laws.[35]

Feminists quickly took up the cause and redefined it as a
women's issue. They asserted the primacy of women's right to
control reproduction and demanded repeal of all abortion laws.
In 1969, for example, the New York NOW chapter formed New
Yorkers for Abortion Law Repeal to mobilize public opinion
and pressure the legislature. Groups from the radical wing of
the women's movement employed dramatic tactics. The radical
feminist group Redstockings disrupted hearings in the New
York legislature, and groups elsewhere in the nation picketed,
demonstrated, engaged in guerrilla theater, and held speak-
outs by women who had had illegal abortions. When the Supreme Court asserted women's right to abortion in *Roe v Wade*

35. Kristin Luker, *Abortion and the Politics of Motherhood* (Berkeley: Univer-
sity of California Press, 1984), pp. 66–91; Barbara Sinclair Deckard, *The
Women's Movement: Political, Socioeconomic, and Psychological Issues* (New
York: Harper and Row, 2nd ed., 1979), pp. 423–24.

in 1973, Alaska, Hawaii, Washington, and New York had already legalized all abortions in the early stages of pregnancy.[36]

Far from settling the abortion issue, the decision unleashed a powerful counterattack that propelled advocates of reproductive freedom into the courts and legislative halls for the rest of the decade and beyond. As we shall see in the next chapter, the anti-abortion lobby began almost immediately to attempt to limit the effects of *Roe* through legislative action. State after state passed laws making it more difficult to obtain abortions by, for example, requiring spousal or parental consent, mandating waiting periods, or placing restrictions on abortion clinics. Although the Supreme Court invalidated most of these restraints in *Planned Parenthood of America v Danforth* in 1976, new laws were passed and litigation continued into the 1980s. The anti-abortion movement failed to win passage of a constitutional amendment to overrule *Roe*, but it did achieve a federal law (commonly called the "Hyde Amendment") that restricted the use of Medicaid funds to pay for abortions. Encouraged by the Supreme Court decision upholding that law, opponents of abortion secured additional measures restricting the use of federal funds for abortions for government personnel.[37]

Limitations on the right to abortion were not the only threats to reproductive freedom. The 1970s saw disclosures of widespread sterilization of women without their informed consent. Most likely to be victims of sterilization abuse were women on welfare, teenagers, and minority and retarded women. The ACLU Women's Rights Project and the Southern Poverty Law Center filed suits against local, state, and federal officials and agencies; and a wide variety of women's organizations, including NOW, WEAL, NWPC, the National Council of Negro Women, the National Women's Health Network, the

36. Deckard, *The Women's Movement,* pp. 424–25; Luker, *Abortion and the Politics of Motherhood,* pp. 92–108; Editorial Research Reports, *The Women's Movement: Achievements and Effects* (Washington, DC: Congressional Quarterly, Inc., 1977), pp. 115–16.

37. Gelb and Palley, *Women and Public Policies,* pp. 130–36, 150; Nancy E. McGlen and Karen O'Connor, *Women's Rights: The Struggle for Equality in the 19th and 20th Centuries* (New York: Praeger, 1983), pp. 303–6.

National Council of Jewish Women, and Church Women United signed on to the campaign against sterilization abuse.[38]

While predominantly white and middle-class women's organizations such as NOW and WEAL joined the attack on sterilization abuse, they still tended to define reproductive rights as the right to prevent childbearing. A number of feminist groups operating primarily on the local level helped to form a more expansive definition of reproductive rights, one which spoke more to the needs of poor women and women of color. The Committee for Abortion Rights and Against Sterilization Abuse (CARASA), was founded by a multiracial group with roots in the women's liberation movement. Unlike the National Abortion Rights Action League, CARASA was as much concerned with protecting women from sterilization abuse as with guaranteeing their right to abortion. In response to litigation and complaints by civil-rights organizations, women's organizations, and feminist groups like CARASA, the Department of Health, Education and Welfare issued more rigorous guidelines, and some states and localities enacted measures requiring strict consent procedures.[39]

RAPE

Women's activism on behalf of reproductive freedom involved politicizing what had previously been a private and individual concern. That kind of transformation also characterized the development of other policy issues that originated at the state and local levels. Before the 1970s, victims of violence, particularly women who were raped or those who suffered physical abuse from their husbands, tended to react with shame and silence. The women's movement and its allies lifted the veil of

38. Rosalind Pollack Petchesky, *Abortion and Woman's Choice: The State, Sexuality, and Reproductive Freedom* (Boston: Northeastern University Press, 1985), pp. 179–80; *New York Times,* July 10, 1973, p. 31; *The Spokeswoman* 4 (September, 1973):1.

39. Adele Clarke, "Subtle Forms of Sterilization Abuse: A Reproductive Rights Analysis," in Rita Arditti, Renate Duelli Klein, and Shelley Minden, eds., *Test-Tube Women: What Future for Motherhood?* (London: Pandora Press, 1984), pp. 188–204.

secrecy from these taboo subjects, pushed them onto the national agenda, and promoted policy initiatives designed to assist the victims and to lessen the incidence of violence against women.

The issue of rape, like abortion law repeal, was first raised by feminism's radical wing. In 1970, New York Radical Feminists held a Rape Speak Out, the first of its kind. Other local groups established rape crisis centers and hot-lines that offered advice and support to victims, and some began offering women training in self-defense. Provision of services to victims led to efforts at institutional changes that would facilitate prosecution of rapists. By 1973, NOW had established a Rape Task Force that collaborated with officials on federal legislation and produced materials instructing local chapters on how to obtain Federal Revenue Sharing funds for rape projects. In 1974, the Massachusetts NOW chapter attracted 300 legal professionals, police, doctors, victims, and legislators to a conference on rape, while the Michigan Women's Task Force on Rape won the support of police and prosecutors' organizations for what became the first comprehensive reform rape legislation in the nation. Above all, feminists were challenging longstanding notions about rape, i.e., that it was a sexual act rather than an act of violence and terrorism, that women were somehow responsible if they were raped, and that rape cases demanded different rules of evidence than other criminal cases.[40]

Rape crisis centers helped to change treatment of victims and prosecution of rapists simply by providing volunteers to accompany victims to hospitals, police stations, and the courts. Staff at the Washington, D.C. Rape Crisis Center noticed that authorities treated victims more humanely when center members were present. In some cities, rape crisis staff members participated in the training of police officers. Eventually many police departments instituted specialized training for women officers working with rape victims.[41]

Women also undertook to change prosecution practices. By the end of the 1970s, forty states had revised or enacted new

40. Deckard, *The Women's Movement*, pp. 429–31; *Do It NOW,* November, 1973, June, 1974, August, 1974; *The Spokeswoman* 4 (June 15, 1974):5.

41. Deckard, *The Women's Movement*, pp. 432–34.

rape statutes. Most states now prohibited cross-examination of the victim about her previous sexual history and eliminated the traditional requirement for corroboration—a witness or proof of victim resistance. New statutes established gradations of rape, and matched the penalty structure to different degrees of assault, as ways to facilitate prosecution and obtain more convictions. A number of women's rights groups joined in the challenge to Georgia's law (*Coker v Georgia*, 1977) providing the death penalty for convicted rapists because they believed that such a drastic sentence reduced the likelihood of convictions. A few laws even eliminated marriage or cohabitation as a defense, thus protecting wives from rape by their husbands.[42]

Because of its nature as a criminal law issue, rape was confronted most extensively at the state and local levels. Nonetheless women did not ignore opportunities for policy development in the federal government. The Center for Women Policy Studies (CWPS) obtained funding from the Law Enforcement Assistance Agency in the Department of Justice to study the needs and treatment of victims and to develop guidelines for agencies dealing with rape. CWPS's research produced a wealth of materials for community-based groups and a newsletter circulated to 35,000 individuals and organizations. In addition, Congress passed a version of the bill NOW had been promoting since 1973: the 1975 Public Health Service Act, which established a National Center for the Prevention and Control of Rape. On the initiative of Elizabeth Holtzman, Congress also helped to shift the stigma from the victim by amending the Federal Rules of Evidence to bar introduction of a victim's sexual history as evidence in a trial.[43]

DOMESTIC VIOLENCE

The issue of domestic violence followed a similar course as it moved on to the public-policy agenda. Although groups related

---

42. Wallace D. Loh, "Q: What Has Reform of Rape Legislation Wrought? A: Truth in Criminal Labelling," *Journal of Social Issues* 37 (1981):28–50; O'Connor, *Women's Organizations' Use of the Courts*, p. 108.

43. Chapman, "Policy Centers," pp. 186–88; Gertzog, *Congressional Women*, p. 156.

to Alcoholics Anonymous had offered some assistance to families of abusive men in the 1960s, it was the activities of radical
feminists that attracted widespread media and public attention
to the problem. The first feminist shelter in the United States
grew out of a consciousness-raising group in St. Paul, Minnesota
in 1971. These women created Women's Advocates and initially set up a hot-line and information service; they soon realized that abused women needed a safe place to live. They
sought funds from the county and private foundations, and
in 1974 they opened a shelter. Local groups in Pittsburgh,
Pasadena, San Francisco, and Cambridge were among the earliest to establish refuges for battered women. NOW created a
Task Force on Battered Women/Household Violence in 1975,
and local chapters began to establish services and to work for
legislative reform. Traditional women's organizations, church
groups, and local civic organizations joined the movement, and
by 1980, 300 shelters were in existence.[44]

Along with establishing shelters, the battered women's
movement put pressure on the political establishment to provide funding for services and to reform laws and practices dealing with domestic violence. By 1978, seven state legislatures
had voted appropriations for shelter projects, and subsequently
states began to levy surtaxes on marriage licenses to provide
funds for domestic-violence programs. By 1979, forty states had
specific remedies for spouse abuse that afforded greater protection to victims and facilitated prosecution of offenders. Among
them were amendments to include cohabitants as well as
spouses; provisions for restraining orders and for warrantless
arrests; and measures allowing women to escape violent homes
without jeopardizing their rights to property or custody of their
children. In several cities, women's lawsuits against local au-

44. Kathleen J. Tierney, "The Battered Women's Movement and the Creation
of the Wife Beating Problem," *Social Problems* 29 (February, 1982):207–8; John
M. Johnson, "Program Enterprise and Official Cooptation in the Battered
Women's Shelter Movement," *American Behavioral Scientist* 24 (July/August
1981):827–31; U.S. Commission on Civil Rights, *Battered Women: Issues of
Public Policy* (Washington, DC: U.S. Commission on Civil Rights, 1978), pp.
400–404. For a thorough account of policy development on domestic violence,
see Elizabeth Pleck, *Domestic Tyranny: The Making of Social Policy against
Family Violence from Colonial Times to the Present* (New York: Oxford University Press, 1987).

thorities led to practices more responsive to the needs and rights of abuse victims.[45]

At the federal level, advocates for battered women lobbied for a bill providing money and assistance to states and communities for a variety of programs. Thwarted by opposition from "pro-family" groups and from legislators who believed that states and communities should be responsible for funding domestic violence programs, the measure was not passed until 1984, and then in a watered-down version. Meanwhile, the Law Enforcement Assistance Agency provided funds for local projects, and the Department of Health, Education and Welfare established an Office on Domestic Violence in 1979. By the late 1970s, assistance to battered women in many localities had shifted from the hands of feminists to social workers, the therapeutic community, and law-and-order officials. While feminists were discouraged to see the attenuation of their woman-centered approach, they could nonetheless take pride in having focused public and official attention on a form of oppression that crippled women from all classes and races.[46]

DISPLACED HOMEMAKERS

A final new policy area introduced by feminists in the 1970s concerned the problems of women displaced by death or divorce from their traditional roles as wives and mothers. In 1970, California initiated divorce law reforms which would spread to nearly every state by the end of the decade. These new measures provided for "no-fault" divorces, eliminating the requirement that one partner show fault before a marriage could be dissolved. Divorce thus became easier and less acrimonious, but women's groups worried about the consequences for women, and NOW opposed no-fault divorce without economic safeguards for women and children. As the divorce rate soared,

45. Pleck, *Domestic Tyranny*, pp. 235–38, 628–35; Sandra Wexler, "Battered Women and Public Policy," in Boneparth, ed., *Women, Power and Policy,* pp. 188–91.

46. June H. Zeitlin, "Domestic Violence: Perspectives from Washington," in Tinker, ed., *Women in Washington,* pp. 263–74; Pleck, *Domestic Tyranny,* pp. 186–200.

women who had entered traditional marriages in which they took care of the home and children while their husbands provided financial support found themselves at mid-life deprived of that security and lacking the skills or experience to enter the labor force.[47]

In response to the crisis of displaced homemakers, feminists joined with other groups to help them become self-supporting and to support their claims to economic justice. They sought to make judges acknowledge women's contributions as homemakers and mothers in the division of marital property, rather than assuming that because the husband's income purchased the property he had a prevailing right to it. Displaced homemakers themselves were politicized by their plight; several, for example, were active in NOW's campaign for a Massachusetts law instructing the courts to consider homemakers' contributions when approving financial settlements in divorce cases. By the 1980s, women were also achieving modest success in their claims not just to tangible assets, but also to "career assets" of their former husbands, including retirement benefits, insurance, and professional degrees and licenses. In 1980, Congresswoman Patricia Schroeder, backed by a women's lobby, successfully sponsored a bill entitling divorced wives of foreign service officers to a share of their former husbands' retirement benefits.[48]

The movement to provide services for displaced homemakers was launched by Tish Sommers, who at fifty-seven was divorced after twenty-three years of housekeeping, motherhood, and volunteer work. In 1973, she founded NOW's Task Force on Older Women, and one year later coined the term "displaced homemakers" to identify women who shared her plight. After forming a coalition of older women, church women, and feminists, she shrewdly organized a lobby to obtain legislation for displaced homemakers from the California legislature. To overcome the governor's opposition to the bill, Sommers

---

47. *The Spokeswoman* 4 (November 16, 1973):4.

48. Priscilla Leith, "Massachusetts NOW Wins Homemaker Rights," *National NOW Times,* February, 1978, p. 13; Lenore J. Weitzman, *The Divorce Revolution: The Unexpected Social and Economic Consequences for Women and Children* (New York: The Free Press, 1985), pp. 110–42; *The Spokeswoman* 10 (October 1980):2.

threatened a sit-in by older feminists. Her efforts achieved a bill providing funds for a pilot project, a multiservice center where widowed and divorced women could come for job training and placement, counseling, and emotional support. With funding from women's religious organizations and NOW, Sommers's associate Laurie Shields criss-crossed the country, publicizing the issue and organizing women to replicate the California program in their own states. By mid-1977, twelve states had displaced homemakers' laws on the books, and in 1978 centers were operating in sixteen states.[49]

The strategy of Sommers and her Alliance for Displaced Homemakers was to work for state legislation as a means of attracting interest in Congress. In 1975, they persuaded California Congresswoman Burke to introduce legislation for federal support of displaced homemakers services. Although Congress failed to pass that bill, it did include displaced homemakers as a targeted group in the Comprehensive Education and Training Act (CETA) passed in 1978 to provide funds for local governments to employ disadvantaged groups. Two years later Congress authorized $5 million through CETA for forty-seven demonstration projects for displaced homemakers.[50]

CONCLUSION

The women's movement and its allies in the 1970s worked a modest revolution in public policy. While the Supreme Court's stance on sex discrimination was ambiguous and failed to match its rigorous scrutiny of legislation regarding race, it had made an abrupt about-face in applying the equal protection clause to laws differentiating men from women. In the legislative arena, in addition to securing state and federal laws banning discrimination in various aspects of employment, education, credit, and military service, women introduced entirely new issues into the public-policy agenda. Politicizing traditionally private issues

49. Laurie Shields, *Displaced Homemakers: Organizing for a New Life* (New York: McGraw-Hill, 1981), pp. 25–64; "Displaced Homemakers Form Network," *Women's Agenda* 3 (December 1978):3.

50. Shields, *Displaced Homemakers,* pp. 47, 117–46; Angela Dodson, "Older Women, New Job Skills," *New York Times,* June 18, 1986.

such as reproduction, rape, domestic violence, sexual harassment, and displaced homemakers, a cluster of women's policy coalitions focused public attention on these issues and compelled officials to act on them.

These accomplishments by no means completed the feminist agenda. Even when strong measures were adopted, such as those banning discrimination in employment, education, and credit, vigorous enforcement did not always follow. Especially in areas where the civil-rights movement had not forged a precedent, government initiatives were limited. Thus, Congress responded to women's demands for action dealing with domestic violence and displaced homemakers with funding sufficient only for a few pilot programs. Efforts to secure a federally supported child-care program failed completely. President Nixon vetoed a comprehensive child-care bill passed by Congress in 1971, and subsequent bills failed even to get out of committee. Some low-income families received services through welfare and antipoverty programs, and some working parents obtained tax credits for child-care expenses. Still, adequate and affordable day care continued to be a critical problem for employed mothers.[51]

Lack of adequate day-care services highlighted a growing dilemma as feminists sought to fashion public policies based on women's needs. Of how much help was equal opportunity in the public sphere for women who continued to bear primary responsibility for the care of their homes and families? What kind of equality did gender-neutral legislation and laws against sex discrimination provide if women were limited by their childbearing role? By the 1970s, a majority of mothers worked outside the home; while husbands were inclined to take on more household responsibilities, shifts in the domestic division of labor were only incremental. Burdened by their "double day," women began to wonder if they could really "have it all," and feminists faced the challenge of effecting public policies that could promote genuine equality, providing women the same opportunity that men had always enjoyed to have both children and jobs.

51. Jill Norgren, "In Search of a National Child Care Policy: Background and Prospects," *Western Political Quarterly* 35 (March 1981):128, 132–37.

Other challenges sobered the buoyant optimism of the early 1970s. Women's public-policy demands fell victim in part to a worsening economic climate, where both inflation and unemployment squeezed government budgets and made lawmakers cool to new programs. Moreover, the diffuse opposition to feminist goals, which had existed since passage of the ERA, developed into a powerful and highly organized movement. That movement not only demonstrated its force in stalling ratification of the ERA, but it mobilized opposition to nearly every measure of concern to feminists.

Chapter 6

The Politics of Antifeminism

By the mid-1970s, a countermobilization had organized to challenge the gains and expanding agenda of the women's movement. Men—especially in New Right and religious organizations—participated as leaders in this counterattack, but some women also took prominent roles; and women constituted the bulk of activists at the grassroots level. Indeed, conservative women dramatically increased their political participation: using both traditional and unconventional tactics, they lobbied office-holders, worked in political campaigns, organized appeals to public opinion, and in a few cases sought public office for themselves. Conservative women aimed most of their fire at the ERA and abortion, but they also mobilized against gay rights, government-sponsored day care, services for battered wives and displaced homemakers, and educational equity reforms.

Opposition to the feminist agenda was not confined to groups on the fringes of the political spectrum. President Jimmy Carter's efforts on behalf of ratification of the ERA did not satisfy feminists in the Democratic party; they were also dismayed at his stand on abortion, and outraged when he fired Bella Abzug from her position as chair of the National Advisory Committee for Women. Most disturbing for the women's movement was the right wing's capture of the 1980 Republican convention and the nomination of Ronald Reagan for president.

THE NEW RIGHT

During the 1970s issues concerning sex roles and women's rights moved to a prominent place on the agenda of right-wing organizations. The resurgence of conservatism drew initial strength from a backlash against the civil-rights revolution, the social and economic reforms of Johnson's Great Society, the antiwar movement, and various forms of cultural and political radicalism of the 1960s. Capitalizing on popular discomfort with these political and social changes, in the mid-1970s conservatives formed a number of new organizations and publications, including the Conservative Caucus, the National Conservative Political Action Committee, and *The New Right Report.*

Two characteristics gave the New Right its novelty. In the 1970s, conservatives' strength was augmented by the growth and increasing politicization of religious fundamentalists led by Jerry Falwell, Pat Robertson, and other ministers of the "electronic church," who preached to vast television audiences. To the longstanding conservative allegiance to states' rights, opposition to a large and intrusive federal government, and concern about international communism and domestic radicalism, the New Right added an emphasis on restoring conventional sex roles and strengthening the traditional family.[1]

WOMEN AGAINST FEMINISM

The shifting emphasis of ultraconservative politics was exemplified by Phyllis Schlafly. Since the 1950s Schlafly had run for office, published books, lectured, and testified before Congress, calling for a stronger national defense and more nuclear weapons, and attacking the federal bureaucracy, public spending on social programs, and other items on the liberal agenda. Indeed, Schlafly's opposition to the ERA, and that of the New Right as well, was linked to a distaste for big government and welfare

1. Allen Hunter, "In the Wings: New Right Ideology and Organization," *Radical America* 15 (Spring 1981):113–36.

state programs, and to concern about what they considered a weak system of national defense. Thus, Schlafly found Article 2 of the ERA, which gave Congress enforcement powers and consequently threatened states rights, as appalling as she found the equality provision. She also argued that the ERA would make women subject to combat duty, and, because women lacked physical and mental qualities for waging war, the United States would become even more vulnerable to its enemies abroad. To a large extent it was the linking of antifeminist goals with issues of longstanding concern to conservatives that made the New Right "new" as it developed its "pro-family" focus in the late 1970s.[2]

Schlafly's ability to mobilize thousands of women against the ERA was especially frustrating and difficult to understand for partisans of the women's movement. The John Birch Society, the American Party, and other ultraconservative organizations mounted early challenges to the amendment and they were joined by male-led New Right groups, but women came quickly to the forefront of the anti-ERA campaign. Although the vast majority of female legislators supported the ERA and its defeat lay in the hands of male legislators in a few states where the margins were slim, women overwhelmingly constituted the troops of lobbyists against the amendment. They probably changed few minds, but they fortified and legitimized opposition to the ERA by calling into question whether it was really in the best interests of women.

The very brevity and simplicity of the amendment furnished ammunition for opponents, for no one could say with absolute certainty how the courts would interpret it. Anti-ERA forces were able to shift the discourse from the abstract principle of equality, with which few Americans could disagree, to predictions about the substantive changes likely to attend adoption of the ERA. In fact, its brevity enabled both sides to exaggerate the consequences, as they had done in the debate over the Nineteenth Amendment. ERA supporters, for example,

2. Carol Felsenthal, *The Sweetheart of the Silent Majority: The Biography of Phyllis Schlafly* (Garden City, NY: Doubleday and Company), pp. 198–231, 235–36; Hunter, "In the Wings," pp. 116–17.

promised that it would close the gap in incomes between men and women. Opponents warned that it would send women into combat, force wives into the labor market, sexually integrate prisons and toilets, encourage homosexuality, and require government to fund abortion on demand.

Overall, Schlafly and her supporters claimed, the ERA would transform the traditional family and the sex roles on which it was based, thereby undermining women's best interests. While feminists saw the ERA as one means to increase women's power and autonomy within the family and to gain identity as individuals both within and outside the home, their opponents clung to a social order in which women's roles were defined by customary family relationships. The sources of women's opposition to the ERA lay primarily in their religious beliefs and in their perceptions of its threat to their own lives. Affirming a literal interpretation of the Bible, women believed that sexual equality violated the God-given authority of men over women, husbands over wives. In contrast to feminists who viewed traditional sex roles as social constructions, anti-ERA women believed that God had endowed men and women with different characteristics appropriate to their different functions in life. Men were ordained to be breadwinners and women to be caretakers of home and family. The ERA, they insisted, would subvert that division of labor and power and absolve men from the responsibility of economic support. Further undermining the traditional family, according to opponents, was the ERA's potential for legalizing homosexual marriages.[3]

In seeking to sustain the traditional family, most anti-ERA activists were defending their own life patterns. Among the general public, marital status did not sharply differentiate supporters from opponents, but a large majority of those active in opposing the ERA were full-time housewives. They also tended to be white, middle-aged, and middle-class, and their views on

3. Susan Harding, "Family Reform Movements: Recent Feminism and Its Opposition," *Feminist Studies* 7 (Spring 1981):57–75; Mariam Darce Frenier, "American Anti-Feminist Women: Comparing the Rhetoric of Opponents of the Equal Rights Amendment with That of Opponents of Women's Suffrage," *Women's Studies International Forum* 7 (1984):460–61.

other issues coincided with those of the New Right. Activist opponents were overwhelmingly religious, the majority belonging to fundamentalist churches. While some amendment opponents had engaged in lobbying and other political activities before, for most it was the ERA that drew women into politics for the first time.[4]

As Barbara Ehrenreich and others have pointed out, conservative women had a direct interest in defeat of the ERA, which they believed would abrogate the duty of men to support their families and, thus, the right of women to be housewives. That threat was especially compelling in an era of a soaring divorce rate and the spread of no-fault divorce laws. The middle-aged full-time housewives who constituted the bulk of ERA opposition had entered conventional marriages where, in exchange for raising children and caring for home and husbands, they expected economic support. Phyllis Schlafly emphasized the unfairness of changing the rules in the middle of the game, noting that "ERA does not even include a 'grandmother clause.' " She also stressed the undesirable qualities of available alternatives to full-time wife- and motherhood. "If you complain about servitude to a husband, servitude to a boss will be more intolerable," she warned, pointing out that most jobs were "just as repetitious, tiresome, and boring" as was housework. Antifeminists turned a deaf ear to feminists' arguments that multitudes of divorced women, even in the absence of an Equal Rights Amendment, were already forced to support themselves and their children with little or no help from former husbands. To anti-ERA women, the amendment threatened "a way of life they had entered in good faith." Thus, women in both camps recognized the precariousness of economic secu-

4. Val Burris, "Who Opposed the ERA? An Analysis of the Social Bases of Antifeminism," *Social Science Quarterly* 64 (June 1983):306, 310; David W. Brady and Kent L. Tedin, "Ladies in Pink: Ideology in the Anti-ERA Movement," *Social Science Quarterly* 56 (March 1976):570–74; Kent L. Tedin, et al., "Social Background and Political Differences Between Pro- and Anti-ERA Activists," *American Politics Quarterly* 5 (July 1977):402–5; Kent L. Tedin, "Religious Preference and Pro/Anti Activism on the Equal Rights Amendment Issue," *Pacific Sociological Review* 21 (January 1978):55–65; Theodore S. Arrington and Patricia A. Kyle, "Equal Rights Amendment Activists in North Carolina," *Signs: Journal of Women in Culture and Society* 3 (Spring 1978): 667–69, 673–75; Janet K. Boles, *The Politics of the Equal Rights Amendment: Conflict and the Decision Process* (New York: Longman, 1979), pp. 82–87.

rity; but while feminists sought to render women self-sustaining, antifeminists wanted men to bear the responsibility for family support.[5]

DERAILING THE ERA

Organized female opposition to the ERA began while the amendment was still under consideration in Congress. In July 1971, Jaquie Davison founded Happiness of Womanhood (HOW) in California, and by the end of 1972, it and a related group, the League of Housewives, claimed 10,000 members in fifty states. Funding for these groups, according to Davison, was provided by members' husbands. In Utah, a group sponsored by the John Birch Society, known as HOTDOGS (Humanitarians Opposed to the Degradation of Our Girls), mounted the original opposition in December 1972, charging that feminists were communists and that the ERA would destroy the family. The Daughters of the American Revolution was one of the few traditional women's organizations in opposition to the ERA; the largest was the National Council of Catholic Women. While it claimed to speak for its members, many Catholic women, including a number of prominent nuns, worked for the amendment, and by 1974 they had formed a national organization, Catholic Women for the ERA.[6]

In contrast to the broad-based feminist movement, leadership of the ERA opposition was concentrated in the hands of one woman, Phyllis Schlafly. In her 1970 congressional campaign she had attacked feminism as "destructive of family living," but had little to say about the ERA until February 1972, when an entire issue of *The Phyllis Schlafly Report* assailed the

5. Barbara Ehrenreich, *The Hearts of Men: American Dreams and the Flight from Commitment* (Garden City, NY: Anchor Press, 1983), pp. 144–49; Felsenthal, *Sweetheart of the Silent Majority,* pp. 236–37; Mark E. Kann, "Legitimation, Consent, and Antifeminism," *Women and Politics* 3 (Spring 1983):13–15; Andrew Hacker, "E.R.A.—R.I.P.: Women, Not Men, Defeated the Amendment for Equal Rights," *Harpers* 261 (September 1980):12.

6. Boles, *The Politics of the Equal Rights Amendment,* pp. 68–71; John Unger Zussman and Shauna M. Adix, "Content and Conjecture in the Equal Rights Amendment Controversy in Utah," *Women's Studies International Forum* 5 (1982):474.

Anti–feminist leader Phyllis
Schlafly. (Bettye Lane)

amendment. In October, she established a national movement,
STOP ERA, and immediately began to mobilize the loyalists she
had attracted through the *Report*, the Eagle Forum, and her
annual political-action leadership conferences. Within months,
Schlafly had constructed a minutely organized campaign which
could respond immediately where action was necessary. Three
telephone lines in her home kept her in constant touch with
state leaders to whom she passed on information and advice.
She traveled extensively and shrewdly exploited the media attention that she attracted as *the* leader of antifeminism.[7]

The anti-ERA campaign utilized most of the tactics common
to interest-group politics. Through mass mailings and public
speeches, leaders mobilized women to write to legislators and
lobby personally in state capitals. The unusual volume of public-
opinion mail on the ERA was a mark of their success. While
Schlafly and others testified before legislative committees,
other antifeminist activists employed unconventional strate-
gems. In an early effort to block ratification in California, HOW

7. Boles, *The Politics of the Equal Rights Amendment,* p. 68; Felsenthal, *Sweetheart of the Silent Majority,* pp. 232, 242–45, 261–67.

members presented senators with mice bearing the message, "Do you want to be a man or a mouse?" A favorite ploy in many states was to present legislators with flowers or home-baked goods. In Illinois, for example, STOP ERA women handed lawmakers apple pies along with poems carrying the appeal:

> My heart and my hand went into this dough
> For the sake of the family please vote "no."

Illinois women also brought baby girls to the Illinois legislature wearing signs which read, "Please don't draft me."[8]

Feminists had constructed an effective lobbying campaign for congressional passage of the Equal Rights Amendment, but they had not developed state-level strategies and would not do so until opposition emerged. Nor did they initially think that such a campaign would be necessary. Witnessing the early rush of state legislatures to ratify, amendment supporters assumed that it would pass smoothly through the required three-fourths of the states. They were taken by surprise when massive resistance began to surface in 1973. As opponents transformed the ERA from a fairly narrow legal rights issue into one with implications that struck at age-old, God-given family and sex-role arrangements, the ratification process stalled. In Utah, for example, Mormon support for the amendment fell from 63 to 31 percent following an opposition editorial in a Mormon newspaper, and Church leaders appealed to members in Utah, Virginia, Arizona, Missouri, and Nevada to organize against ratification.[9]

In 1974 only three states joined the thirty that had already ratified; by very close votes two more states approved the amendment in 1975 and 1977. The strongest warning that the ERA was in trouble occurred in 1975 when New York and New Jersey rejected state equal-rights referenda. Both had easily ratified the ERA, but New Jersey voters defeated the state measure by a narrow margin and in New York opponents marshalled a surplus of more than 400,000 votes. Intense campaigns

8. Boles, *The Politics of the Equal Rights Amendment*, pp. 8, 27, 104–5, 112–17, 126.

9. Janet K. Boles, "Building Support for the ERA: A Case of 'Too Much, Too Late,'" *PS* 15 (Fall 1982):573; Zussman and Adix, "Content and Conjecture in the ERA Contest in Utah," pp. 476–81.

by ERA opponents played upon the usual fears of homosexuality, unisex toilets, and subjecting women to the draft. Feminists' success in obtaining antidiscrimination laws worked against them, as opponents argued that women could obtain their rights without changing the Constitution and predicted that an equal rights amendment would cost them dearly. Above all, they appealed to housewives' fears that they would not only lose their right to remain at home, but would suffer status loss as well. Expressing the threat to traditional roles posed by the feminist movement, Annette Stern, leader of anti-ERA group WUNDER (Women United to Defend Equal Rights), insisted, "I'm not going to stand for having my role denigrated."[10]

Feminists redoubled their efforts after the New York and New Jersey referenda. To pressure recalcitrant legislatures, in 1977 NOW called for an economic boycott of all unratified states. More than 350 organizations joined the boycott, refusing to hold meetings in states that had not approved the ERA. As we have seen, supporters were also successful in getting Congress to extend the time limit for ratification until June 1982. Having made the ERA its highest priority, NOW increased its membership from 55,000 to over 200,000 between 1977 and 1982. Its coffers swelled, too, as NOW raised one million dollars a month in the first half of 1982. Despite these achievements, when time ran out on the amendment in June 1982, the ratification effort fell three states short of the necessary thirty-eight. Most of the unratified states were in the South or Southwest; Illinois was the only northern industrial state that withheld approval.[11]

The anti-ERA movement defeated a measure that a majority of the general public, even in most unratified states, consistently favored. Public support for the ERA peaked at 74 percent in 1974, and it never fell below 52 percent. Opposition never surpassed 31 percent. Moreover, a poll taken in Utah suggested that many people who said they were against the

10. Boles, *The Politics of the Equal Rights Amendment,* pp. 2–3, 180; Marion K. Sanders, "Requiem for ERA," *The New Republic* 173 (November 29, 1975): 20–21.

11. Janet K. Boles, "The Equal Rights Amendment as a Non-Zero-Sum Game," in Joan Hoff Wilson, ed., *Rights of Passage: The Past and Future of the ERA* (Bloomington: Indiana University Press, 1986), pp. 58–59.

amendment actually agreed with its substance. Only one-third of the respondents reported that they were for the ERA, but when the text of Article 1 was read to them ("Equality of rights under the law shall not be denied or abridged by the United States or by any State on account of sex"), more than two-thirds said they favored it. The Utah poll indicated in part a general confusion about the measure. More importantly, it demonstrated that Americans tended to favor equality in principle, while simultaneously opposing substantive changes in sex roles. The success of the opposition movement depended upon its ability to persuade people that the amendment would bring about a host of undesirable substantive changes.[12]

Indeed, anti-ERA activists fashioned the amendment into a highly charged symbol, making a number of claims, which while frequently dubious, played on popular attachment to traditional sex roles and fears of social change. They threatened homemakers with the prospect of losing their right to economic support and being forced into the labor market. Linking the ERA with a number of controversial issues, opponents of the amendment warned that it would place mothers on the front lines of military combat, legalize homosexual marriages, solidify forever women's right to obtain abortions, and force the integration of public toilets. In the context of recent unexpected and unpopular Supreme Court decisions regarding pornography, criminals' rights, school prayer, school busing, and abortion, opponents' arguments that the ERA would give the Court a blank check to mandate radical changes struck home.[13]

Opponents also benefited when the Soviet Union invaded Afghanistan and changes in military policy claimed the attention of national policymakers. In 1980, Congress passed a law mandating registration for the draft, but it rejected President Carter's proposal that registration include women. While most

12. Mark R. Daniels, Robert Darcy, and Joseph W. Westphal, "The ERA Won—At Least in the Opinion Polls," *PS* (Fall 1982):578–84; Zussman and Adix, "Content and Conjecture in the Equal Rights Amendment Controversy in Utah," pp. 481–86; Jane J. Mansbridge, *Why We Lost the ERA* (Chicago: University of Illinois Press, 1986), pp. 20–26.

13. Jane Dehart Mathews and Donald Mathews, "The Cultural Politics of the ERA's Defeat," In Wilson, ed., *Rights of Passage*, pp. 44–62; Mansbridge, *Why We Lost the ERA*, pp. 26–28.

feminist and other women's organizations opposed any draft, NOW, WEAL, the AAUW, BPW, and other groups took the position that if registration were required for men, the principle of gender-neutrality required that women too be included. In response to a suit challenging all-male registration as discriminatory, the Supreme Court upheld the law, thereby adding fuel to anti-ERA fire. If the Court had decided that the existing Constitution required gender neutrality in military policies, ERA opponents would have lost one of their most compelling arguments. With judicial affirmation of Congress's right to treat men and women differently with respect to military service in the absence of an Equal Rights amendment, anti-ERA forces' claims that the amendment would threaten women's historic privilege took on greater force.[14]

Opponents of the ERA had by far the easier job in mobilizing opposition. As advocates of change, ERA supporters bore the burden of proof that the amendment was necessary and desirable; feminists were often hard-pressed to spell out protections that had not already been enacted into federal law. Opponents, on the other hand, had only to sow seeds of reasonable doubt about its potential effects. The variety of issues that opponents were able to tie to the ERA provided them considerable flexibility. If the unisex toilets argument didn't work, they could shift attention to the draft, to abortion, or to homosexual marriages. Moreover, as Zillah Eisenstein has pointed out, opponents were "more singly committed to the defeat of the ERA than feminists have been singly committed to its ratification." To most supporters, the ERA was only one of a multitude of changes necessary to achieve sexual equality, and many feminists assigned it relatively low priority. In contrast, to opponents its defeat was absolutely crucial to defending both their most deeply held values and the life situations in which they found themselves. In addition, feminists' concentration on national politics left them unprepared to mount aggressive ratification

14. Mansbridge, *Why We Lost the ERA*, pp. 67–86; Gilbert Y. Steiner, *Constitutional Inequality: The Political Fortunes of the Equal Rights Amendment* (Washington, DC: Brookings Institution, 1985), pp. 72–74.

campaigns in the states before the opposition had time to mobilize.[15]

Above all, opponents had the advantage because they needed only a margin of one vote in just a minority of state legislatures. That male legislators cast the vast majority of opposition votes should not obscure the importance of women in defeating the amendment. The ability of Phyllis Schlafly and others to mobilize women to lobby against the ERA furnished male lawmakers the compelling rationale for blocking ratification, while it diminished the threat of retribution at the polls for legislators who voted no. Whatever their own reasons for opposing the amendment, male legislators could insist that it was not in women's best interests, by pointing to the substantial numbers of women in active opposition. The dedicated minority of women who worked against ratification thus provided legitimation for the decisions of the male legislators who defeated the ERA.

THE ANTI-ABORTION MOVEMENT

Political mobilization against abortion, the other major issue of the women's movement, was more complex than opposition to the ERA. As with the ERA, the New Right saw abortion as a means to expand its appeal, and it made opposition to abortion a central element of its "pro-family" thrust. The Catholic Church played a critical role in the politics of abortion, but some Protestant denominations, Orthodox Jews, and Mormons were also active. Although men directed much of the anti-abortion campaign, some women assumed leadership roles, and women contributed a mass constituency, many of them activated into politics for the first time by this issue. The "pro-life" movement even included a few self-identified feminists who created Feminists for Life and similar groups.

Unlike the anti-ERA movement, opponents of abortion

15. Boles, *The Politics of the Equal Rights Amendment*, p. 18; Elizabeth Pleck, "Failed Strategies; Renewed Hope," in Wilson, ed., *Rights of Passage*, pp. 108–19; Zillah R. Eisenstein, *Feminism and Sexual Equality: Crisis in Liberal America* (New York: Monthly Review Press, 1984), p. 181.

failed in their ultimate goal, thanks largely to the federal courts. Yet the anti-abortion movement was able to make abortion a prominent issue in the 1970s and beyond. It mobilized massive pressure on political officials and in some cases defeated candidates who failed to take a "pro-life" position. The right-to-life (RTL) movement claimed inordinate attention from Congress and state legislatures, and though failing to end abortion, it succeeded in imposing limitations on women's reproductive rights. Moreover, it shifted the focus of debate from women's reproductive rights to the rights of embryos.

The Catholic Church and other abortion opponents had entered the political arena in the late 1960s and early 1970s in efforts to block liberalization laws in state legislatures. The early anti-abortion movement, however, was largely male and composed of political elites. It was the Supreme Court decision that legalized abortion throughout the nation in January 1973 that sparked a mass movement. That year the National Council of Catholic Bishops (NCCB) created the National Committee for a Human Life Amendment to lobby for a constitutional amendment to overturn the Supreme Court decision. Two years later the NCCB issued the *Pastoral Plan for Pro-Life Activities* with detailed instructions on how to organize pro-life groups in every congressional district. While the goal of the *Pastoral Plan* was a constitutional amendment, grass-roots organizations were also to lobby for laws and administrative rules to restrict abortions and to monitor elected officials and candidates on their positions on abortion. Catholic women were active in RTL mobilization. Randy Engel of Pennsylvania had established a secular organization, the U.S. Coalition for Life, and before adoption of the *Pastoral Plan* had criticized the Catholic hierarchy for being insufficiently aggressive in organizing RTL activities.[16]

Other women assumed leadership roles in the RTL movement. The largest anti-abortion coalition was the secular National Right to Life Committee (NRLC), an umbrella organization that claimed 11 million supporters. Mildred Jefferson and Carolyn Gerster both served as president of the NRLC, Judie Brown and Anne O'Donnell held the post of director, and

16. Robert J. Spitzer, *The Right to Life Movement and Third Party Politics* (Westport, CT: Greenwood Press, 1987), pp. 58–59, 68.

Thea Rossi Barron worked as chief Washington lobbyist. Ellen McCormack led the Right-to-Life Party (RTLP) in New York, and as a contender for the Democratic Party presidential nomination in 1976, she ran in eighteen state primaries and qualified for federal matching funds. Like most of the RTLP leaders and members, McCormack was a novice in politics, activated by her profound opposition to abortion.[17]

As it did with other single-issue causes, the New Right grasped the abortion issue as a vehicle for broadening its political base. It also identified abortion with the emancipated woman, the erosion of customary sex roles, and the destruction of the traditional family, which to the New Right was the very bulwark of a stable and conservative society. Cooperating with religious and secular RTL groups, the New Right also established its own organizations, such as the American Life Lobby.[18]

The success of all of these RTL organizations depended upon their ability to mobilize women at the grass-roots level. And in fact, a national survey of RTL activists found that 80 percent of them were women. A study of these women in California indicated that they bore some resemblance to anti-ERA women. Many were newcomers to political activism. The majority were not employed, and only 14 percent of the married women were in the labor force. More than two-thirds reported that religion was very important in their lives, though, unlike women in the anti-ERA movement, almost 80 percent of the pro-lifers belonged to the Catholic Church. They also reported lower family incomes than either ERA opponents or women in the pro-choice movement.[19]

Claiming that human life began at conception, opponents of abortion insisted that the rights of the fetus were paramount. However, as Kristin Luker has argued, the meaning and role of motherhood in women's lives was central to women activated

17. Frederick S. Jaffe, Barbara L. Lindheim, and Philip R. Lee, *Abortion Politics: Private Morality and Public Policy* (New York: McGraw-Hill, 1981), pp. 73–77.

18. Rosalind Pollack Petchesky, *Abortion and Woman's Choice: The State, Sexuality, and Reproductive Freedom* (Boston: Northeastern University Press, 1984), pp. 241–57.

19. Kristen Luker, *Abortion and the Politics of Motherhood* (Berkeley: University of California Press, 1984), pp. 194–97.

by the abortion issue. Like those in the anti-ERA campaigns, women in the anti-abortion movement believed that God and nature had ordained sharp distinctions between women and men in biological and psychological make-up and in social roles. Motherhood was paramount in women's lives, and no other interest or activity should take precedence. RTL women believed that abortion devalued motherhood and reduced male responsibility to protect and support women. Since most anti-abortion activists were themselves dependent on men for economic support and had focused their energies on motherhood, abortion threatened the meaning and value of their own lives. In this way, anti-abortion activities not only coincided with these women's religious beliefs, but, as for ERA opponents, their political activism represented a defense of their own life patterns.[20]

Tactics employed by the RTL movement ran the gamut from the conventional to the extreme. Writing letters and making phone calls to public officials, using "telephone trees" to mobilize women for specific efforts, and voting for "pro-life" candidates were activities that home-bound women could accommodate to their domestic responsibilities. For many women, however, RTL activism took them outside the home. Every January thousands of women traveled to Washington for the March for Life, organized by lawyer and former WAC corporal Nellie Gray, to protest the 1973 Supreme Court decision. Others regularly picketed abortion clinics throughout the country and some even tried to intercept women entering clinics for abortions. By the 1980s direct action had escalated into arson, bombings, and other forms of violence against clinics in a number of communities. While abortion clinic actions tended to be directed by men, who also constituted a large portion of the protesters, women also participated and spent time in jail for what they claimed were acts of civil disobedience.[21]

Although clinic actions may have deterred few women from obtaining abortions, the RTL movement enjoyed considerable success in the traditional realms of politics. Joining forces with

20. *Ibid.*, pp. 145, 159–62, 193, 200, 217.

21. *Ibid.*, pp. 219–22; Jaffe, et al., *Abortion Politics*, pp. 77, 137; Bill Smith, "The Abortion Wars," *St. Louis Post-Dispatch*, July 13 and 14, 1986.

elements of the New Right, opponents of abortion won a plank in the 1976 Republican Party platform calling for a constitutional amendment to "restore the protection of the right to life for unborn children." In 1978, RTL political action committees helped defeat two pro-choice legislators, Iowa Senator Dick Clark and Minnesota Representative Donald Fraser. Two years later, the National Conservative Political Action Committee and the Life Amendment Political Action Committee targeted twelve members of Congress for defeat and claimed victories when liberal Democrats Birch Bayh (Indiana), George McGovern (South Dakota), and Frank Church (Idaho) lost their Senate seats to RTL-supported challengers.[22]

Increasingly successful in injecting the abortion issue into campaign politics, the RTL movement also forced Congress and state legislatures to pay it an inordinate amount of attention. In fact, in 1977 the abortion issue paralyzed Congress for several months, moving one Representative to call abortion "an albatross on all legislation." The question before Congress in 1977 involved efforts by the anti-abortion movement to restrict the use of federal funds for abortion services. For five months the appropriations bill for the departments of Labor and Health, Education and Welfare was stalled as legislators fought over proposed anti-abortion riders. The final compromise—called the Hyde amendment—prohibited the use of federal Medicaid funds for abortions except in cases of rape and incest when reported immediately, or in cases where the life of the pregnant woman was endangered. Protracted argument in subsequent years resulted in even tighter restrictions on federal funding of abortions for poor women as well as bans on government-funded abortions for military personnel, Peace Corps volunteers, and other federal employees.[23]

Equally vigorous efforts to restrict abortion were carried on at the state and local levels. Among various ordinances and laws

22. Joyce Gelb and Marian Lief Palley, *Women and Public Policies* (Princeton, NJ: Princeton University Press, 1982), p. 138–39; Jaffe, et al., *Abortion Politics*, pp. 120–22.

23. Jaffe, et al., *Abortion Politics*, pp. 128–34; Gelb and Palley, *Women and Public Policies*, pp. 130–37; Susan J. Tolchin, "The Impact of the Hyde Amendment on Congress: Effects of Single Issue Politics on Legislative Dysfunction, June 1977–June 1978," *Women and Politics* 5 (Spring 1985):91–106.

Anti–feminist demonstration at the National Women's Conference, Houston, November 1977. (Bettye Lane)

won by the RTL movement were those prohibiting municipally funded hospitals from providing abortions; revising zoning restrictions to bar abortion clinics; requiring husbands' consent or parental consent in the case of minors; mandating a twenty-four-hour waiting period; requiring doctors to inform pregnant women that the fetus was a human life; restricting abortions to licensed hospitals; and prohibiting commonly used techniques for abortions. Although the federal courts struck down most of these regulations, they upheld the right of public hospitals to refuse to provide abortion services except where the woman's life or health was endangered; allowed federal and state governments to exclude abortions from government-funded medical services; and retained laws requiring minors to have parental consent or a court authorization before obtaining an abortion.[24]

24. Jaffe, et al., *Abortion Politics*, pp. 135–37; Petchesky, *Abortion and Woman's Choice*, pp. 293–316.

A GROWING CHALLENGE TO THE FEMINIST AGENDA

The Equal Rights Amendment and abortion were the most volatile issues over which women clashed in the political arena, but they were not the only ones. In 1977, antifeminists showed their strength in state meetings to elect delegates to the National Women's Conference, which Phyllis Schlafly derided as "Federal Financing of a Foolish Festival for Frustrated Feminists." Sponsored by antiabortion groups, fundamentalist churches, STOP-ERA, the Eagle Forum, and the John Birch Society, busloads of women opposed to change attended delegate-selection conferences. They gained control in eleven states and won around 20 percent of the seats at the Houston meeting, while hundreds of "pro-family" representatives staged a counter-convention nearby. The Right's forces at the National Women's Conference were insufficient to block any of the resolutions proposed by feminists, but they demonstrated again their power to mobilize women at the state level, even controlling delegations from some states that had ratified the ERA.[25]

Conservative women and their New Right allies also achieved some success in thwarting activities of state commissions on the status of women. Between 1977 and 1980, nine states abolished their commissions, and in others conservatives gained a majority of the seats. In Massachusetts, for example, conservative Democratic Governor Edward King dismissed commission members and appointed a new body that included leaders of anti-ERA and anti-abortion organizations. Reflecting its conservative domination, New Hampshire's Commission on the Status of Women opposed the ERA, abortion rights, and shelters for battered women; its major positive accomplishment in 1977 was sponsorship of a law making the ladybug the state insect.[26]

Acknowledging the existence of wife battering, conserva-

25. Lindsay Van Gelder, "Countdown to Houston," *Ms.* 6 (November, 1977): 60–62, 107–8.

26. *Women's Agenda* 2 (November 1977):13; Rina Rosenberg, "Representing Women at the State and Local Levels: Commissions on the Status of Women," in Ellen Boneparth, ed., *Women, Power and Policy* (New York: Pergamon, 1982), pp. 42–43.

tives nonetheless opposed government-supported shelters, which they felt were "indoctrination centers" run by feminists. "The federal government should not fund missionaries who would war on the traditional family or on local values," argued conservative Republican Senator Gordon Humphrey. The New Right believed that publicly funded shelters represented "an unwarranted federal intrusion into family matters," and preferred that churches and other private institutions deal with the problem by offering counseling. A fifty-state lobbying campaign conducted by the Reverend Jerry Falwell's "pro-family" Moral Majority inundated lawmakers and blocked passage of the Domestic Violence Bill in 1980. Referring to the Right's characterization of domestic violence programs as "antifamily," columnist Ellen Goodman remarked, "Apparently an intact family with a broken wife is better than a broken family with an intact ex-wife."[27]

Two of the issues that aroused conservative opposition to battered women's shelters—the use of federal funds and the feminist principles that informed victim services and advocacy—were also prominent in the Right's attack on centers for displaced homemakers. Phyllis Schlafly couched her position in the context of opposition to federal funding for any social programs. However, she also claimed that centers for displaced homemakers were "nothing but indoctrination and training centers for women's lib. The feminists who run such centers use them to push ERA, abortion, federal child care, lesbian privileges . . . at the taxpayers' expense."[28]

Right wingers also mobilized against homosexual rights, a cause which NOW and other feminist organizations had moved to their agendas by the mid-1970s. Women in leadership positions in the gay and lesbian rights movement had counterparts in the groups opposed to laws protecting homo-

27. Elizabeth Pleck, *Domestic Tyranny: The Making of American Social Policy against Family Violence from Colonial Times to the Present* (New York: Oxford University Press, 1987), pp. 196–98; June H. Zeitlin, "Domestic Violence: Perspectives from Washington," in Irene Tinker, ed., *Women in Washington: Advocates for Public Policy* (Beverly Hills, CA: Sage Publications, 1983), pp. 265–73; Ellen Goodman, "Broken Wives Battered Bill," *Spokeswoman* 10 (November 1980):16.

28. Laurie Shields, *Displaced Homemakers: Organizing for a New Life* (New York: McGraw-Hill, 1981), p. 130.

sexuals from discrimination. When more than thirty localities passed ordinances banning discrimination against homosexuals in employment, housing, and public accommodations, the New Right sought their overturn by popular referenda. Anita Bryant, gospel singer and publicist for the Florida Citrus Commission, was the most visible woman in the countermovement, but women such as Michelle Barton and Lynn Green of VOICE of the People, an anti-gay group in Eugene, Oregon, served as leaders and spokeswomen in several localities. In 1977, Bryant's Protect America's Children organization led a successful campaign to repeal a gay-rights measure in Dade County, Florida, claiming "the will of the American people is to return this country to pro-family, Bible morality." Bryant's victory was followed by similar successes in St. Paul, Wichita, and Eugene.[29]

Conservatives' abhorrence of homosexuality was of a piece with their opposition to the ERA and abortion. Each, they felt, was a violation of divine law and threatened to obliterate familiar sex roles and to devalue women's primary role as mothers. Yet by becoming politically involved in defense of traditional sex roles, conservative women were themselves crossing over the customary dividing line between activities they considered appropriate to men and women. Therefore, conservative women's increasing politicization appeared to contradict their vigorous defense of woman's traditional place. Yet, as Virginia Sapiro and Barbara G. Farah have pointed out, the political activism of right-wing women was compatible with their firmly held beliefs: "The elements of politics which are thought to be unfeminine are competition and *visible* dominance." When political activities were "non-competitive, service oriented, and not in conflict with home and child," Sapiro and Farah argued, conservative women could at once defend tradition and increase their own presence in the formerly male stronghold of politics.[30]

29. "Voting Against Gay Rights," *Time*, May 22, 1978, pp. 21–22; "Anita and the Gays," *Newsweek*, March 13, 1978, pp. 14–16.

30. Virginia Sapiro and Barbara G. Farah, "New Pride and Old Prejudice: Political Ambition and Role Orientations among Female Partisan Elites," *Women and Politics* 1 (Spring 1980):17–18.

FEMINISTS AND THE CARTER ADMINISTRATION

If feminists were dismayed to face resistance to their goals among women themselves, they were also frustrated by the Carter administration's lack of vigorous support for some of their objectives and outright opposition to others. Leaders of the women's movement compromised on some of their objectives, but they came away from the 1976 Democratic National Convention satisfied with the concessions they had won from Carter, and many worked hard for his election. Once in office, Carter appointed more women to high-level administrative posts and to the federal judiciary than had his predecessors. Still, the NWPC's Coalition for Women's Appointments and other feminist groups maintained throughout his term that he had not done enough to increase women's representation in the highest ranks of the executive branch.[31]

The same was true for ERA ratification. Carter surpassed the efforts of his predecessors, but he failed to meet the expectations of feminists. He supported extension of the ratification deadline, made telephone calls to key legislators in unratified states, and even urged ratification in person before the Illinois General Assembly. This was not enough for feminists, who felt that Carter relied too much on ERA efforts by his wife and daughter-in-law instead of doing more himself. They were angry at his refusal to visit other crucial states and his unwillingness to have the federal government join the boycott of unratified states, and they could not understand why he was unable to get his own state of Georgia to ratify. Furthermore, feminists believed that Carter should have used the promise or threat of removal of federal grants to pressure recalcitrant states.[32]

Even more dismaying to the women's movement was Carter's position on abortion. Personally opposed to abortion except in cases of rape, incest, or when a woman's life was endangered, he approved a platform plank that called a consti-

---

31. Susan J. Carroll, "Women Appointed to the Carter Administration: More or Less Qualified?" *Polity* 18 (Summer 1986):696–97.

32. Bella Abzug with Mim Kelber, *Gender Gap: Bella Abzug's Guide to Political Power for American Women* (Boston: Houghton Mifflin, 1984), pp. 63, 77–79.

tutional amendment to overturn *Roe v Wade* "undesirable."
But he supported the Hyde Amendment, countering arguments that denial of Medicaid funds for abortions was unfair to
poor women with the statement, "There are many things in life
that are not fair, that wealthy people can afford and that poor
people can't." Moreover, he promised strict enforcement of the
Hyde Amendment and his Secretary of Health, Education and
Welfare, Joseph Califano, issued regulations making it extremely difficult for women to qualify for the exceptions that
permitted use of Medicaid funds for abortions.[33]

Jimmy Carter's sharpest clash with leaders of the women's
movement came in 1979 when he removed Bella Abzug from
her post as co-chair of the National Advisory Committee for
Women (NACW). Appointed to that position after she lost her
bid for the United States Senate, Abzug and other members of
the advisory committee viewed with alarm the administration's
economic and defense policies, particularly its plan to curb
inflation and rising unemployment by cutting $15 million from
the domestic budget while increasing military spending. In January, the NACW drafted a paper demonstrating the disproportionate impact the cuts would have on women and issued a
statement to that effect to the press. Immediately following a
meeting with the president to discuss the statement, Abzug was
informed that he had decided to replace her. In protest over
Abzug's firing a substantial number of committee members
handed in their resignations. Although Carter reconstituted the
committee, the breach with a major segment of the women's
movement was irrevocable.[34]

The firing of Bella Abzug, called by Gloria Steinem "the
Friday night massacre," reflected the political maturation of the
women's movement, its expanded definition of "women's issues," and the growing opposition to its goals. By the mid-1970s
the women's movement had achieved considerable success in
obtaining laws and policies to promote equal opportunity for
women in the public sphere. Regardless of their personal predi-
lections, it was difficult for political officials publicly to oppose

33. *Ibid.*, pp. 46–47, 64–65; Gelb and Palley, *Women and Public Policy*, pp.
133–34.
34. Abzug, *Gender Gap*, pp. 65–75.

feminists when they made claims to individual rights. But it was another matter when feminists moved from equal opportunity to women's deprivations that were deeply embedded in the current distribution of national resources and the customary division of power and roles within the family.

In stressing how economically disadvantaged women would suffer from the Hyde amendment and Carter's budget cuts, the NACW reflected—as had the National Plan of Action approved at the Houston conference—the increasing inclusivity of the women's movement and its determination to address the needs of all women. However, as the feminist agenda broadened to include issues that affected personal and family matters and that involved decisions about national economic priorities, feminists confronted opposition not just from the right wing, but from mainstream politicians. With a Republican party on its way to being captivated by the Right, and a Democratic leadership unresponsive to its expanding agenda, the women's movement faced its greatest challenge since its rebirth.

Chapter 7

The 1980s: Challenges and Changes

In the aftermath of the 1980 elections, political commentators debated the meaning of voter choices. Some argued that a new Republican electoral majority had emerged, while others pointed to a "dealignment"—the defection of large numbers of voters from party loyalty altogether—and to the presence of a high degree of volatility in electoral behavior.[1] Whether or not 1980 marked a general watershed in politics, the election both signaled and promoted shifts in the relationship between women and politics. For the first time, the major parties differed sharply over women's issues, and that polarization took concrete form in the generally antifeminist policies and practices of the Reagan administration. Thrown on the defensive, women's advocates sought to maintain the gains of the 1970s, focusing on electoral politics and on public-policy objectives deemed more conducive to success in a conservative climate.

The general voting patterns of women converged with those of men in many respects, but their electoral choices and opinions on issues reflected important differences and spawned widespread discussion of a "gender gap." As the women's movement concentrated more attention on electoral politics, it developed sophisticated new strategies for fund raising that met with considerable success. Women experienced small gains in numbers of elected and appointed officials primarily at

1. Everett Carll Ladd, "The Brittle Mandate: Electoral Dealignment and the 1980 Presidential Election," *Political Science Quarterly* 96 (Spring 1981):1–25.

the local and state levels. National political leadership continued to elude women's grasp, but the nomination of Geraldine Ferraro for the vice presidency on the Democratic ticket in 1984 signified the clout of women activists and felled one more barrier to female representation at the highest levels of government.

THE 1980 ELECTIONS AND THE GENDER GAP

While feminists had always more strongly identified with the Democratic party, the 1980 election was the first time that the major parties differed markedly on women's issues. At the Republican convention, the ascendancy of conservative forces produced the nomination of Ronald Reagan and a platform opposing the two major goals of the women's movement. Right-to-life forces won a plank calling for a constitutional amendment to ban abortion and for the appointment of judges who "respect . . . the sanctity of innocent human life." A second plank committed the party to equality for women, but Republicans abandoned their longstanding commitment to the Equal Rights Amendment, recognizing both support for and opposition to the ERA as "legitimate." Far outnumbered at the convention by their conservative sisters, women in the moderate and liberal wings of the Republican party, dressed in the traditional white of the suffragists, marched outside the convention hall to show their displeasure with their party's new stance on women's issues.[2]

Democratic women, on the other hand, exerted unprecedented influence at their party's convention. For the first time, women constituted 50 percent of the delegates, as mandated by rules adopted in 1976. More than 200 of these delegates were NOW members, and another several hundred were members

2. Theodore H. White, *America in Search of Itself: The Making of the President, 1956–1980* (New York: Harper and Row, 1982), pp. 317–19, 351; Zillah R. Eisenstein, *Feminism and Sexual Equality: Crisis in Liberal America* (New York: Monthly Review Press, 1984), p. 27; Bella Abzug with Mim Kelber, *Gender Gap: Bella Abzug's Guide to Political Power for American Women* (Boston: Houghton Mifflin, 1984), pp 81–82.

of the National Women's Political Caucus and the National Abortion Rights Action League. Platform decisions reflected this feminist strength. When Carter forces on the platform committee defeated two feminist planks, the women took their fight to the floor. By voice vote, they won a provision that denied party financial support and technical campaign assistance to candidates opposed to the ERA; and by a two-thirds majority, they obtained party endorsement of Medicaid financing of abortions.[3]

Despite the party polarization over women's issues, the 1980 election was not contested on that basis. Although they had won a favorable platform from the Democrats, feminists remained cool towards Jimmy Carter, and NOW refused to endorse him. Neither Carter nor Reagan attempted to mobilize voters on the basis of women's issues, focusing instead on the economy, foreign policy, and defense. Reagan's antifeminist positions were important to the New Right, but most of his support came from voters who held Carter responsible for rampant inflation and rising unemployment and for the national humiliation experienced when Iran seized the American embassy in November 1979 and held American hostages through the 1980 election campaign.[4]

If the 1980 election did not represent a referendum on women's issues, it did disclose significant voting differences between men and women, who for the first time in peacetime turned out at the same rate as men. Exit polls taken in 1976 had shown men and women voting identically, 50 to 48 percent for Carter against Ford. But in 1980, while both men and women voted for third-party candidate John Anderson at the rate of 7 percent, men favored Reagan over Carter 54 to 37 percent, while women gave Reagan only the slim margin, 46 percent, to 45 percent for Carter.[5]

Bella Abzug and other feminists immediately seized on the eight-point difference between male and female voters. This

3. White, *America in Search of Itself,* p. 339; Abzug, *Gender Gap,* pp. 83–84.

4. Mary Fainsod Katzenstein, "Feminism and the Meaning of the Vote," *Signs: Journal of Women in Culture and Society* 10 (Autumn 1984):21; Ethel Klein, *Gender Politics: From Consciousness to Mass Politics* (Cambridge, MA: Harvard University Press, 1984), pp. 158–60.

5. *New York Times,* November 9, 1980, p. 18.

"gender gap," they argued, demonstrated that women acted on distinct interests and were developing leverage at the polls, forcing politicians to take their concerns seriously. Abzug noted that Reagan was not the first choice of the majority of women voters, and that even among Republicans, 13 percent of the women favored either Carter or Anderson.[6]

The gender gap, however, turned less on concern for women's legal and reproductive rights than on issues of peace, the environment, the economy, and the government's responsibility for social welfare. For example, 38 percent of men but only 28 percent of women favored reducing government spending on social services, while 73 percent of men but only 61 percent of women favored increasing military spending. Thus in some ways the gender gap of 1980 harked back to differences between male and female voters which had been recognized by pollsters in the 1950s. Moreover, the gender gap did not mean that women were becoming more liberal or Democratic, for women had cast 50 percent of their votes for the Democratic ticket in 1976, but only 45 percent in 1980. Rather, it signified that men had moved towards the Republican party and conservative values in considerably larger numbers than women.[7]

Political differences between men and women persisted as the Reagan administration presented them with concrete actions on which to base their preferences. Sharp cuts in domestic expenditures disproportionately disadvantaged women, who constituted the majority of both clients and employees in welfare and social service programs. Women tended to be more critical of the Reagan administration during the 1982 recession, which added millions of people to the unemployment rolls and the poverty population. Women were less likely to favor the sharp increases in defense spending, and when the Administration invaded Grenada during a revolution there in 1983, only 45 percent of women approved, in contrast to 69 percent of men. Considerable volatility characterized these polls, and

6. Abzug, *Gender Gap*, pp. 89–95; Christine R. Riddiough, "Women, Feminism, and the 1980 Elections," *Socialist Review* 56 (March–April 1981):41.

7. Klein, *Gender Politics*, pp. 158–59; Kathleen A. Frankovic, "Sex and Politics—New Alignments, Old Issues," *P.S.* 15 (Summer 1982):441–44; Daniel Wirls, "Reinterpreting the Gender Gap," *Public Opinion Quarterly* 50 (Fall 1986): 317–29.

opinion tended to shift from year to year, but every poll taken during the 1980s indicated significant differences between men and women. The most consistent features of voter attitudes were women's greater loyalty to the Democratic party and their stronger support for peace and for protection of the environment.[8]

Although the gender gap in voting narrowed slightly, exit polls taken during the 1982 elections revealed that women favored Democratic candidates over Republicans 53 to 47 percent, while for men the opposite was true. Moreover, women's votes made the difference in several key races, including the gubernatorial victories of Mario Cuomo in New York and James Blanchard in Michigan, whose running mate for Lieutenant Governor was former congresswoman Martha Griffiths. In Texas, Democrat Mark White defeated the incumbent governor by 7.6 percentage points, and exit polls showed women's support for White at 8 points higher than that of men. White's running mate, Ann W. Richards, won the race for state treasurer, outpolling all the other Democrats in statewide races.[9]

The gender gap narrowed to around four percentage points in the Reagan landslide of 1984, but continued to make a critical difference to Democrats in several congressional races. Women's votes were decisive in the election of Madeline Kunin as governor of Vermont, and in the Senate victories of Paul Simon in Illinois and John Kerry in Massachusetts. Moreover, in 1986 women provided the margin of victory in nine senatorial races, favoring the Democratic candidates by between five and nine percentage points. By tipping the balance in these states, women's ballots altered national politics and gave the Democrats control of the Senate (55–45) for the first time since the election of 1980.[10]

8. Frances Fox Piven, "Women and the State: Ideology, Power, and the Welfare State," *Socialist Review* 74 (March–April 1984):13–19; *New York Times*, June 30, 1982, November 27, 1983; Abzug, *Gender Gap*, pp. 116–26; Wirls, "Reinterpreting the Gender Gap," pp. 324. 327–28; Frankovic, "Sex and Politics," p. 444.

9. Abzug, *Gender Gap*, pp. 97–101; Sara Sanborn, "Ann Richard's Success Story," *Ms.* 12 (June 1984):88, 92.

10. *New York Times*, November 8, 1984, December 15, 1985, November 7, 1986; Judy Mann, "Assessing the Women's Vote," *Graduate Woman* 79 (January 1985):7.

THE WOMEN'S MOVEMENT IN THE REAGAN ERA

The women's movement retained and even increased its organizational diversity in the 1980s. The press tended to present NOW as the exemplar of the women's movement. Nonetheless, as was true in the 1970s, most of the public-policy initiatives for women were pushed by a broad range of groups, including new feminist groups and older women's organizations. Although less frequently in the limelight, traditional women's groups such as the BPW, LWV, and AAUW, newer organizations such as the Older Women's League and the National Women's Health Network, and leadership bodies such as the Center for Women Policy Studies and the National Coalition for Women and Girls in Education frequently played more important roles than NOW in defining issues and influencing policy.[11]

That breadth and diversity was all the more valuable to a women's movement facing the most hostile climate since its rebirth. In that conservative atmosphere, feminists adjusted their strategies and goals. They did not abandon the two most prominent issues of the women's movement, an Equal Rights Amendment and the right to abortion. And they waged determined fights in defense of antidiscrimination measures and affirmative action, which were also in jeopardy during the Reagan administration. Nonetheless, in the 1980s the national women's lobby shifted its emphasis from equity issues to women's economic and family problems that had not been touched by antidiscrimination measures.

Of major concern to feminists was the fact that, despite all the antidiscrimination legislation of the 1960s and 1970s, women's income still lagged far below that of men. In 1980, women employed in full-time jobs earned only about 60 percent of what men earned. This pay gap reflected the fact that while some women had made inroads into traditionally male fields, the vast majority of women continued to work in pre-

11. Marion Lief Palley, "The Women's Movement in Recent American Politics," in Sara E. Rix, ed., *The American Woman 1987–88: A Report in Depth* (New York: Norton, 1987), pp. 164–73; Marjorie Williams, "Ten Years After the Women's Conference," *Washington Post National Weekly Edition,* December 7, 1987, pp. 8–9.

dominantly female occupations that had always been under-valued and underpaid. Feminists argued that many of these jobs required similar or greater amounts of skill, effort, and responsibility than male occupations, but that they were under-valued because women filled them. On the average, a licensed practical nurse, for example, earned less than a truck driver, and a child-care worker less than an unskilled construction worker. The women's movement called for compensation based on the worth of the work, not the sex of the worker. Equal pay for work of comparable worth—pay equity—became a major focus of feminist efforts in the 1980s.[12]

Other economic problems of women were attacked in a comprehensive measure, the Economic Equity bill, supported by a broad range of women's organizations, including NOW and WEAL as well as the AAUW, the BPW, and the LWV. Intro-duced in every Congress throughout the 1980s, the bill dealt with pensions and retirement, displaced homemakers, nondis-crimination in insurance, child-support enforcement, and care of children and other dependents. Many of its provisions were aimed at homemakers and women on the lower rungs of the economic ladder. The new agenda reflected the increased range of issues included in the women's movement, and the efforts of women of color, poor, and working-class women who had struggled within the movement to bring these issues to the fore.[13]

The emphasis on women's economic problems was in part a recognition of the "feminization of poverty" that began to claim national attention in the 1980s. (Many feminists disliked the term and preferred "the pauperization of women," to sig-nify that women and their children constituted the vast major-ity of the poverty population, and that the disproportionate representation of women among the poor was increasing.) De-signed to combat poverty among women, by emphasizing issues like child-support and care of children and other depen-

12. Nancy Barrett, "Women and the Economy," in Rix, *The American Woman 1987–88*, pp. 124–34.

13. Nadine Cohodas, "Women Shift Focus on Hill to Economic Equity Issues," *Congressional Quarterly Weekly Report* 41 (1983):781–83, 786; Geraldine A. Ferraro, with Linda Bird Franke, *Ferraro: My Story* (New York: Bantam Books, 1985), pp. 44–45.

dents, the new feminist agenda also challenged the New Right's claim to be the sole voice for the homemaker and the family. The shift in priorities also reflected the strains experienced by a growing number of women of every race and class struggling to combine employment outside the home with their age-old responsibilities in the family.

In expanding its agenda, the women's movement entered into more complicated territory. Coalitions had been easy to form around relatively simple anti-discrimination measures, but feminists did not agree on measures to resolve the conflicts between women's family roles and their employment outside the home. Some feminists argued that equal treatment under the law sometimes worked against women and that for women to have equality in substance, they would have to be treated differently. For example, they argued, special measures such as maternity leave and job protection during pregnancy were necessary if women were to have the same opportunities for both parenthood and employment outside the home as men did. The Pregnancy Disability Act of 1978 prevented an employer from discriminating against pregnant women, but it did not require employers to offer pregnant women any benefits not offered to all employees.

Some states, however, went further than federal law and enacted measures requiring employers to provide job protection and disability leave for childbirth even though they did not offer similar provisions for other conditions requiring an employee's temporary absence from work. When California's law was tested in the courts, feminists were found on both sides of the debate. The ACLU, the LWV, NOW, and other feminist groups opposed preferential treatment for pregnancy. They argued that protective labor legislation had limited women's employment opportunities in the past, that the need to provide special benefits for women would discourage the hiring of women, and that the women's movement would lose credibility by asking for equality and special treatment at the same time. Defenders, who included local chapters of NOW and the ACLU, replied that special treatment was necessary if women were in fact to achieve the same opportunities as men for jobs and families.[14]

14. *New York Times,* July 22, 1985, January 14, 1987.

Early in 1987, the Supreme Court ruled in favor of the California law. Preferential treatment of pregnancy, it said "promotes equal employment opportunity" by allowing "women, as well as men, to have families without losing their jobs." After the decision, feminists who had been on both sides of the issue called for a redoubling of efforts to enact a national *parental* leave law. The Family and Medical Leave bill, spearheaded by Colorado Democrat Patricia Schroeder and supported by nearly every women's organization, would require employers to allow *any* employee to take unpaid medical leave for him- or herself or to take unpaid leave to care for a new born or newly adopted child or for a seriously ill dependent. The proposed law united the women's movement because it was gender-neutral while at the same time enabling women to become mothers without risking their jobs. Because the bill would provide leave for fathers as well as mothers, supporters hoped that it would encourage men to take a greater part in childrearing. Finally, the proposed measure spoke to an additional stress for employed women—their growing responsibility for the care of elderly parents.[15]

To advance legislation on economic and family issues, feminists could turn to a new vehicle within Congress. The Congresswomen's Caucus had been crippled by the refusal of several Republican women to join after Reagan's election and by the reluctance of those who did join to challenge the president. Therefore, in 1981 the caucus reorganized, changing its name to the Congressional Caucus for Women's Issues and opening its doors to men. Only women served on the executive committee, but more than one hundred men joined, making it one of the largest caucuses on the Hill. This reorganization reflected the growing propensity of the women's movement for coalition building, as well as its efforts to promote the idea that women's issues should be of concern to men as well as women.[16]

Along with a new public policy agenda, two other features characterized the women's movement in the 1980s. It became more heavily involved in efforts to elect feminists to office, and it put more emphasis on organizing at the state level. To be

---

15. *New York Times*, January 14, 1987, February 3, 1987.

16. Ferraro, *Ferraro: My Story*, pp. 46–47; Cohodas, "Women Shift Focus on Hill," p. 786.

Co–chairs of the Congressional Caucus for Women's Issues, *(left)* Olympia Snowe (Republican-Maine) and Patricia Schroeder (Democrat-Colorado), May 1984. (Wide World Photos)

sure, feminists had been involved in electoral and state politics since the early 1970s. But defeat of ERA ratification highlighted the importance of organizing at the state level and of electing legislators who would support feminist goals. Similarly, the conservative climate in the nation's capital prompted feminists to look more to state legislatures for policy advances.

PUBLIC POLICIES IN THE REAGAN ADMINISTRATION

The gender gap worried Republican leaders, and during his first term Reagan's political advisers initiated efforts to increase his appeal to women voters. Yet in terms of the women's policy agenda, these initiatives were little more than cosmetic. Reagan appointed the first woman, Sandra Day O'Connor, to the Supreme Court, and selected Jeane Kirkpatrick as United Nations Ambassador. In 1983, he named two female cabinet members, Margaret Heckler as Secretary of Health and Human Services, and Elizabeth Dole as Secretary of Transportation. And, late in his second term Reagan appointed Ann Dore McLaughlin as Secretary of Labor. But these highly visible appointments neither compensated for the general decline of numbers of women in high-level government posts nor quelled criticism from women. Even the "showcasing" of women declined after the 1984 elections, as Kirkpatrick and Heckler were replaced with men, and the White House staff became even more a male preserve. Of serious long-range consequence was the decline of female appointments to the federal judiciary.[17]

Opportunities for women outside government were also limited by the Reagan administration, whose officials sought to eliminate initiatives on behalf of equity and affirmative action. Protests from civil-rights and feminist groups blocked the complete dismantling of affirmative action, but federal government officials relaxed compliance requirements for employers. As we will see, the Justice Department in the Grove City case obtained a Supreme Court decision severely crippling enforcement of Title IX, the measure that promoted educational equity. To implement his opposition to affirmative action, Reagan was even willing to alienate prominent Republican women. For example, in an effort to bring the historically independent U.S. Commission on Civil Rights into line with administration views, in 1983 the president removed women's rights advocates Jill Ruckelshaus and Mary Louise Smith from the commission.[18]

The Reagan administration failed, however, to achieve the major goal of the right-to-life movement, congressional passage of a human life amendment. The coalition in defense of reproductive freedom grew as both the League of Women Voters and the National Federation of Business and Professional Women's Clubs abandoned their former neutrality and directly endorsed women's right to abortion. Even more heartening to feminists was the Supreme Court's reaffirmation of *Roe v Wade*

17. Abzug, *Gender Gap*, pp. 133–36; *Washington Post*, March 3, 1985; *Wall Street Journal*, September 10, 1985; Lois Romano, "Women in the White House," *Washington Post National Weekly Edition*, February 24, 1986, pp. 6–8; *New York Times*, November 4, 1987; Lynn R. Holmes, "Law," in Mary Drake McFeely, ed., *The Women's Annual, Number 5: 1984–1985* (Boston: G. K. Hall, 1985), p. 65.

18. Cynthia E. Harrison, "Politics and Law," in Sarah M. Pritchard, ed., *The Women's Annual, Number 4: 1983–1984* (Boston: G. K. Hall, 1984), pp. 148–53.

in June 1983. Rejecting arguments of Reagan's solicitor general, the Court in a 6–3 decision not only struck down a series of local restrictions on abortion, but seized the opportunity to reiterate its commitment to women's right to decide whether to terminate a pregnancy. The only bright spot in the decision for the administration was Sandra Day O'Connor's dissent, which the president publicly praised.[19]

On a few issues, which upheld women's customary roles, the women's movement and the Reagan administration found themselves in agreement. Thus, some provisions of the Economic Equity bill became law. In 1984 Congress enacted the Child Support Enforcement Amendments, designed to assist parents in obtaining court-ordered child-support payments. Because most of the parents entitled to child support were women, the law promised some relief for single and divorced mothers supporting children alone. It applied to families at all income levels, provided means to locate absent fathers, and required the interception of tax refunds and the garnishment of wages to collect past due child support.[20]

A second measure of the bill, the Retirement Equity Act of 1984, addressed the problems of older women. Taking into account women's more frequent movement in and out of the labor force due to childbearing and family responsibilities, the law enabled women to qualify more easily for private pension plans. It also strengthened the claims of divorced or widowed women on their husbands' pensions. As Mary Berry has pointed out, these laws did not challenge women's customary roles of wife and mother. On the contrary, they "encouraged women to play traditional maternal and housewife roles while making provisions for the sometimes traumatic economic consequences that ensued."[21]

Other items on the feminist agenda got nowhere. Opposed by a million-dollar lobby managed by the insurance industry, a

19. *New York Times,* June 19, 1983, p. E7; *St. Louis Post-Dispatch,* August 23, 1985.

20. Lenore J. Weitzman, *The Divorce Revolution: The Unexpected Social and Economic Consequences for Women and Children in America* (New York: Free Press, 1985), pp. 262–64, 307–9.

21. Mary Frances Berry, *Why ERA Failed: Politics, Women's Rights, and the Amending Process of the Constitution* (Bloomington: Indiana University Press, 1986), pp. 109–10.

bill to abolish gender-based actuarial ratings failed to receive committee support. Congress refused also to increase tax deductions for child care expenses and to provide tax credits to businesses employing displaced homemakers. And proposals to promote pay equity, i.e., to mandate equal pay rates for women and men in jobs of comparable worth, met a similar fate. Arguing that market conditions rather than government should regulate wage rates, Reagan's chair of the U.S. Civil Rights Commission Clarence Pendleton dismissed pay equity as "the looniest idea since Looney Tunes came on the screen."[22]

Resisting much of the women's movement's public-policy agenda, the Reagan administration also moved to turn back advances already won. Along with federal budget cuts in welfare, child-care subsidies, and other social services, the most serious challenges came in the area of educational equity. Congress resisted the administration's efforts to eliminate funding for the Women's Educational Equity Act Program (WEEA), but the administration found another way to cripple the program. Reagan simply appointed conservative opponents of WEEA to oversee its activities.[23]

The Administration also sought to limit coverage of Title IX of the Education Amendments of 1972, the measure that promoted sex equity in education by providing that institutions that discriminated against women could not receive federal funds. The White House wanted the measure to apply only to those programs within the institution that actually received the federal funds. Thus, for example, if a university did not receive federal funding for athletic programs—and most did not—it could practice sex discrimination in athletics but continue to receive federal monies for other purposes. The administration failed to get Congress to agree, but it succeeded in the courts. Concurring with a brief filed by the Justice Department, the Supreme Court in *Grove City College v Bell* (1984), ruled that a college could receive federal support for activities in which it did not practice discrimination, even though it discriminated in other areas.[24]

The effects of the *Grove City* decision reached beyond sex

22. *Ibid.*, pp. 108–9, 110–12.
23. Holmes, "Law," pp. 63–64.
24. *Ibid.*

discrimination, narrowing antidiscrimination protections for racial minorities, the disabled, and the elderly. Because of the decision, within three years the Department of Education had dropped or curtailed more than 600 complaints of discrimination. At the same time, however, feminist and civil-rights groups organized a broad coalition pushing for passage of the Civil Rights Restoration bill, which would not only overturn the effects of *Grove City* but also insure that institution-wide coverage of antidiscrimination measures applied to state and local governments, corporations, churches, synagogues and other private organizations that received federal funds. Conflicts over attempts to attach anti-abortion riders and opposition in the Republican-controlled Senate stalled the bill until 1988. An amendment making clear that the law did not require any institution receiving federal funds to perform or pay for abortions was adopted, and both houses passed the bill by large majorities. Support for the Civil Rights Restoration bill withstood a presidential veto as the House voted to override, 315–98, and the Senate, 75–14. Feminists decried the sacrifice of abortion rights necessary to secure passage, while taking satisfaction in the defeat of the Reagan administration's efforts to derail anti-discrimination policy.[25]

Apart from the *Grove City* case, the Supreme Court proved a valuable ally to the women's movement. In contrast to the 1970s when Congress had been their champion, feminists now won more of their victories in the Supreme Court. Still refusing to consider sex a "suspect" classification, as it did race, the Court nonetheless issued decisions promoting economic equity. In 1983, it ruled that employers could not pay women lower retirement benefits than men who had contributed the same amounts, although the Court did not require retroactive relief to victims of discrimination. In 1984, the justices found that Title VII of the Civil Rights Act of 1964, which prohibited discrimination in employment, applied to law firms' decisions to name partners; and in a series of cases the Court ruled that the United States Jaycees, Rotary International, and other businessmen's clubs could not bar women from membership. The Supreme Court also assisted women's efforts against sexual

25. *Washington Post,* March 7, 1988; *New York Times,* March 23, 1988.

harassment, ruling in 1986 that such harassment constituted an illegal form of sex discrimination.[26]

Most heartening to feminists was the Court's decision one year later in *Johnson v Transportation Agency, Santa Clara County*. Rebuffing Reagan administration lawyers, the Supreme Court issued a broad decision on affirmative action, rejecting the "reverse-discrimination" charge of a man who lost a promotion to a woman. Both were fully qualified for the position, but the man had scored slightly higher on an oral examination. The Court, in a 6–3 vote, for the first time upheld affirmative action for women, and also for the first time ruled that employers could practice affirmative action even when evidence of past discrimination within their organization was absent. Preference for qualified women and minorities was legal, the Court said, to correct "a conspicuous imbalance in traditionally segregated job categories." Feminists were jubilant as the Court seemed to close the door on the relentless efforts of the Reagan administration to destroy affirmative action. That many corporate spokesmen also lauded the decision and pronounced affirmative action good personnel practice testified to the extent to which feminist goals had penetrated major institutions.[27]

PUBLIC POLICIES AT STATE AND LOCAL LEVELS

Both feminists and their opponents sought to achieve on the state level what eluded them in Congress or the courts. The anti-abortion movement pursued restrictions on abortion through popular referenda in Arkansas, Massachusetts, Rhode Island, and Oregon in 1986. In every case reproductive rights forces were the victors. While these elections by no means laid to rest the abortion issue, they did indicate that anti-abortion groups had lost the initiative.[28]

Although pay equity got nowhere in Congress, its advocates

26. Berry, *Why ERA Failed*, pp. 112–14; *New York Times*, November 9, 1986.
27. *Washington Post*, March 27, 1987; *New York Times*, March 26, 1987.
28. *New York Times*, November 13, 1986.

made significant gains at the state and local levels. These efforts concentrated on employees in the public sector, and labor unions served as feminists' most important allies. The AFL-CIO and the Coalition of Labor Union Women strongly endorsed equal pay for work of comparable worth, and several unions, most prominently the American Federation of State, County, and Municipal Employees (AFSCME) and the Service Employees International Union (SEIU), promoted it vigorously through contract negotiations, litigation, and lobbying.

The campaign for pay equity was pioneered in the state of Washington, where AFCSME played the leading role. When state officials declined to act upon job-classification studies documenting underpayment in female occupations, AFSCME filed a federal suit in 1982. Backed by feminist groups and labor unions, women legislators then pushed through legislation providing a modest appropriation to begin reduction of the pay differentials. In 1983, AFSCME won a favorable decision in the federal district court but suffered a reversal in the appeals court. In exchange for agreeing not to appeal to the Supreme Court, AFSCME negotiated a settlement, with the state allocating an estimated $482 million in raises for workers identified in job studies as underpaid. Meanwhile, other states had jumped on the pay equity bandwagon. In 1982, New York reached an agreement with employee unions to work toward equal pay for jobs of comparable worth, and the Minnesota legislature appropriated $22 million to begin elimination of wage differentials. In 1984, Minnesota extended pay equity to cities, counties, and school districts. By 1987, twenty-seven states had begun to study pay scales, and fifteen states had begun to implement, pay adjustments.[29]

City governments, too, began to respond to demands for pay equity. The first to do so was San Jose, California, termed "the feminist capital of the nation" because of its female mayor from 1975 to 1982, Janet Gray Hayes, and female majorities on both

29. Helen Remick, "Major Issues in *a priori* Applications," in Helen Remick, ed., *Comparable Worth and Wage Discrimination: Technical Possibilities and Political Realities* (Philadelphia: Temple University Press, 1984), pp. 101–6; Elaine Johansen, *Comparable Worth: The Myth and the Movement* (Boulder, CO: Westview Press, 1984), pp. 80–84, 106–9; *New York Times,* September 8, 1985, January 27, 1986, February 10, 1986; Judy Mann, "Progress on Pay Equity," *Washington Post,* January 27, 1987, p. B3.

the San Jose City Council and the Santa Clara County Board of Supervisors. By 1984, more than a dozen cities in California, Colorado, Minnesota, Vermont, Virginia, and Washington had undertaken pay equity activities. The first popular referendum on the issue occurred in San Francisco in 1986, when voters approved a measure requiring annual comparable-worth studies and implementation.[30]

San Francisco also took the lead in addressing another major problem of employed women—child care. With a woman in the mayor's office and women constituting a majority of the city's board of supervisors, that body adopted an ordinance requiring developers of large commercial projects to provide free space for child care or pay for the construction of such space nearby. This would increase the availability of child care, make the costs to parents less expensive, and provide facilities near the parents' workplaces.[31]

Feminists were also successful at the state level in promoting measures to reduce violence against women. In the 1970s, rape law reform had focused on more effective prosecution and greater sensitivity to victims. Most state laws retained the marital exemption, which prevented wives from bringing rape charges against husbands. By the mid-1980s, however, twenty-three states had made it a crime for a man to force his wife to have sexual relations. In most states changes were enacted by the legislature, although in New York it was the state supreme court that ruled the marital exemption unconstitutional, finding "no rational basis for distinguishing between marital rape and non-marital rape." As rape continued to be the most rapidly increasing crime, states also benefited from the Victims of Crime Act of 1984, which provided federal revenues to every state for rape crisis centers.[32]

Although national domestic-violence legislation was a dead

30. Janet A. Flammang, "Female Officials in the Feminist Capital: The Case of Santa Clara County," *Western Political Quarterly* 38 (March 1985):94–95; Lisa Portman, Joy Ann Grune, and Eve Johnson, "The Role of Labor," in Remick, *Comparable Worth and Wage Discrimination*, p. 233; Johansen, *Comparable Worth*, p. 141; *New York Times*, November 9, 1986.

31. Ellen Goodman, "San Francisco Cares for Kids," *St. Louis Post-Dispatch*, December 6, 1985, p. 10H.

32. "Marital Rape Now a Crime in New York," *off our backs*, February, 1985, p. 3; *National Plan of Action UPDATE* (Washington, DC: National Women's Conference Committee, 1986), pp. 26–27.

issue in the 1980s, and federal support for shelters and other services for battered women shrunk with the Reagan budget cuts, the movement against wife abuse persisted in the states and localities. Municipal and county police forces increasingly established spousal abuse or domestic-violence units to promote investigation and prosecution of abusers. The Illinois legislature passed a comprehensive domestic-violence act in 1981—even while it voted down the ERA. By 1986, every state had domestic-violence legislation; seven states had laws mandating arrests in cases of probable assault, even if the victim was unwilling to sign a complaint; and more than 750 shelters existed, though large numbers of women still could not be accommodated. One of the stiffest domestic-violence measures was passed in Connecticut in 1986: it mandated arrests, required prompt court hearings, provided court-appointed lawyers for victims, established family-violence intervention units, and appropriated $2.7 million for training programs, social services, and shelters for battered women. The Connecticut law and other reforms indicated a major shift in official treatment of domestic violence from an emphasis on reconciliation between spouses to prosecution of the abuser.[33]

The most prominent failure of feminists at the state level was defeat of a state equal rights amendment in Vermont in 1986. That state appeared to provide an auspicious setting for a popular referendum. Vermont had a woman governor and a strong women's movement, and all the major candidates endorsed the amendment. A coalition of fifty organizations engaged in a heated battle which brought Phyllis Schlafly and her Eagle Forum to the state. In the end, voters defeated the amendment by a margin of around 3 percent.[34]

Schlafly called prospects for a federal ERA "absolutely dead" after the Vermont referendum, and some feminists believed that the women's movement should concentrate on economic issues and resign the ERA to the back burner until more

33. Joyce Gelb, "The Politics of Wife Abuse," in Irene Diamond and Mary Lyndon Shanley, eds., *Families, Politics, and Public Policy: A Feminist Dialogue on Women and the State* (New York: Longman, 1983), pp. 254–60; *New York Times*, June 15, 1986; *St. Louis Post-Dispatch*, July 7, 1986; *National Plan of Action UPDATE*, p. 5.

34. *New York Times*, November 6, 1986.

propitious times. Thus, while a new amendment was routinely introduced in Congress, it only reached the floor once, in 1983, when it failed to get a two-thirds majority in the House. Some activists, and especially the leadership of NOW, saw the ERA as a powerful mobilizing tool and insisted on the need to keep it in the public consciousness. However, the women's movement as a whole, while maintaining the ERA on its agenda, focused its energies elsewhere.

THE WOMEN'S MOVEMENT AND ELECTORAL POLITICS

Feminists believed that more significant public-policy gains depended upon electing more women to office, but progress was modest throughout the 1980s. Women inched their way into elective office at the state and local levels, constituting around 15 percent of these positions by the mid-1980s. Three new women governors took office in Kentucky, Nebraska, and Vermont, and women headed four of the one hundred largest cities in 1985. But the pace at which women entered Congress remained glacially slow. In 1986, women held twenty-five seats, the highest number ever and up from fifteen in the early 1970s, but just five more than their previous peak of twenty in 1960. Three women held Senate seats in the 1980s, but no more than two at the same time. While four black congresswomen had served in the 1970s, only Cardiss Collins of Illinois remained. Nearly as problematical as their small numbers was the complete turnover of Congresswomen between 1972 and 1984, since power and influence depended on seniority.[35]

Sobered by the slow pace of progress at the state level and the near intractability of higher office to women's claims, activists in the the 1980s settled in for a long struggle and focused more attention on the nuts-and-bolts of practical politics. The biggest barrier to women seemed to be incumbency. It was extremely difficult for any candidate, male or female, to defeat

35. Fact Sheets of the Center for the American Woman and Politics: "Women in State Government," April 1986; "Women in Municipal Office," May 1986; "Women in the U.S. Congress," January 1 1986.

an incumbent, so for women to make substantial gains, that problem had to be tackled.

The Women's Campaign Fund, which had previously concentrated on congressional races, began to pay more attention to getting women into the pipeline at the local and state levels. Launching a new project under the not-for-profit, tax-deductible Women's Campaign Research Fund (WCRF), it identified congressional seats for which incumbents were not expected to run in future elections. Simultaneously, the WCRF developed a Talent Bank of potential female candidates and organized a Candidate Training Program so that women would be prepared to run for these open seats.[36]

The movement's increasing attention to fundraising also began to pay off. In 1984, its tenth-anniversary year, the Women's Campaign Fund expended almost half a million dollars. By then it had been joined by more than twenty local and national political action committees (PACs). In addition to PACs established by NOW, the NWPC, and other national women's organizations, there were a variety of independent groups raising money for female and feminist candidates. The Los Angeles Women's Campaign Fund, for example, collected annual memberships of $250 or $1,000. In contrast, the Women's Political Action Committee of New Jersey had only $10,000 to disburse in 1984, but small sums could make an impact on local races where campaign budgets were usually modest.[37]

Another new organization demonstrated activists' skill at maximizing the financial bases of candidates while complying with federal election law. EMILY's List was founded in 1985 to raise money for Democratic woman candidates for the House and Senate. EMILY was an acronym for Early Money Is Like Yeast—"It makes the dough rise"—and reflected the importance of providing substantial monetary backing in the early

36. "WCRF Helps Candidates Prepare Winning Campaigns," *Moving Up* 1 (Winter 1987):1, 6.

37. Katherine E. Kleeman, "Women's PACs," Report of the Center for the American Woman and Politics, 1983, pp. 3–8; Kathy Stanwick, "Women's PACs," *News and Notes About Women Public Officials* 4 (August 1968):8–19; Letter from Janis Berman, Los Angeles Women's Campaign Fund, to the author, May 29, 1986; Letter from Patricia Connolly Gentile, president, Women's Political Action Committee of New Jersey, to the author, June 30, 1986.

stages of a campaign. By November 1986, EMILY's List had recruited 1,500 members who paid dues of $100 and pledged to give $100 more to at least two candidates endorsed by the fund. The fund channeled $350,000 to two senatorial candidates, Harriet F. Woods of Missouri and Barbara Mikulski of Maryland. Woods lost her race, but Mikulski became the first Democratic woman elected to the Senate who did not follow her husband. EMILY's List members had contributed 20 percent of her early money.[38]

Mikulski's victory testified to the importance of the women's movement's new concentration on "pipeline politics." The five-term Representative was a visible feminist who had served first on the Baltimore City Council and had lost an earlier Senate bid. In the 1986 race, Mikulski won more than 50 percent of the primary vote in a three-way race against two strong Democrats, and then overcame lesbian-baiting to defeat Republican Linda Chavez. Mikulski called herself a "20-year overnight success story," referring to her long apprenticeship in politics and holding out the prospect of high office for other women willing to start from the bottom, bounce back after defeats, and devote the years necessary to building a base of voter support.[39]

THE CANDIDACY OF GERALDINE FERRARO

The most spectacular breakthrough for women in politics was the nomination of Geraldine Ferraro for vice president on the 1984 Democratic ticket. In just her third term as Representative from Queens, New York, Ferraro had overcome the limitations of low seniority with a large assist from House Speaker Tip O'Neill, under whose tutelage she gained influence and visibility as member of the Democratic Committee for Party Effectiveness and the Hunt Commission on Presidential Nominations, as secretary of the Democratic Caucus in the House,

38. *Notes from Emily,* April, 1986, pp. 1, 2; "Women's Money in the 1986 Election: An Interview with Ellen Malcolm," *News and Notes About Women Public Officials* 5 (December 1986):4–5.

39. *Washington Post,* September 11, 1986; Ellen Goodman, "Mikulski a '20-year Overnight Success Story,'" *The Columbus Dispatch,* October 31, 1986, p. 11A.

and as chair of the 1984 Democratic Platform Committee. A supporter of most of the feminist agenda, Ferraro had the reputation of a moderate, and as an Italian-American Catholic wife and mother of three, she could appeal to voters concerned about "family values."[40]

Ferraro's nomination reflected the women's movement's increasing focus on electoral politics. Convinced that ratification of a new ERA and adoption of other feminist programs depended on electing more women to office, and heartened by the appearance of the gender gap in 1980, NOW shifted its strategy from the mobilization of pressure on elected officials to the mobilization and election of feminist candidates. Late in 1983, NOW abandoned its nonpartisanship, endorsing Walter Mondale for the presidency, and it called for a woman vice president, a demand echoed by the National Women's Political Caucus.

In August 1983, a small group of women with experience as congressional staffers and abortion rights and labor activists, who represented the American Nurses Association, the Women's Vote Project, and the National Abortion Rights Action League, constituted themselves into "Team A." Their purpose was to promote nomination of a woman for vice president on the Democratic ticket. They persuaded Ferraro to cooperate and helped to generate extensive press coverage about a woman on the ticket. By the spring of 1984 a number of male politicians and officials and several labor unions had expressed approval of a woman nominee, and Tip O'Neill specifically endorsed Ferraro.[41]

Presidential nominee Walter Mondale's choice of Ferraro electrified the Democratic convention and many women throughout the country. NOW had already committed its support to the Democratic ticket, and for the first time the NWPC abandoned its nonpartisanship in national elections to endorse Mondale and Ferraro. Despite her limited political background, Ferraro proved an able campaigner who drew large and enthusiastic crowds. She held her own in a televised debate

40. Ferraro, *Ferraro: My Story,* pp. 15, 49–50, 76–78; Peggy Simpson, "Politics," in McFeely, *The Women's Annual, Number 5,* pp. 87–88.
41. Ferraro, *Ferraro: My Story,* pp. 67–68, 71–79, 85–90.

Democratic presidential nominee Walter Mondale and his running mate Geraldine Ferraro at the podium of the Democratic National Convention in San Francisco, July 1984. (Wide World Photos)

with Vice President George Bush, and she withstood disclosures about her husband's questionable real estate dealings and a challenge from the Catholic Church hierarchy to her prochoice position on abortion. The issue of John Zaccaro's financial dealings and the abortion controversy, however, cost the Democrats momentum and votes, though they contributed only marginally to the overwhelming defeat of the Mondale-Ferraro ticket.[42]

Team A and others promoting Ferraro's nomination had argued that she would put Reagan on the defensive about women's issues and encourage voters to look more closely at the Democratic ticket. In a close election, they suggested, Ferraro could attract a female vote large enough to put the Democrats over the top. Women did support the Democratic ticket by around five percentage points more than men, but the election was not close and Team A's prediction could not be tested.

42. Simpson, "Politics," pp. 88–95.

Post mortems on the role of Ferraro's candidacy in the Democratic defeat abounded. Some male party leaders, pointing to Ferraro's limited political experience, felt that she was nominated only because she was a woman. They believed that some voters were put off by the appearance that feminists had bullied Mondale into choosing a woman. Other Democratic officials saw disclosures over Ferraro's family finances as a serious liability to the Democratic campaign.[43]

Feminists, on the other hand, charged that the Mondale campaign had neglected to capitalize on the potential women's vote. Campaign advertising failed to target women, and local campaign officials seemed indifferent to grass-roots organizing and to the eager women who called campaign headquarters to volunteer. Feminists also criticized the decision, endorsed by Ferraro, not to focus on women's issues. The gender gap was small, they argued, because the candidates did not appeal to women on the issues in which they had a critical stake. Neither side, however, gave sufficient emphasis to a truism of American politics—that voters make their choices on their perceptions of the presidential candidates, and that their running mates have never had much influence on the decisions of the electorate.[44]

Despite the stinging defeat, Ferraro's nomination was an important breakthrough. While her candidacy did not fulfill feminists' hopes that a woman would grasp victory for the Democrats, it did demonstrate women's ability to attract substantial contributions, and it offered hope and inspiration to other women with political aspirations. It also provided lessons, among them that the next female candidate should have already developed high national visibility and should have seen that her husband's business dealings and family financial arrangements were in impeccable order. Since the next woman on a national ticket would not be a novelty, it was unlikely that she would have to endure the intense media scrutiny about her appearance, style, and other characteristics irrelevant to her qualifications for high political office that dogged Ferraro.

43. Maureen Dowd, "Reassessing Women's Political Role: The Lasting Impact of Geraldine Ferraro," *New York Times Magazine,* December 30, 1984, pp. 19, 32.

44. *Ibid.,* p. 32; Ferraro, *Ferraro: My Story,* p. 282.

RUPTURES IN THE WOMEN'S POLITICAL MOVEMENT

In contrast to white feminists, euphoric over their influence in the 1984 Democratic convention, black women were stung by how little support they could marshal for their particular concerns. Before the convention, NOW had supported a number of planks advanced by black presidential candidate Jesse Jackson. Once Ferraro was chosen, however, the feminist coalition at the convention, which included representatives from NOW, the NWPC, and other women's groups, simply dismantled its organization. The Jackson campaign had expected the women's caucus to use its whip system to support his minority platform planks, and black women especially felt abandoned by their white sisters. They were also dismayed when Ferraro's initial appointments to her campaign staff were all white. Convinced that an independent base was necessary, they organized the National Political Congress of Black Women in August 1984. Although it did not directly challenge white-dominated women's organizations, its existence reflected shortcomings in the ability of the women's movement to sustain essential political alliances.[45]

Moreover, while the women's movement presented a united front in opposition to Reagan in the 1984 campaign, and the more politically oriented groups gave official endorsements to the Mondale-Ferraro ticket, unanimity in endorsements of state and local candidates proved more difficult. Women disagreed over whether it was more important to support women regardless of their stand on issues or to endorse candidates of either sex who took pro-feminist stands. As the Reagan administration pursued conservative economic and military policies, some women believed it essential to defeat any candidates— even women with good records on women's rights—whose election would increase the likelihood of congressional approval of Republican policies.[46]

The endorsement dilemma was played out most dramati-

---

45. Berry, *Why ERA Failed*, p. 116; *Washington Post*, August 6, 1984.

46. Myra Marx Ferree and Beth B. Hess, *Controversy and Coalition: The New Feminist Movement* (Boston: Twayne Publishers, 1985), pp. 108–9.

cally in the campaign of Republican Representative Millicent Fenwick, who sought a Senate seat in 1982. Fenwick, a moderate Republican, had steadfastly championed women's rights and other issues important to the women's movement, but she had voted for some of Reagan's economic policies, and, even more importantly, her election would increase Republican numbers in the Senate. On these grounds New Jersey NOW endorsed her opponent, Frank Lautenberg, who took a strong anti-Reagan position while vigorously supporting women's rights. The NWPC, on the other hand, endorsed Fenwick, who lost by a fairly small margin.[47]

Even when two men were running, women's organizations did not always agree. In Connecticut, the state NOW endorsed the more progressive candidate, while national NOW supported Republican Lowell Weicker, a moderate Republican and strong proponent of abortion rights. Women's organizations did achieve unanimity in supporting the male challenger to Margaret Heckler, Republican Representative from Massachusetts. Although Heckler was a consistent advocate for most women's issues, she opposed abortion and had supported most of Reagan's budget proposals. Heckler's defeat removed from the House one of the oldest and strongest Republican voices for feminist concerns.[48]

Women's political organizations continued to endorse Republicans as well as Democrats, but the longstanding tendency of feminists to identify with the Democratic party intensified in response to the explicit antifeminism of the Reagan administration. While some Republican feminists, such as Kathy Wilson who headed the NWPC during Reagan's first term, did not hesitate to oppose the president, others were alienated by the increasing partisanship of the women's movement. NWPC leader Bobbie Green Kilberg, for example, broke with the caucus over its increasing identification with liberal causes and the Democratic party. Although she was committed to the ERA and abortion rights, Kilberg believed that simply getting women into office should command highest priority and was dismayed when women's groups helped defeat Fenwick

47. Abzug, *Gender Gap*, pp. 189–92.
48. *Ibid.*

and Heckler. Despite similar disaffections, by the mid-1980s the woman's political movement had clearly ranked election of progressive and feminist candidates ahead of electing more women regardless of their position on issues.[49]

CONCLUSION

The election and reelection of Ronald Reagan posed the strongest challenge to the women's movement since its resurgence in the 1960s. Defeat of the ERA and emasculation of Title IX were bitter blows, and the women's movement was compelled to expend enormous resources simply trying to maintain the status quo. Yet women demonstrated their staying power in the political arena even when the political climate was no longer hospitable to feminist goals and when the media pronounced the arrival of a "post-feminist" era.

Broadening its agenda to tackle economic and employment problems not amenable to resolution through simple antidiscrimination measures, the women's movement defended successfully most of the public-policy iniatives of the 1970s and even enjoyed some modest progress. Women held on to their rights to reproductive freedom and to affirmative action and obtained federal assistance in the areas of pension rights and child support. State and local governments strengthened their efforts to protect women from rape and domestic violence. And a coalition of women's organizations and labor unions turned the attention of state and local assemblies to the issue of equal pay for work of comparable worth.

Women continued to impress pollsters with their more liberal stands on major issues, and in every election year they demonstrated the potential of the gender gap in a number of statewide races. Although the nomination of Geraldine Ferraro failed to fulfill feminists' expectations about her potential to mobilize female voters, it did register the clout of women in the Democratic party, demonstrate that women were capable of

49. Margaret W. Freivogel, "Activist Chose Children over Job with Clout," *St. Louis Post-Dispatch*, December 15, 1984, p. B1.

running for the highest offices, and accustom voters to the idea of a woman on a national ticket. Aside from a handful of "firsts," women made no dramatic gains as political candidates in the 1980s, but they sustained the previous pace of increase in office-holding and, perfected the tools for getting women into the political pipeline and preparing them for higher office.

Epilogue

After gaining the vote in 1920, it took American women more than half a century to become a distinct, sustained, and forceful presence in the nation's policymaking and politics. By the end of the 1980s women were voting in greater numbers than men, and their votes at times provided the critical margin in close elections. Women continued to lag far behind men in holding office, but they were steadily increasing their numbers, and they had developed sophisticated means to step up that pace. Even without an equal presence in legislative bodies, women had advanced their particular interests on the nation's public-policy agenda, and they had dramatically recast the assumptions which for centuries had underlain the law.

These changes rested to a large extent on massive social and economic forces that altered the material bases of women's lives. The movement of women into the labor force, their increasing educational levels, the declining birth rate, the rising level of divorce and single motherhood began before and contributed to the resurgence of a women's movement. That movement in turn shaped these new experiences into a political force. Feminists analyzed these changes from women's perspective, articulated policies to make these forces work in women's favor, and marshalled a constituency to bring women and their concerns to the center of policymaking.

The resurgence and staying power of the women's movement itself depended considerably on specific features of the American political system. The declining influence of political parties and the strong role of interest groups in American politics facilitated women's ability to claim attention in the corridors of power. The social movements of the 1960s raised women's consciousness about their own oppression and gave legitimacy and inspiration to the politics of protest. And the

181

black freedom struggle provided not only a model of organized protest, but also a legal framework and precedent on which women could build policies to redress their own grievances.

ELECTORAL POLITICS AND OFFICE-HOLDING

At the elite level of politics, women's participation changed dramatically between the late 1960s and the late 1980s. Women developed their own political organizations aimed at putting women and feminists into office, and they also achieved prominence in male-dominated organizations where they had previously done the routine jobs of canvassing, getting out mail, and holding coffees for candidates. In 1988, candidates for both major parties' presidential nominations employed women in powerful positions. Susan Estrich served as campaign manager for Democratic candidate Michael Dukakis, and other women served as press secretary, deputy campaign manager, and political director for various candidates. Women had moved to central positions in presidential campaigns.[1]

Women's prospects for gaining political office themselves had increased substantially by the 1980s. Public opinion polls found that 82 percent of the population would vote for a qualified woman for president, up from around 50 percent two decades earlier. Geraldine Ferraro's pathbreaking nomination and campaign for the vice presidency in 1984 drove a large wedge into the male monopoly at the highest level of politics. In 1988, Democrat Patricia Schroeder and Republican Jeane J. Kirkpatrick carefully considered presidential races and were taken seriously by the media. By the end of the 1980s, it was no longer a foregone conclusion that genuine contenders for the presidency would all be male.

Most presidential candidates came from congressional or gubernatorial service, and the pool of women in these offices grew, though at a snail's pace. At the end of the 1980s women constituted just 2 percent of the Senate and 4.5 percent of the House. That representation left them far behind women in

1. *New York Times,* December 29, 1987.

many industrialized democracies, such as Norway and Sweden, where women constituted more than 30 percent of the national legislatures, and Australia, Canada, and New Zealand where they claimed around 10 percent of the legislative seats. Qualitative changes were more impressive than quantitative ones. Virtually all women legislators had entered politics on their own, instead of following in their husbands' footsteps. And, once in office, they tended to coalesce around women's issues and to obtain more diverse committee assignments and positions of power than the women who had served in the 1940s and 1950s. Most Congresswomen elected in the 1980s had moved up from substantial state legislative service, and the women's political movement began to direct its considerable skills and energies to getting women into the pipeline at lower levels.[2]

Although the pace of women's entrance into the pipeline remained slow, every election since the 1960s witnessed some progress. In 1985, women claimed 14 percent of all municipal offices, an increase of 260 percent over the previous decade. Most of these women held council seats, but among the hundred largest cities, ten served as mayors. Loretta Glickman, elected as mayor of Pasadena, California in 1982, was the first black woman to head a city larger than 100,000. Her victory was followed by the election of black women as mayors of Little Rock, Arkansas, Newport News, Virginia, and Hartford, Connecticut.[3]

Similarly, women continued to edge into state elective office. In 1987, women held 15.5 percent of seats in state legislatures, a quadrupling of their presence since 1969. Although black women constituted only 7.8 percent of all women serving in statehouses, they held 22.8 percent of all black seats, a better representation relative to men of their race than was the case for white women. Hispanic women were most poorly represented, with just twelve serving in statehouses, occupying only

2. "Women in Government Around the World," Fact Sheet of the Center for the American Woman and Politics, April 1987, p. 1; "Women Candidates Gain Ground in November Elections," *Women's Times* 1 (November 14 1986):5–7.

3. "Women in Municipal Office," Fact Sheet of the Center for the American Woman and Politics, May 1986, pp. 1–2; "Women in Elective Office, 1987," Fact Sheet of the Center for the American Woman in Politics, June 1987, p. 2; *New York Times*, October 29, 1987, November 5, 1987.

1 percent of all female seats and 10 percent of all Hispanic seats.[4]

Women's presence in state legislatures ranged from 33 percent in New Hampshire to 2.3 percent in Mississippi, while in eleven states, they formed a critical mass, occupying at least 20 percent of all seats. Only one woman served as speaker in a state legislature, but women held some form of leadership position in around half the states. Women did nearly as well in elective statewide office as they did in legislatures, serving in 15 percent of such positions. In addition to an attorney general and five lieutenant governors, three women held the highest state office in 1987, Martha Layne Collins in Kentucky, Madeleine Kunin in Vermont, and Kay Orr in Nebraska. Native American women enjoyed a "first" when Wilma P. Mankiller was sworn in as chief of the Cherokee Nation, the second largest American Indian tribe in the United States.[5]

By the 1980s feminist activists realized that more equal representation of women in elective office would require a long struggle. The women's movement focused more attention on electoral politics, and activists paid increasing attention to fund-raising. In the 1980s more than twenty women's political action committees raised money for the campaigns of women and men who supported feminist goals. And the oldest women's fund-raising organization, the Women's Campaign Fund, had developed a comprehensive program to predict openings where women would have good chances of winning and to prepare them to run. "Pipeline politics" became the strategy of the women's political movement.

Besides dealing with the problem of incumbency, female candidates still encountered barriers not faced by men. Attitudes about women in office had becomed markedly more positive since the 1960s, but voter prejudice lingered. In a survey taken in 1987, half of the respondents believed women to be as capable to serve as president as men. Eight percent believed

---

4. "Women in State Legislatures, 1987," Fact Sheet of the Center for the American Woman in Politics, p. 1.

5. *Ibid.;* "Elected Women in Statewide Executive Office, 1987," Fact Sheet of the Center for the American Woman and Politics, May 1987, p. 1; David Broder, "This Woman's Place Is in the House," *St. Louis Post-Dispatch,* March 2, 1985; *New York Times,* December 15, 1985.

that women would be better, but 31 percent said that women would not do as good a job as men, leaving women at a 23-point disadvantage. While women were rated better than men as potential school board members, for every other office ranging from city council member to U.S. vice president, women suffered a net disavantage in voters' beliefs about their capabilities.[6]

PUBLIC POLICIES

After twenty years, one great defeat continued to dog the women's movement—failure to obtain the Equal Rights Amendment. The leadership of NOW believed it essential to continue to press for constitutional equality. Other feminists wanted to concentrate on policies such as day care and parental leave where they perceived the need more pressing and success more likely. Most of the largest organizations in the women's policy network, however, agreed that it was important to keep the ERA alive so that it could be vigorously promoted when the political climate improved. As the nation celebrated the bicentennial of its Constitution in 1987, sixteen national women's organizations announced a drive to press for congressional hearings on the ERA. Calling itself the Council of Presidents, the coalition included explicitly feminist groups like NOW and the NWPC, as well as the LWC, the BPW, the AAUW, and other traditional women's organizations.[7]

Revival of the ERA was just one of eight goals agreed upon by the Council of Presidents. Other issues included reproductive rights and government funding of reproductive health care for all women; equal pay for work of comparable worth; a federal policy of unpaid leave for men and women for disability, childbirth, adoption, or to care for ill dependents; an increase in the minimum wage; a federal child-care program; welfare reform to include adequate job training, income maintenance, and medical care; and passage of the Civil Rights Restoration

6. *New York Times,* December 12, 1984; *Washington Post,* August 13, 1987.
7. *Washington Post,* January 17, 1987; *St. Louis Post-Dispatch,* January 18, 1987.

bill to overrule the Supreme Court decision in the Grove City case and restore institution-wide coverage of civil-rights laws.[8]

A comparison of the Council of Presidents' agenda with the eight-point Bill of Rights proposed by NOW two decades earlier indicates both the intractability and the responsiveness of public policy to women's concerns. On the one hand, twenty years of agitation had not brought about constitutional equality nor adequate day-care facilities. The welfare system continued to serve women badly, and the impoverishment of women had actually grown since the 1960s.

On the other hand, significant gains had occurred in three areas: educational equity, equality in employment opportunity, and reproductive freedom. In some cases, these gains were under attack or had been curtailed. Reproductive freedom, for example, had been undermined for poor women and for civil service personnel and other employed women whose medical benefits did not cover abortions. Moreover, pro-choice forces had been forced to commit massive resources to preserving abortion rights. Similarly, the Grove City decision had severely weakened women's claim to protection against discrimination in education. It took four years to obtain the Civil Rights Restoration Act, itself flawed by a provision that compromised women's access to abortion.

Laws against sex discrimination in employment remained intact, and the Supreme Court had bolstered affirmative action in the Johnson case. Due to the efforts of feminists, the federal courts had also defined sexual harassment as a form of sex discrimination and ruled that employers could be held responsible when it occurred in the workplace. The law had taken an enormous leap from the early 1960s when it was perfectly legal for employers to refuse to hire women, pay them less than men, and treat them differently in the workplace.

Yet feminists discovered that antidiscrimination and affirmative action policies, while of critical importance, failed to address the complexity of women's inferior position in the work force. The historical undervaluation of occupations monopo-

8. *St. Louis Post-Dispatch,* January 18, 1987.

lized by women proved largely immune to remedy through the Equal Pay Act and Title VII. And all the antidiscrimination measures on the books could not overcome the disadvantages suffered by women workers who attempted to combine employment with motherhood.

Pay equity, or equal pay for work of comparable worth, a national leave policy for childbearing and adoption, and substantial federal support for day-care services became the focal points for activists concerned with women's employment in the 1980s. While pressing for federal policies in these areas, feminists enjoyed a measure of success at the state level. Pay equity laws were passed in more than a dozen states and localities, and in 1987 Minnesota and Oregon became the first states to require employers to provide mothers or fathers unpaid leave following the birth or adoption of a child.[9]

What the 1967 NOW Bill of Rights and the 1987 agenda of the Council of Presidents do not reveal are policy changes initiated and addressed largely at the state level. Women activists not only focused public and official attention on rape and wife-battering, but they redefined these issues from a feminist perspective, compelled legal changes, and improved treatment of and services for victims of these crimes. Due largely to the women's movement, states and the federal government also addressed the problems of divorced women and other displaced homemakers, granting increasing recognition to their work as wives and mothers, and taking those contributions into account in divorce and pension policies.

In no other period had American women's legal status changed so dramatically as in the years since 1960. Instead of defining women primarily as wives and mothers, as American law had done throughout history, the new policies defined women as autonomous individuals entitled to equal treatment in the public sphere. Equally significant, legislation and court rulings of the 1970s and 1980s mitigated the effects of women's historic dependence on men by promoting their well-being and independence within the family.

9. *New York Times*, June 18, 1987.

THE WOMEN'S MOVEMENT AFTER TWENTY YEARS

The women's movement could take considerable credit for these policy changes. Feminist activists encouraged women to understand the political, economic, and social sources of what they had formerly considered to be their personal problems. Activists mobilized this new consciousness into a mass, grass-roots movement which policymakers could not ignore. They created dozens of new organizations. Some, like the Older Women's League, the Coalition of Labor Union Women, and the National Political Congress of Black Women, were formed around the interests of discrete groups of women. Others, such as the National Abortion Rights Action League and the Alliance for Displaced Homemakers worked on a particular cluster of issues. And some new organizations like the Women's Campaign Fund and the National Women's Political Caucus concentrated on getting women and feminists into policymaking positions.

Working alongside the new groups were traditional women's organizations such as the League of Women Voters, the National Council of Negro Women, the American Association of University Women, the National Federation of Business and Professional Women, and women's religious organizations. The new or intensified commitment of these groups to a feminist agenda was in itself striking testimony to how extensively attitudes about women's roles and rights had been transformed since the 1960s. That commitment was also absolutely crucial to the ability of the women's movement to sustain a national focus on women's public policy issues.

The pluralistic nature of the women's movement made it possible to mobilize large numbers of women with divergent experiences and interests. Activists disagreed about priorities as well as substantive issues, such as laws treating pregnant workers differently than other workers. Yet the size and diversity of the women's movement kept such differences from weakening its impact. Regardless of disagreements, women's organizations usually did not squander resources fighting each other. Rather, they formed coalitions whenever possible and left individual groups to focus on the concerns they deemed most important. More than fifty organizations, for example, endorsed the Economic Equity bill, but each was free to concentrate on provisions of greatest concern to its members.[10]

The Economic Equity bill, with its provisions for child care, pay equity, health and pension benefits, and welfare reform denoted the flexibility and maturity of the women's movement. Its early emphasis on equal rights and opportunities had assisted primarily those privileged women who had the resources to capitalize on equal opportunity. Women of color, working-class women, and others had struggled within the women's movement and criticized it from without for its white, middle-class orientation. By the 1980s, the women's movement had become more inclusive, recognizing the effects of class and race on women's status and pursuing an agenda that would improve the lives of clerical workers and welfare mothers as well as aspiring professionals.

Such an agenda was also suited to an economic and political environment characterized by the increasing impoverishment of women, and in which a powerful reaction against the changes in women's roles over the previous two decades was taking place. Moreover, that agenda spoke to the reality of the lives of a majority of American women, who struggled with the dual burdens of paid employment and family responsibilities. Finally, the women's movement's agenda of the 1980s furnished prospects for widespread support through coalitions with labor unions, civil-rights organizations, social welfare groups, and others.

The media frequently characterized the 1980s as the "post-feminist generation." The resurgence of conservativism, defeat of the ERA, and diffidence among many younger women towards organized feminism lent some validity to that label. Yet the progress of women into mainstream politics, both as office-holders and as an interest group shaping public policy, had not subsided. At the grass-roots level, the gender gap in voting persisted and alerted politicians that they would have to continue to take women's aspirations seriously. The larger forces

10. "1987 'Economic Equity Act,' Seen As 'Blueprint' for Meeting Women's Needs," *Women's Times* 2 (June 16, 1987):1–6.

that had altered women's position in the work force, the family, and politics had not abated, and a credible women's movement, which had articulated an agenda in response to those developments, persevered. More than twenty years after its commencement, the third era of women's political participation had not yet run its course.

Suggestions for Further Reading

Until very recently studies in women's political history were as scarce as were the presence of women and their concerns in formal political arenas. As the resurgent feminist movement stimulated women's political activism and increased their representation in governing bodies, it also stimulated research on women's relationships with politics and government. While historians and sociologists have pioneered in this explosion of knowledge about women—in part because women are relatively well represented as scholars in those disciplines—political scientists have also begun to study women in a systematic way. Research on women has closed gaps in our knowledge by examining a hitherto neglected population. Even more important, it has begun to remedy inaccuracies and distortions resulting from the use of male data to construct theories and generalizations and from the assumption of male behavior as normative.

The displacement of women as subjects of inquiry was based most obviously on their historical absence from the electorate and from institutionalized power. It derived as well from the tendency of male scholars to value male experience over female and to treat the male experience as if it subsumed all humanity. Finally, the scholarly neglect of women reflected a rather narrow conception of politics and government, one which focused on the state and formal power structures and overlooked particularly female forms of political involvement—in communities and in grass-roots movements.

A number of scholars have examined the distinctly female contributions to government and politics during the first four decades of enfranchisement. J. Stanley Lemons, *The Woman Citizen: Social Feminism in the 1920s,* University of Illinois Press, Urbana, 1973, analyzes the initial impact of women armed with the vote. Felice D. Gordon, *After Winning: The*

Legacy of the New Jersey Suffragists, 1920–1947, Rutgers University Press, New Brunswick, New Jersey, 1986, focuses on post-suffrage developments in a single state. Susan Ware has written two important studies of women in national government and politics: *Beyond Suffrage: Women in the New Deal,* Harvard University Press, Cambridge, 1981 and *Partner and I: Molly Dewson, Feminism, and New Deal Politics,* Yale University Press, 1987. Sandra Baxter and Marjorie Lansing, eds., *Women and Politics: The Visible Majority,* University of Michigan Press, Ann Arbor, rev. ed., 1987, contains several articles that present statistical data and analyses of women's mass political behavior and attitudes.

There are several excellent studies that focus on feminism between the suffrage era and the contemporary women's movement: Nancy Cott, *The Grounding of Modern Feminism,* Yale University Press, New Haven, 1987; Lois Scharf, *To Work and to Wed: Female Employment, Feminism and the Great Depression,* Greenwood Press, Westport, Connecticut, 1980; Leila J. Rupp and Verta Taylor, *Survival in the Doldrums: The American Women's Rights Movement, 1945 to the 1960s,* Oxford University Press, New York, 1987; Cynthia E. Harrison, *On Account of Sex: The Politics of Women's Issues, 1945 to 1968,* University of California Press, Berkeley, 1988; and Lois Scharf and Joan M. Jensen, eds., *Decades of Discontent: The Women's Movement, 1920–1940,* Greenwood Press, Westport, Connecticut, 1983. Scharf and Jensen contains an illuminating study of black women's activism by Rosalyn Terborg-Penn, "Discontented Black Feminists: Prelude and Postscript to the Nineteenth Amendment." Paula Giddings, *When and Where I Enter: The Impact of Black Women on Race and Sex in America,* Bantam Books, New York, 1985, provides the best account of black women's political activism from the nineteenth century through the 1970s.

Most of the studies of social movements in the 1960s thus far suffer from the conventional assumption that men were the only subjects worthy of serious attention. A few, however, adopt gender as an important category of analysis and explore women's roles in social activism and the effects of that participation on women: Aldon Morris, *The Origins of the Civil Rights Movement: Black Communities Organizing for Change,* The

Free Press, New York, 1984; Nancy Zaroulis and Gerald Sullivan, *Who Spoke Up? American Protest Against the War in Vietnam,* Doubleday, Garden City, New York, 1984; Guida West, *The National Welfare Rights Movement: The Social Protest of Poor Women,* Praeger, New York, 1981; and Sara Evans, *Personal Politics: The Roots of Women's Liberation in the Civil Rights Movement and the New Left,* Random House, New York, 1979.

Firsthand accounts of their participation in social movements have been recorded by a number of women. For the civil-rights movement, see Anne Moody, *Coming of Age in Mississippi,* Dial Press, New York, 1965; David J. Garrow, ed., *The Montgomery Boycott and the Women Who Started It: The Memoir of Jo Ann Gibson Robinson,* University of Tennessee Press, Knoxville, 1987; Septima Clark, *Echo in My Soul,* E. P. Dutton, New York, 1962; Angela Davis, *An Autobiography,* Random House, New York, 1974; Mary King, *Freedom Song: A Personal Story of the 1960s Civil Rights Movement,* William Morrow, New York, 1987; and Pauli Murray, *Song in a Weary Throat: An American Pilgrimage,* Harper and Row, New York, 1987, which also discusses Murray's role in the resurgence of the women's movement. Ellen Cantarow, *Moving the Mountain: Women Working for Social Change,* The Feminist Press, Old Westbury, New York, 1980, contains oral histories of Ella Baker and Jessie Lopez De La Cruz.

The most useful survey of the origins and development of the women's movement is Myra Marx Ferree and Beth B. Hess, *Controversy and Coalition: The New Feminist Movement,* Twayne Publishers, Boston, 1985. Jo Freeman, *The Politics of Liberation: A Case Study of an Emerging Movement and Its Relation to the Policy Process,* David McKay, New York, 1975, provides the best analysis of the resurgence of feminism and its early impact on public policies. Scholars should also consult Winifred D. Wandersee, *On the Move: American Women in the 1970s,* Twayne Publishers, Boston, 1988, and Ethel Klein, *Gender Politics: From Consciousness to Mass Politics,* Harvard University Press, Cambridge, 1984. For a first-person account by a key individual in the launching of the women's movement, see Betty Friedan, *It Changed My Life: Writings on the Women's Movement,* Random House, New York, 1976.

Studies of policy developments that predated and spurred the formation of a mass women's movement include Patricia Zelman, *Women, Work, and National Policy: The Kennedy-Johnson Years,* UMI Research Press, Ann Arbor, Michigan, 1982; and Carl Brauer, "Women Activists, Southern Conservatives, and the Prohibition of Sex Discrimination in Title VII of the 1964 Civil Rights Act," *Journal of Southern History* 49 (February 1983): 37–56. Harrison, and Rupp and Taylor, cited above, document the connections between women's pre-1960s activism and the resurgent feminist movement.

Although no extended, systematic study yet exists of the National Organization for Women or the National Women's Political Caucus, a number of works deal with the mobilization of female pressure on the parties and government. For a discussion of the women's movement and political parties, see Anne N. Costain and W. Douglas Costain, "Strategy and Tactics of the Women's Movement in the United States: The Role of Political Parties," and Jo Freeman, "Whom You Know versus Whom You Represent: Feminist Influence in the Democratic and Republican Parties," in Mary Fainsod Katzenstein and Carol McClurg Mueller, eds., *The Women's Movements of the United States and Western Europe: Consciousness, Political Opportunity, and Public Policy,* Temple University Press, Philadelphia, 1987.

Feminists' efforts to promote women's interests in Congress and the executive branch are examined in Joyce Gelb and Marian Lief Palley, *Women and Public Policies,* Princeton University Press, rev. ed., 1987; Anne N. Costain, "The Struggle for a National Women's Lobby: Organizing a Diffuse Interest," *Western Political Quarterly* 33 (December 1980): 476–91; and Anne N. Costain, "Representing Women: The Transition from Social Movement to Interest Group," *Western Political Quarterly* 34 (March 1981): 100–112. Susan and Martin Tolchin, *Clout: Womanpower and Politics,* G. P. Putnam's Sons, New York, 1974, provides a lively account of women's pressure politics; and Irene Tinker, ed., *Women in Washington: Advocates for Public Policy,* Sage Publications, Beverly Hills, California, 1983, contains articles about a variety of women's networks and coalitions. For an excellent analysis of the shifting strategies of the women's movement, see Mary Fainsod Katzenstein, "Feminism and the Meaning of the Vote," *Signs: Journal of Women in Culture and Society* 10 (Autumn 1984): 4–26.

Litigation efforts on behalf of women are analyzed in Karen O'Connor, *Women's Organizations' Use of the Courts,* Lexington Books, Lexington, Massachusetts, 1980; Margaret A. Berger, *Litigation on Behalf of Women,* The Ford Foundation, New York, 1980; and Wendy W. Williams and Judith L. Lichtman, "Closing the Law's Gender Gap," *The Nation* 239 (September 29, 1984): 281–284.

The most extensive and analytical account of women's engagement in the public-policy process is Gelb and Palley, noted above, which is organized around the issues of credit, education, pregnancy discrimination, and reproductive freedom. Useful collections of articles about women's policy issues include: Ellen Boneparth, ed., *Women, Power and Policy,* Pergamon Press, New York, 1982; and Irene Diamond and Mary Lyndon Shanley, eds., *Families, Politics and Public Policy: A Feminist Dialogue on Women and the State,* Longman, New York, 1983.

Among the public-policy concerns of women, the largest body of research has been done on the Equal Rights Amendment. Janet K. Boles, *The Politics of the Equal Rights Amendment: Conflict and the Decision Process,* Longman, New York, 1979 provides case studies of ratification efforts in several states. The central concern of the following studies is to explain why ratification failed: Janet K. Boles, "Building Support for the ERA: A Case of 'Too Much, Too Late,' " *PS* 15 (Fall 1982): 572–78; Gilbert Y. Steiner, *Constitutional Inequality: The Political Fortunes of the Equal Rights Amendment,* The Brookings Institution, Washington, DC, 1985; Mary Frances Berry, *Why ERA Failed: Politics, Women's Rights, and the Amending Process of the Constitution,* Indiana University Press, Bloomington, 1986; and Jane J. Mansbridge, *Why We Lost the ERA,* University of Chicago Press, Chicago, 1986. Joan Hoff Wilson, ed., *Rights of Passage: The Past and Future of the ERA,* Indiana University Press, Bloomington, 1986, is a collection of articles that document the history of the ERA from its inception to 1982.

The issue of equal pay for work of comparable worth is embedded in controversy concerning explanations of the income gap between men and women and appropriate remedies. For women's activism around the issue of pay equity, see Helen Remick, ed., *Comparable Worth and Wage Discrimination: Technical Possibilities and Political Realities,* Temple University Press, Philadelphia, 1984; and Elaine Johansen, *Comparable Worth: The Myth and the Movement,* Westview Press, Boulder, Colorado, 1984.

Other studies of specific policy issues include Jane Roberts Chapman and Margaret Gates, eds., *The Victimization of Women,* Sage Publications, Beverly Hills, California, 1978; Elizabeth Pleck, *Domestic Tyranny: The Making of American Social Policy Against Family Violence from Colonial Times to the Present,* Oxford University Press, New York, 1987; Patricia Huckle, "The Womb Factor: Pregnancy Policies and Employment of Women," *Western Political Quarterly* 34 (March 1981): 114–26; Jill Norgren, "In Search of a National Child Care Policy: Background and Prospects," *Western Political Quarterly* 34 (March 1981): 127–42; Kathleen J. Tierney, "The Battered Women's Movement and the Creation of the Wife Beating Problem," *Social Problems* 29 (February 1982): 207–20; and Wallace D. Loh, "Q: What Has Reform of Rape Legislation Wrought? A: Truth in Labelling," *Journal of Social Issues* 37 (1981): 28–52.

Studies of abortion policy have tended to focus on partisans in the controversy. Kristen Luker, *Abortion and the Politics of Motherhood,* University of California, Berkeley, 1984, provides an excellent analysis of California activists on both sides. Other studies, which concentrate on abortion opponents, include Frederick Jaffe, Barbara L. Lindheim, and Philip R. Lee, *Abortion Politics: Private Morality and Public Policy,* McGraw-Hill, New York, 1981; and Rosalind Pollack Petchesky, *Abortion and Woman's Choice: The State, Sexuality, and Reproductive Freedom,* Northeastern University Press, Boston, 1984.

Women in the antifeminist camp have been the subject of a number of studies. Rebecca E. Klatch, *Women of the New Right,* Temple University Press, Philadelphia, 1987, examines motivations, values, and self-perceptions of conservative women, emphasizing their diversity and exploring their views on the role of government and their anticommunism as well as their antifeminism. See also Susan Harding, "Family Reform

Movements: Recent Feminism and Its Opposition," *Feminist Studies* 7 (Spring 1981): 57–75. There is no scholarly biography of Phyllis Schlafly, but considerable information about her career can be found in the journalistic account by Carol Felsenthal, *The Sweetheart of the Silent Majority: The Biography of Phyllis Schlafly*, Doubleday, Garden City, New York, 1981. For an extensive quantitative analysis of antifeminism, see Pamela Conover and Virginia Gray, *Feminism and the New Right: Conflict over the American Family*, Praeger, New York, 1983.

Opposition to the Equal Rights Amendment has received considerable scholarly attention. Activists in particular states are examined by Theodore S. Arrington and Patricia A. Kyle, "Equal Rights Amendment Activists in North Carolina," *Signs: Journal of Women in Culture and Society* 3 (Spring 1978): 666–80; Texas is looked at in Kent L. Tedin, et al., "Social Background and Political Differences Between Pro- and Anti-ERA Activists," *American Politics Quarterly* 5 (July 1977): 395–408; and Massachusetts is examined in Carol Mueller and Thomas Dimieri, "The Structure of Belief Systems among Contending ERA Activists," *Social Forces* 60 (March 1982): 657–75. Opposition to the ERA among the public at large is analyzed by Val Burris, "Who Opposed the ERA? An Analysis of the Social Bases of Antifeminism," *Social Science Quarterly* 64 (June 1983): 305–17; and by Joan Huber, Cynthia Rexroad, and Glenna Spitze, "A Crucible of Opinion on Women's Status: ERA in Illinois," *Social Forces* 57 (December 1978): 549–65.

The best studies of recent patterns in women's mass-level political participation are Baxter and Lansing, noted above, and Karen Leigh Beckwith, *American Women and Political Participation: The Impacts of Work, Generation, and Feminism*, Greenwood, Westport, Connecticut, 1986. Baxter and Lansing, and Carol M. Mueller, ed., *The Politics of the Gender Gap*, Sage Publications, Beverly Hills, CA, 1988 present a valuable analysis of the gender gap in voting and policy preferences, but see also Ethel Klein, *Gender Politics: From Consciousness to Mass Politics*, Harvard University Press, Cambridge, 1984; Kathleen A. Frankovic, "Sex and Politics—New Alignments, Old Issues," *P.S.* 15 (Summer 1982): 441–44; Daniel Wirls, "Reinterpreting the Gender Gap," *Public Opinion Quarterly* 50 (Fall 1986): 317–29; Robert Y. Shapiro and Harpreet Mahajan, "Trends in

Gender Differences in Policy Preferences," *Public Opinion Quarterly* 50 (Spring 1986): 42–61; and Bella Abzug with Mim Kelber, *Gender Gap: Bella Abzug's Guide to Political Power for American Women,* Houghton Mifflin, Boston, 1984.

Women as candidates for political office are examined in Ruth B. Mandel, *In the Running: The New Woman Candidate,* Beacon Press, Boston, 1981; and Susan J. Carroll, *Women as Candidates in American Politics,* Indiana University Press, Bloomington, 1985. For a recent study of voter attitudes towards female candidates see Susan Welch, et al., "The Effect of Candidate Gender on Electoral Outcomes in State Legislative Races," *Western Political Quarterly* 38 (September 1985): 464–73. Campaign financing is treated in Carole Jean Uhlaner and Kay Lehman Schlozman, "Candidate Gender and Congressional Campaign Receipts," *Journal of Politics* 48 (1986): 30–50; Barbara C. Burrell, "Women's and Men's Campaigns for the U.S. House of Representatives, 1972–1982: A Finance Gap?" *American Politics Quarterly* 13 (July 1985): 251–72; and Katherine E. Kleeman, *Women's PACs,* Report of the Center for the American Woman and Politics, New Brunswick, N.J., 1983. The problem of incumbency is discussed by Kristi Andersen and Stuart J. Thorson, "Congressional Turnover and the Election of Women," *Western Political Quarterly* 37 (March 1984): 143–56.

Scholarly analyses of women as office-holders began with Jeane J. Kirkpatrick, *Political Woman,* Basic Books, New York, 1974, and Irene Diamond, *Sex Roles in the State House,* Yale University Press, New Haven, 1977. For accounts of the "new" woman legislator, see *Women State Legislators: Report from a Conference, June 17–20, 1982,* Center for the American Woman and Politics, n.d.; Carol Mueller, "Feminism and the New Woman in Public Office," *Women and Politics* 2 (Fall 1982): 7–21; and Irwin N. Gertzog, *Congressional Women: Their Recruitment, Treatment, and Behavior,* Praeger, New York, 1984. Research on black women office-holders is reported in Jewel L. Prestage, "Black Women State Legislators," in Marianne Githens and Jewel L. Prestage, eds., *A Portrait of Marginality: The Political Behavior of American Women,* David McKay, New York, 1977.

Memoirs, autobiographies, and biographies of women active

in politics and government include Bella Abzug, *Bella! Ms. Abzug Goes to Washington,* Saturday Review Press, New York, 1972; Shirley Chisholm, *Unbought and Unbossed,* Avon Books, New York, 1971; Shirley Chisholm, *The Good Fight,* Harper and Row, New York, 1973; Geraldine A. Ferraro with Linda Bird Francke, *Ferraro: My Story,* Bantam Books, New York, 1985; Judith Patterson, *Be Somebody: A Biography of Marguerite Rawalt,* Eakin Press, Austin, Texas, 1986; and Emily George, *Martha Griffiths,* University Press of America, Lanham, Md., 1983.

For insights into American women's political experiences gleaned from an international perspective, see Drude Dahlerup, ed., *The New Women's Movement: Feminism and Political Power in Europe and the USA,* Sage Publications, London, 1986; Joni Lovenduski, *Women and European Politics: Contemporary Feminism and Public Policy,* University of Massachusetts Press, Amherst, 1986; and Katzenstein and Mueller, cited above.

For current information on women and politics, scholars should consult the Center for the Study of the American Woman and Politics (CAWP) at Rutgers University, New Brunswick, New Jersey. Established in 1971 as a unit of the Eagleton Institute of Politics, the center has published a number of studies on women in public office and maintains a National Information Bank on Women in Public Office. Besides sponsoring conferences and other research and educational programs and maintaining a collection of books, articles, periodicals, working papers, and clippings, CAWP publishes *News and Notes,* a newsletter about women and politics, and fact sheets that contain current information about women in public life.

Glossary of Organizations

American Association of University Women Founded in 1882 as the Association of Collegiate Alumnae, the **AAUW** unites more than 150,000 college-educated women to promote sex equity and the advancement of women, education, progressive societal change, and self-development among its members. It contributed significantly to the promotion of women's policy issues in the 1970s and 1980s.

Center for Women Policy Studies One of the first feminist policy centers, the **CWPS** was founded in Washington, D.C. in 1972 to promote improvements in women's legal and economic status by providing research and advice to policy makers. The Center has paid particular attention to issues of social security equity, domestic violence, and sexual assault.

Citizens' Advisory Council on the Status of Women The **CACSW** was established in 1963 as successor to the President's Commission on the Status of Women. It investigated women's status, recommended policy, and helped to mobilize women's organizations around particular issues. During the Carter administration, the CACSW was succeeded by the National Advisory Committee for Women in 1978 and by the President's Advisory Committee for Women in 1979. Ronald Reagan failed to appoint a successor body.

Congressional Caucus for Women's Issues Democratic and Republican women legislators created the Congresswomen's Caucus in 1977 to work for public policies that would eliminate sex discrimination and advance women's welfare. In 1982 it changed its name and opened its membership to men, and by the end of the decade counted more than 100 legislators among its membership.

Eagle Forum   Founded by Phyllis Schlafly in 1975 to work against ratification of the Equal Rights Amendment, abortion, and other issues considered by its membership to threaten the traditional family, the Eagle Forum counted 80,000 members in the 1980s.

League of Women Voters   Successor to the National Woman Suffrage Association, the **LWV** was founded in 1920 as a non-partisan organization to encourage informed citizen participation in government and politics. The League was particularly active in promoting public policy to improve women's status in the 1920s and again in the 1970s and 1980s when its membership exceeded 100,000.

National Abortion Rights Action League   **NARAL** was established by feminists in 1969 as the National Association to Repeal Abortion Laws whose purpose was to eliminate anti-abortion laws in the states. After the 1973 Supreme Court decision on abortion, it changed its name and through litigation, lobbying, and mobilizing grass-roots campaigns, it has concentrated on safeguarding women's right to control their reproduction. Its membership consisted of nearly 100,000 health activists, medical professionals, and feminists in 1980.

National Council of Jewish Women   The **NCJW** was founded in 1893 and works for the betterment of the Jewish community in the United States and Israel. Women's issues have always been part of its program, and it was one of the traditional women's organizations promoting feminist goals during the 1970s and 1980s.

National Council of Negro Women   Founded by Mary McLeod Bethune in 1935, the **NCNW** is a federation of more than twenty national organizations and dozens of local councils. Its major purpose is to meet the economic, educational, and social needs of minority and low-income women, and it lobbied for women's policy issues in the 1970s and 1980s.

National Federation of Business and Professional Women's Clubs   Founded in 1919, the **BPW** has concentrated on improving opportunities for employed women, who comprise most of its 125,000 members. An early proponent of the Equal Rights Amendment, the BPW formed a link between the older women's rights movement and contemporary feminism and played an active role in the women's lobby of the 1970s and 1980s.

National Organization for Women Since its birth in 1967, **NOW** has been the major feminist advocacy organization, with a membership of around 150,000 in the mid-1980s, and chapters at the state and local levels.

National Women's Party The **NWP** was founded in 1916 as the militant wing of the women's suffrage movement. In 1923, it called for an Equal Rights Amendment, and its small but intensely committed membership has continued to pursue that goal.

National Women's Political Caucus The **NWPC** was established in 1971 to increase women's participation in politics and government, to support feminist candidates for political office, and to direct attention to issues of concern to women. It counted around 75,000 members and chapters in 44 states during the 1980s.

President's Commission on the Status of Women The **PCSW** was established by John F. Kennedy in 1961 as the first official body to examine women's status and recommend ways to combat discrimination against women. Chaired by Eleanor Roosevelt, the Commission's membership included government officials and leaders from labor, business, and voluntary organizations.

Women's Campaign Fund Established in 1974, the **WCF** supports female candidates for office who are committed to women's rights. The Fund furnishes technical assistance, training seminars, and money for the candidates it endorses.

Women's Equity Action League **WEAL** was organized in 1968 as a "moderate" alternative to NOW. Composed primarily of executive and professional women, it does not seek a mass membership. Its research, litigation, and advocacy have focused on women's education, women's employment and other economic issues, and women in the military.

Women's Rights Project of the American Civil Liberties Union
The **WRP** was established in 1972 with a grant from the Ford Foundation and subsequent support from other foundations and individuals. Its staff of four lawyers pursues litigation on behalf of sex equity.

Index

About the Author

Susan M. Hartmann is Professor of History and Director of the Center for Women's Studies at Ohio State University. She has taught at the University of Missouri—St. Louis as well as Boston University, and has received fellowships from the Rockefeller Foundation and the National Endowment for the Humanities. Her publications include *Truman and the 80th Congress* (1971), which won the David D. Lloyd Award, *The Home Front and Beyond: American Women in the 1940s* (1982), and articles on various aspects of women's history.

A Note on the Type

The text of this book is set in CALEDONIA, originally a Linotype face designed by W. A. Dwiggins. It belongs to the family of printing types called "modern face" by printers—a term used to mark the change in style of type-letters that occurred about 1800. Caledonia borders on the general design of Scotch Modern, but is more freely drawn than that letter.

This book was composed by ComCom, Allentown, Pa., and printed and bound by R. R. Donnelley & Sons Co., **Harrisonburg, Virginia.**